SOWETO
A History

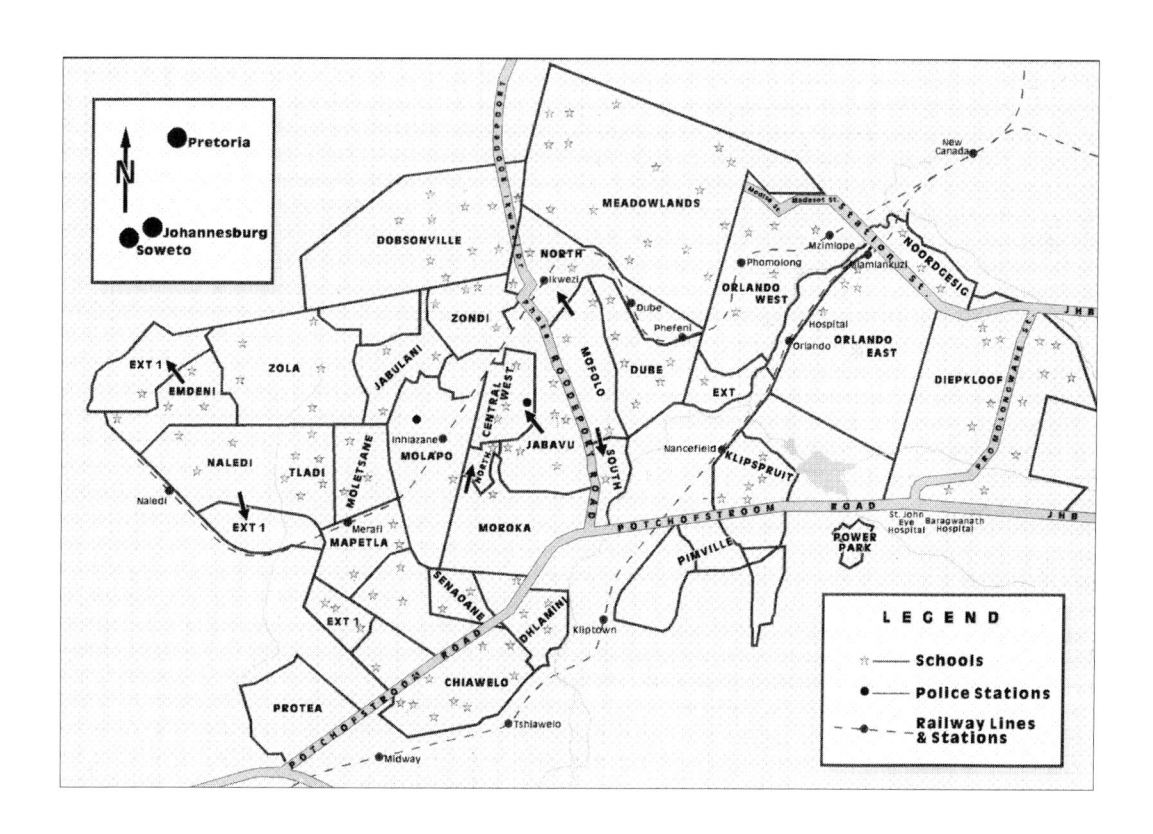

Philip Bonner and Lauren Segal

MASKEW MILLER LONGMAN

Maskew Miller Longman (Pty) Ltd,
Forest Drive, Pinelands, Cape Town

Offices in Johannesburg, Durban, Kimberley, King William's Town, Polokwane, Bloemfontein, representatives in Mafikeng and companies throughout southern and central Africa.

website: www.mml.co.za

© Maskew Miller Longman (Pty) Ltd 1998

All rights reserved. No part of this publication may be reproduced, stored in a retrieval system, or transmitted in any form or by any means, electronic, mechanical, photocopying, recording, or otherwise, without the prior written permission of the copyright holder.

First published in 1998
Third impression 2005

ISBN 0 636 03033 4

Edited by Sean Fraser
Concept and cover design by Karli Hadingham
DTP design by Mandy Mckay
Reproduction by Grapco Processing
Printed and bound by CTP Book Printers, Cape
RK5334/25956

Contents

Acknowledgements	5
Foreword: Walter Sisulu	7
Building Matchbox City	8
Divide and Rule	32
The Loaded Pause	54
This is Our Day	76
At War	102
New Beginnings	132
Bibliography	160

Acknowledgements

The vision of the film series *Soweto – A History* was first conceived by the History Workshop at the University of the Witwatersrand in 1986, and the project represents an important part of its quest to accord a central place within the writing of South African history to the experiences of the often silenced black population. Among the most resounding of these silences surrounds the history of South Africa's major black city, Soweto, about which nothing systematic or comprehensive had been written or documented. In 1987, Philip Bonner, Peter Delius and Denise Moys established contact with Free Film Makers, a group of film makers who were also committed to telling South Africa's untold stories on film. Angus Gibson joined the project as director, Nicola Galombik as producer, Jonathan Miller as executive producer and Lauren Segal as film and document researcher and subsequently as associate producer. They were joined by Patrick Shai, Ramalao Makhene and Mtutuzeli Matshoba to set the project in motion and they, in turn, were joined by Teboho Mahlatsi, Motsamai Kabi and Dingaan Kapa.

Symptomatic of the times, the History Workshop and Free Film Makers experienced major difficulties in raising funds: big business in South Africa was not interested and the SABC's commissioning editors were unwilling to invest money in the project. It took the commitment of Channel Four Television in Britain and SBS Television in Australia to realise the value of the enterprise and provide the major financial backing. We also have to thank the Joseph Rowntree Charitable Trust, which not only contributed to finishing the films but also provided the main sponsorship for the book. The Anglo American and De Beers Chairman's Fund also helped make this book possible. Because of financial constraints, the filming often hiccuped and, in the end, the six half-hour films took almost five years to complete.

While *Soweto – A History* had its starting point in the university, much of the work happened in the township. In conjunction with the film team and historians, young Sowetans set out to find ordinary people who could tell the story of their home from its very beginning. Steve Lebello, Steve Mokoena and Jon-Jon Mkhonza began the process and were joined, over the years, by Steven Tshabalala, Mtutuzeli Matshoba, Ma Matshoba, Theboho Mohapi, Sergeant Kekana, Thomas Mathole, Sipho Mchunu. They spent many hours listening to the untold stories of the young and old which were to provide the basis for the television series and this book. Prior to funding becoming available, many of these people were willing to do this work for little or no pay. To tell the history of South Africa's most famous township was seen as a duty, part of the activist spirit of the day. Thank you to the researchers for their invaluable contribution.

The film and picture research was an equally far-reaching process. There is an amazing paucity of images of Soweto in South African archives, especially before the 1980s. Much of the moving archive of Soweto in the series came from overseas archives, usually from films that were not directly about Soweto itself. Many of the photographs in both the film and this book also had to be dug from a wide range of sources. Researchers drew on the personal archives of Sowetans and spent much time tracing photographers who owned or worked in studios in Soweto and the city centre from the beginning of the century. Luli Callinicos generously supplied photographs from her personal collection; David Goldblatt provided many of his images for the films and book; Marie Human helped us with research in Bailey's Archive, as did Kerri Nkosi in the Africana Museum. Michele Rowe assisted in the photograph research.

The richness of all this material suggested a need for a book to accompany the series and fill in those parts of the story that the medium of film was unable to convey. We are grateful to Maskew Miller Longman for their enthusiastic support for the book project. A special thanks is due to the publisher Orenna Krut who spent many hours reading the manuscript. Her sharp insights and careful editing shaped the chapters that emerged. Thanks also to Inga Norenius who has spent many hours nursing the final manuscript; Sean Fraser who has given up his weekends to comment on and edit the manuscript so carefully and intelligently; Pat Swanepoel who tirelessly collected the original photographs to reprint here; and Mandy McKay who executed Karli Hadingham's striking concept design and typeset these pages.

Thank you to Candice Harrison who helped gather some of the additional archival and interview research for the process of writing, and to Mandhu Kanji who provided administrative back-up and support. Many others were involved in the compilation of both the film and book projects and have not been mentioned here. Thank you to them all.

Philip Bonner and Lauren Segal
May 1998

Foreword

Not much has been written about the history of Soweto – about the perspectives, the construction of the place, its growth and the people who lived and struggled within its parameters. Not much has been written about Soweto – yet it is known the world over as a symbol of apartheid terror and as a symbol of the heroic struggles of its people against that terror. This book is, therefore, so welcome as it begins the process of filling that void.

The history of South Africa cannot be understood outside the history of Soweto. Certainly, the history of Soweto is the history of South Africa. The development of the township, and the trials and tribulations of its people are a microcosm of the history of this country. Industrialisation, apartheid policies and the struggles of South African people all find their expression in that place called Soweto. Indeed, this book is a welcome companion in our journey to selfhood.

Soweto – A History finds its place among the many texts that have helped to rewrite the history of our country. For generations, the history of the black people in South Africa has either been written from a perspective that undermines the nuances of a rich and vibrant past or completely removes the many voices that make up the black communities in South Africa. That time of exclusion and marginalisation is now over.

The rewriting of our history is deeply bound to the reconstruction of South Africa, but reconstruction does not simply refer to the material upliftment of the majority of people in our country. It also refers critically to the reconstruction of our cultural resources and attaching value to the ideas and attitudes that have for so long been sidelined and hidden from institutional historical narratives. As we begin defining a new South African identity for ourselves, the memory of what informs us and the resources of our past need to be captured.

Not only does *Soweto – A History* begin to alter the content of our formal history, but its form is also superlative in its attempt to forge a unity between the different sources of historical narrative. It has beautifully combined oral and written records as it constructs its story. It is unique in that it does not privilege one source over the other. Many stories are told, and all are woven together in a coherent and fine narrative about our past. There are also various wonderful pictures and photographs that constantly complement the written story. In this way, the story may be accessed by many people with varied interests.

This book, *Soweto – A History*, bears testimony to the bold resilience of the people of this country to not only survive the extremities of repression and the violence of apartheid, but to create a vibrant, caring, communal environment that reinforced humanity in conditions of pronounced inhumanity. The people of Soweto refused to let their spirit die, and it is that spirit which contributed to the demise of apartheid. That spirit is also captured in the pages of this book and will live on partly through its existence.

I am delighted that this book has been written and am privileged to have been a part of its making through the interviews the authors have conducted with me.

Walter Sisulu

Cape Town
May 1998

BUILDING MATCHBOX CITY

'*It has been said that the path through Africa runs through Soweto; that Soweto is a microcosm, or the soul of South Africa; that Soweto is a shining example of neglect and exploitation: that Soweto means many things to many people.*'

Louis Rive, 'The Significance of Soweto', address given at the annual general meeting of the National Development and Management Foundation, Johannesburg, November 1980

Soweto — A History

(Below, top)
A homestead stands among the hills of the Witwatersrand in the early 1880s, the site on which the city of Johannesburg later developed.

(Below, bottom)
Miners underground.

Soweto. To millions of people beyond the borders of South Africa, the name is the very symbol of the black struggle for freedom in South Africa. To South Africans, it signifies the country's main black metropolis and the leading centre of black urban culture. Beyond that, for outsiders and South Africans alike, Soweto's history remains somewhat of a blank. When was it constructed? Why was it built? Where did its residents come from? Why did people flock in vast numbers to such an inhospitable setting? This book sets out to answer some of those questions and to tell the story of Soweto through the eyes of its residents.

Most of Soweto was built in the 1950s and early 1960s and, within a remarkably short space of time, it became home to half a million people. The area was only given its present name in 1963, but the first African township in modern Soweto was established as far back as 1905. In those days it was called Klipspruit, but was subsequently called Pimville, and it is by this latter name that the original township of Soweto is known today. Many of Klipspruit's first residents had already lived and worked in Johannesburg for many years and, to tell their story, we go back to the very first strike of gold on the Rand.

'Egoli' — the golden city

Looking at modern Johannesburg, it is difficult to believe it is little more than 100 years old. In 1880, the land on which the city stands was bare veld. Only a handful of African homesteads and Boer farmhouses lay within 50 kilometres of what was to become the city centre.

This desolate landscape, however, hid great wealth. Reefs of gold ore slanted up to the earth's surface and contained the largest volumes of this precious metal discovered anywhere in the world. One of the first nuggets of gold ore was found in 1886, and thousands of treasure seekers streamed in by ox wagon and on foot to seek their fortune. Within 10 years, the original mining camp population of 3 000 swelled to over 100 000 people. Smaller claim holders were absorbed into the huge mining groups like Gold Fields and Wernher Beit/Eckstein, which were financed largely by British, German and American investors to dig deeper and deeper into the earth.

In its early days, Johannesburg was no different to mining camps anywhere else in the world. Its population was overwhelmingly male and mostly temporary. Both blacks and whites arrived in search of short-term financial reward after which they had every intention of moving on. Social life reflected the temporary character of the population. Virtually the entire population of male miners lived first in tents and then in crude corrugated iron structures. This is how a visitor to the area in 1886 described it:

Building Matchbox City

'...galvanised iron shanties were to be seen in their hundreds. Streets were tracks over the sandy soil and dense dust pervaded the whole place'. For recreation and leisure, there were bars, shebeens, gambling dens and brothels. The insecurity and fears of mining life are captured in a Swazi song which the migrants sang as they tramped overland to the mines. The song asks 'Whose place am I going to sleep at tonight among all that rough lot in Johannesburg?' and it speaks of the wives who had been left behind.

It was only in the early 1900s, after it had become clear that there were huge reserves of gold hidden deep underground, that Johannesburg began to acquire a more stable and settled character.

By this time, almost 60 000 Africans were employed on the mines and the gold output was worth £20 million a year. Buildings were erected along the town's main streets and around the market square, and the wealthy mine owners began to build palatial homes on the ridges to the north of the town. As production expanded, the mine managers began to feel the need for a more stable, reliable and sober workforce who would not partake in the 'social evils' of Johannesburg life. White miners were encouraged to marry and new white suburbs were established to house the growing number of families. Between 1897 and 1902, the number of 'European' mine employees who were married and accompanied by their families nearly doubled.

Black miners, however, faced an entirely different prospect. They were made to enter into short-term labour contracts of between 6 and 18 months, and to leave their wives and families behind in the rural areas while they worked underground. Although black workers were often lured to the mines with a promise of high wages, in reality, life on the mines was tough for black labourers. They lived on the mining property in tightly controlled single-sex barracks surrounded by high compound walls and the conditions inside were squalid. Migrant labourers were also forced to carry an identity document, known as a 'pass', which detailed their work contracts and enabled the authorities to exert control over their movements.

A miner with his family outside the mine's white married quarters.

Concrete bunks serve as beds in the living quarters allocated to black migrant workers at Crown Mines near Johannesburg.

13 kilometres into town each day, and they were forced to travel in cattle trucks which had been converted into 'carriages'. In the end, the chief reason why Klipspruit was built where it was, was to have it as far as possible removed from any neighbourhood inhabited by Europeans.

Not surprisingly, slum dwellers resisted being sent to Klipspruit. Many of their employers also objected to the move because workers now arrived late to work and were no longer available for overtime or evening work. The mounting opposition thus forced the Council to grant special licences to employers which allowed them to house their workers in compounds on their own premises or in hired accommodation in the towns. Within almost every warehouse, foundry and factory in central Johannesburg, small private compounds sprang up. The system was very difficult to police, however, and thousands of Africans continued to live in privately rented rooms in the slumyards of the inner city.

By 1919, 105 000 Africans lived in Johannesburg. Of these, approximately half were employed and accommodated by the mines, 30 000 domestic workers lived on the premises of their white employers, while only 4 000 lived in municipal locations and compounds such as Klipspruit. The remaining 17 000 workers lived in the slums, and the population here continued to rise during most of the 1920s, when every imaginable space was filled by people desperate for accommodation. Landlords grew rich by renting out rooms. By 1927, over 40 000 people lived in the unregulated, unhygienic and boisterous world of the slums.

An African woman living in the Rooiyard slum brews a drum of 'skokiaan' (beer) to serve the shebeen's clients.

The Marabi era

Marabi was the name given to the exuberant new urban culture created by the slum-dwellers in the 1920s. Destined to influence greatly the cultural world of black Sowetans, its most distinct feature was its racial mix. In the slums Africans, Indians, coloureds, Chinese and whites of many diverse origins (British, Boers, Lebanese, East European Jews) lived side by side and borrowed many elements from one another's social lives and cultures. For example, the shebeens — unlicensed drinking houses selling home-brewed beer — were transported from Ireland to the Cape before finally being introduced in modified form in the slums. Similarly, the slumyard dialect of *flaaitaal* combined elements of Afrikaans, English and African languages, while Marabi was a music style blending African, Afrikaans, coloured and black American musical forms into a melodic mix. So influential was this style that it gave its name to the urban culture taking shape in the slums — the music, dance parties, and thriving beer trade. In *Fight Where We Stand*, jazz saxophonist Wilson 'King Force' Silgee describes Marabi:

❝ Marabi: that was the environment. It was either organ but mostly piano. You get there, you pay your ten cents, you get your share of whatever concoction there is and you dance. It used to start from Friday night right through to Sunday evening. ❞

The slums, however, continued to alarm Johannesburg society. Fears of infection, racial mixing and a lack of control led many sections of the white communities – and some sections of black society – to call for the segregation and clearance of the slumyards. Local newspapers frequently carried letters expressing the concern of the white community. One of the best known of these slums was in Doornfontein, on the site of what is today the Ellis Park sporting complex and rugby stadium, much of which was demolished only in the 1970s and 1980s. Another well-known slum area, Prospect Township, from which many first-generation Sowetan residents were moved, stood on the site of present-day Kazerne railway goods depot, which may still be seen as you enter Johannesburg on the M2 East.

> Our inner city slums are veritable dens of vice, harbouring within their congested, ramshackle buildings and intricate underground passages, criminals of all kinds. We need to find a solution.
>
> This slum-like property swarms with low-class white and coloured people and their children; their habits are swinish in their filthiness.
>
> Letter
> Susan Parnell, 'Johannesburg's Slums', 1993

The government takes action

The 1923 Native Urban Areas Act was the first attempt by Smuts's government to deal with the growing problem. According to TRH Davenport's 'The Beginning of Urban Segregation', it felt that 'the Native should only be allowed to enter urban areas, which are essentially the white man's creation, when he is willing to administer to the needs of the white man, and should depart from them when he ceases to so minister'.

The reason for passing the Act was so that the government could rid the urban areas of liquor sellers, criminals and the unemployed, thereby eradicating the promiscuous multiracial environment in which they lived and forcing the remaining African labour force on the Rand to live in townships and single-sex compounds.

The problem for the Johannesburg City Council, however, was that it required a substantial initial investment of money to build houses for Africans – and its white ratepayers were reluctant to provide sufficient money for this purpose. As a result, it simply expelled African residents from the slums without providing adequate alternative housing in the newly built Western and Eastern Native Townships. Both slum landlords and the African tenants responded by challenging the legality of these actions in the courts on the grounds that alternative housing had to be provided before evictions could take place. In 1925, the courts declared the Council's actions invalid and the African residents flooded back. In 1927, the Native Affairs Committee was established under the control of the JCC, and its main task was to solve the housing problem of the city's African population. By 1930, an estimated 27 000 Africans had been placed in compounds and locations, but another 40 000 still needed government housing and were living in the slums.

In the early 1930s, however, the situation began to change and this is the period in which the origins of modern Soweto are to be found. In 1930, the Great Depression hit South Africa and crippled white agriculture. Thousands of destitute Afrikaner farmers began to stream into the cities amid increasing fears among officials of further inter-racial mixing in the slums. To overcome the legal obstacles with which they had been faced in creating segregated cities, the urban municipalities secured changes to the Urban Areas Act. These changes freed the JCC from the obligation to provide alternative housing to African workers evicted from inner-city slums. Additional legislation in the form of the Slums Act of 1934 also aided the clearance of slum areas. From 1932, also, an increase in the price of gold gave the South African economy and industry the huge boost it so desperately needed. The higher gold price provided the incentive to prospect and develop deeper level mines, and the expansion of mining provided expanded markets for manufacturing companies. The urban centres suddenly prospered. Slum lands became valuable for industrial sites and Johannesburg's income grew to a point where the city was sufficiently wealthy to build African (and poor white) houses.

In 1931, the new African township of Orlando was constructed in the heart of modern Soweto, 15 kilometres southwest of Johannesburg and adjacent to the main road to Potchefstroom. Again, the prime consideration governing its location was its distance away from white urban areas. In the 1930s, much of the African slumyard population was forcibly removed from the slums, and a new era had begun.

Slum clearance at Prospect Township, before removal to Orlando.

Orlando in the early days, showing its rural beginnings.

The building of Orlando

In 1930, the Johannesburg City Council bought land on the farm Klipspruit Number 8, which was situated near the Pimville location, and then organised a massive competition – offering a prize of £500 – for the best layout of the proposed township, which they claimed would be the 'biggest and finest township in the Union of South Africa'. The entrants were specifically instructed to avoid the 'smallness and similarity of the houses' in the Western Native Township and the Council stressed that it was building the township for the needs of the 'better-class native, the new Bantu who has a sense of beauty and proportion. Like other people, they appreciate variety'. (*Umteteli wa Bantu*, 30 January 1932) All early comments on the location emphasised the aesthetic appeal of the Council's plans. 'This will undoubtedly be somewhat of a paradise,' wrote the *Bantu World* newspaper, 'and to a greater extent will enhance the status of the Bantu within the ambit of progress and civilisation.' (*Bantu World*, 14 May 1932)

Named after the first chairman of the Native Affairs Committee, Councillor Edwin Orlando Leake, work on the new Orlando township began in 1931. 'Each house has a neat veranda and either two or three airy apartments, such as many Europeans would not despise,' wrote a reporter on *The Star* newspaper of the new buildings.

The first 300 houses were completed by October of that year but only 70 were immediately occupied. Many of those who had voluntarily moved to Orlando were relatively wealthy Africans who could afford the extra transport costs and the advance of two months' rent required by the Council. The new residents were allowed to choose their own houses and some families even moved from house to house before they finally made the decision on where to settle. One resident whose parents moved to Orlando East in 1932, explains:

People were choosing a house because of certain things. Some wanted to be near the station. Others wanted to be near the road so that people could easily get to their house. My father chose house number 435 because the houses had no tap inside and the tap for the whole street was in front of house 435.

The City Council, eager for the other slum-dwellers to move, arranged for a special train to take people to Orlando on a Sunday where they conducted tours of the area and distributed pictures of happy families sitting outside their new homes. The new township clearly differed, however, from the image of 'paradise' painted by the Council. The two- or three-bedroomed identical houses, which were packed close together, were built cheaply. Nelson Botile describes his new home:

Orlando East, circa 1935.

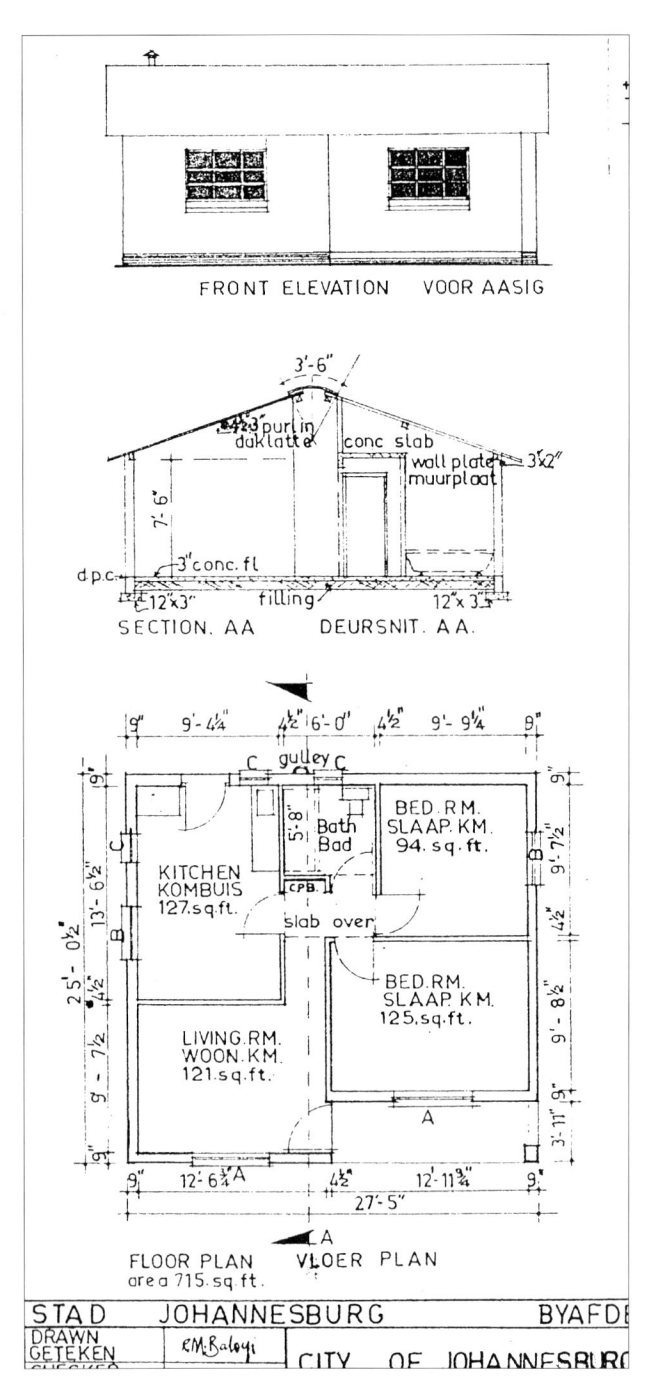

" The walls were not plastered, they were rough and the floor was just grass. It was not cemented. My father started plastering the house once we were inside. The houses had no taps. We didn't have sewerage – we had what was called the bucket system and we had these people coming at night to remove the sanitation. The streets were not tarred and they had no names. The houses only had numbers. "

Besides the poor standard of accommodation, other community facilities were equally poor. Orlando had no parks, sports grounds, hairdressers, clothing shops, or banks. All shopping had to be done in the city, there was schooling for only a small minority of the township's children, and there was not a single electric light or tarred road. The regulated uniformity of the township of Orlando also compared unfavourably in other ways with the areas which Orlando residents were originally forced to leave. In E Koch's 'Doornfontein and its African Working Class', Modikwe Dikobe, a leading writer about slum and township life, compared the two communities:

" Marabi parties could not take place in Orlando, because the community spirit was lost. The Orlando people were isolated from one another. In Doornfontein, we lived closely together, we helped each other in everything. Quite a lot of people preferred Doornfontein because selling beer there was a profitable business. In Orlando there were no customers – it was known as a place of hunger. "

Clement Twala confirms that it was for these reasons that his parents resisted the move from Prospect Township:

" In Prospect Township, they used to make money out of umquomboti – the African liquor brewed out of corn. In Prospect Township, we were close to a mine called City Deep and used to have a flood of customers from the mine compound. In Orlando East, the compounds were very far away so it was difficult for the customers who used to support the old people to come and buy. "

The plans of the houses, usually called 'matchboxes', illustrate their monotonous layout. The total internal floorspace was about the size of the average living room in a white middle-class home.

However, by far the most important reason why slum-dwellers resisted the move was the distance which separated the township from greater Johannesburg. While the slums were close to the workplace, Orlando was miles from the city. Public transport was entirely inadequate and very expensive. 'People didn't want to go at first because of the distance,' writes Dikobe. 'They would have to take trams to town and spend 2 shillings and 6 pence on transport while earning only 21 shillings a month. They felt the pinch.' And very few trams ran each day.

By 1936, only 12 000 people lived in Orlando and, even after the Council initiated a slums clearance programme and began forcing people to move from the inner-city areas, they still screened slum-dwellers to see if they were 'suitable residents'. Orlando had clearly failed to become the 'model' township the Council had hoped it would be.

The Second World War

The Second World War marked a turning point in the history of Soweto and the general movement of Africans to the country's towns. During the war, in which the South African government fought with the British against Nazi Germany, the number of African families moving from the rural areas to the towns increased dramatically. Until this point, it was mainly the men who had moved to Johannesburg on a migrant basis and had returned to their families in the rural areas after a limited period of employment.

A survey of African pass records in Johannesburg conducted in 1946 showed, for example, that between 1936 and 1944, 50 per cent of jobs for African workers lasted less than 12 months and only 10 per cent for more than two years. This meant that Johannesburg's male African labour force replaced itself every 20 months. Large-scale migrancy by males also slowed the movement of African women to the town, and hence the growth of African urban family units. In 1900, of the 60 000 Africans in the city, the ratio of males to females was 12:1. By 1927, with a population of 136 000, the ratio was 6:1. At the outbreak of the war, however, the ratio was 3:1 and, by 1967, it was equal. When women did migrate to the towns, however, they did so overwhelmingly on a permanent basis. Several factors caused more permanent family settlement of Africans in Johannesburg by the mid-1940s. Firstly, the Second World War led to the massive expansion of manufacturing in and around Johannesburg and there were many more jobs available. Secondly, these new manufacturing jobs offered unskilled and semi-skilled African workers far higher wages than they were getting in the mining and farming sectors, which provided a minimum income on which to support a family. Thirdly, over 150 000 white men fought in the war, leaving vacancies for better paying semi-skilled jobs for black workers. And, fourthly, pass laws were relaxed in the middle of the war, partly to assist the flow of black workers to the towns. By the end of the war, Johannesburg's black population had increased by over half a million. The waiting list for houses in Orlando climbed from 143 in 1939 to 4 500 two years later and 16 000 in 1945. Nevertheless, few new units were built during the last years of the war as the government claimed that it was using all its resources to support the war effort. New arrivals in the city during these years were forced to cram in as subtenants in the houses or backyards of the already established township dwellers.

The movement of black people into the cities during the Second World War was often depicted in local newspapers as an invasion.

Ethel Leisa describes how the houses in Orlando East were 'so small but they had to accommodate other people who had no accommodation, because you would find that two families are staying in a two-roomed house'. Walter Sisulu, African National Congress (ANC) leader and Robben Island prisoner with Nelson Mandela, who was living in Orlando at the time, remarks: 'Take my own house, a two-roomed house. I had relatives who came to stay with me. My uncle and his family came to stay with me, and my cousins also came to stay with me.'

The Council thus had no option but to overlook the presence of lodgers. Overcrowded conditions meant that there was no privacy, and personal and familial relationships were severely strained. Moreover, lodgers were charged exorbitant rents and had little power to challenge their landlords. As a result, migrant workers found it increasingly difficult to send money home so that their relationships with their families in the rural areas also came under strain. The communal spirit that had characterised the earlier period of black urban life was slowly being replaced by bitterness and resentment between the long-established urban folk and the new arrivals in the townships.

A letter written to the House of Assembly captured the situation in Orlando:

> There is bitter discontent amongst the older Natives. If this is a model township... then God preserve the Natives from the repetition of such a monstrosity. I am driven to the conclusion that a colossal crime has been perpetrated by the white races against the Natives. Johannesburg will reap what it has sown.
>
> Letter
> Kevin French, 'James Mpanza', 1983

Soweto's 'Messiah'

Amidst the growing crisis in Orlando, an individual emerged who was to change the course of the township's history. He was James Sofasonke Mpanza, the flamboyant founder and leader of the Sofasonke Party in Orlando. His slogan demanded 'Housing and Shelter for all', and he has often been referred to as the 'man who founded Soweto'. Mpanza was a rather colourful character with a criminal past. In 1915, he had been sentenced to life imprisonment for murder but, while in jail, had had a vision and converted to Christianity. He started preaching from his cell, trying to convert other prisoners to his new-found faith, and was released from prison after just 15 years. He came to live – and preach – in Johannesburg.

Mpanza was described by one observer as a 'fighter, lover of race horses, fluent in English, educated, keen on soccer, popular with women, astute and experienced with law, a persuasive preacher and a jack of many other trades'.

1940s' Orlando East houses.

'He has a small shrill voice and is five foot six inches high,' wrote another newspaper of Mpanza. 'At first sight, he looks a very tired man, an unimpressive figure, but on closer acquaintance one cannot but be impressed with the man's resourcefulness and profound knowledge of human nature.' (Kevin French, 'James Mpanza and the Sofasonke Party', 1983)

Mpanza arrived in Orlando in 1934, after he had been forced out of Bertrams – northeast of today's Ellis Park Stadium – when the Council declared the whole of Johannesburg a white area under the Urban Areas Act. He moved into Number 957, Pheele Street, one of the first houses built in Orlando and, before long, he was elected to the Advisory Board in the township. This board was the only official form of representation for black people living in Orlando and was set up to liaise between the residents and the Johannesburg City Council. 'The Advisory Board had no powers as you can hear from the word advisory,' says Nelson Botile of this structure. 'All they did was get complaints from the residents, then they'd go and advise the JCC. The Board would meet the Manager of the Non-European Affairs Department who was chairman of the Board. He'd make recommendations to the JCC.'

The most important criticism of the Board was that it was unrepresentative and only registered male tenants in the location were allowed to vote in elections. This left both women and subtenants disenfranchised, so it was to this voiceless, voteless mass that Mpanza increasingly devoted his attention. His precise motives, however, remain unclear. It seems likely that he saw in this anonymous mass, who until that point had been mostly ignored by the main black political parties such as the ANC and the CPSA, a source of personal and political gain. At the same time, there can be little doubt that he was also genuinely concerned about their plight. Whatever his reasons, Mpanza began to plot a means of securing housing for the tens of thousands of homeless families now congregating on the Reef. For several years, he wrote to the Minister of Native Affairs alerting the department to the chronic housing shortage, but his letters met with no response.

Mpanza, nevertheless, evoked very strong and often contradictory opinions about who he was and what he was doing. Government officials loathed Mpanza, attributing to him all kinds of moral failings and crimes. To Walter Sisulu, on the other hand, he was 'a brilliant chap; he was a thinker and a man who was very stylish, too, in his action. He could be devastating when he dealt with the opposition'.

Clement Twala remembers Mpanza with equal admiration:

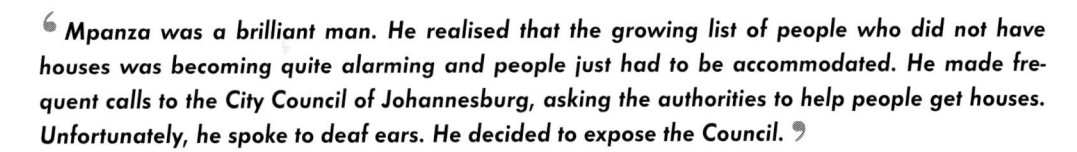

❝ Mpanza was a brilliant man. He realised that the growing list of people who did not have houses was becoming quite alarming and people just had to be accommodated. He made frequent calls to the City Council of Johannesburg, asking the authorities to help people get houses. Unfortunately, he spoke to deaf ears. He decided to expose the Council. ❞

For the young Nelson Botile, Mpanza was an imposing figure:

❝ Mpanza would not easily be convinced by a young man with no experience. When you stand up, as a young man, to raise your point of view, he would ask you, "Do you have a house?" If you say, "No, I don't have a house", Mpanza would say, "You can't talk in this meeting because you don't know anything about life, my son. Sit down. We'll give you a chance one day when you are old." What I liked about Mpanza is that he stood for the people. ❞

By 1943, Mpanza's behaviour had become more assertive and, as recorded in an affidavit in the Central Archives Depot, he declared himself a messiah figure:

James Sofasonke Mpanza.

Soweto — A History

> ❝ I am a messenger sent by God. The Municipality has taken on itself the duty of providing us with houses. But it has not carried out that duty. There are no houses for us. We can no longer wait for them to put a roof over our heads. I am taking possession of the authority's vacant land and I am building shacks for the people who have no houses. ❞

Initiated by James Sofasonke Mpanza, the first shacks are erected beyond the demarcated boundaries of Orlando Township.

James Sofasonke Mpanza prepares to administer strokes in a court that he had established in Shantytown.

On Saturday, 20 March 1944, the small figure of James Mpanza, perched on his horse, led the sub-tenants of Orlando on a 20th-century exodus to a vacant stretch of land across the river in Orlando West. Mpanza compared himself to Moses who had led the children of Israel out of bondage and announced that they were about to cross the River Jordan. *Sofasonke nengwevu baba* (we shall die together with our father) sang his followers as they walked. Violet Khanyeza describes her experience of that day:

> ❝ We moved out with our blankets and our children on the back. Our husbands were not there. We were only women and babies and children. When we got there, there were no houses. Everyone was drawing their own room, everyone was digging. And in the evening, when our husbands came back from work, they asked the owners of the house, "Where are our wives?" and the owners said, "Your wife has gone to build a house for herself." And they all went to Mpanza's office and they were calling our names, "Violet! Violet!" ❞

Jane Khanyeza describes how, 'it was all mixed up, there were no streets. Some of the people built nice shacks, some built bad shacks and when it rained some had water in the shacks'. Five days later, there were more than 1 500 residents of Shantytown, better known as Masakeng, 'the place of sacks' after the materials used by people to build their simple shelters. Each new day saw long queues of women line up outside 'the office' to pay their admission fee to Mpanza's Sofasonke Party so they could join the camp.

From a start of 500 families and 250 shacks, Shantytown grew at an average of 300 families per day.

The residents now included backyard dwellers from the city who were tired of being constantly harassed by the police for living in supposedly illegal spaces. At its peak, Shantytown had over 4 000 registered shacks, and women and children spent a large part of the day hunting for poles, sacks, corrugated iron and other materials with which new arrivals could build their homes.

From his office, James Mpanza controlled all aspects of the squatter camp and unashamedly took over what should have been the responsibility of the Council. He employed 28 of his own policemen, set up his own courts and meted out punishment to those who disturbed the neighbourhood peace. Mpanza boasted that his was the only crime-free area in Soweto.

Mpanza and his committee also saw to the day-to-day needs of the people. In an attempt to overcome the extreme material hardships faced by the squatters, the committee handed out coal, firewood and milk bought with funds from the Sofasonke Party. Sympathetic township residents and well-wishers also donated food and money to the camp. Jane Khanyeza, who was a young girl at the time, remembers that Mpanza was treated with a respect that bordered on reverence. 'We little children liked to sing for him when he came. We drank soup and he gave us a slice of bread with peanut butter on it. When he came we all sang standing up, singing for Mpanza, he was like a king.'

'We used to make a procession and we all went there and we would sing and dance,' recounts Jane's mother, Violet Khanyeza. 'It was nice. He gave us some things to eat and we were dancing for him. We put on red belts so that when we jive he must see them. It was very nice.'

At a time when the government tightly regulated trading laws in the township and prohibited the selling of home-brewed beer, Mpanza's camp became a safe hideaway for frustrated traders. Mpanza sold traders' licences and, in contrast to the municipally controlled townships, they were then free to do business as they wished. It was virtually impossible for the municipal police to penetrate the tightly packed, unnumbered and haphazardly sited shanties in order to stop illegal trading activities and business flourished in Shantytown.

The Council had been caught off guard by Mpanza's bold move, so its first response was to prosecute the camps' residents and have them removed by the police. But neither the government nor the police agreed to this course of action as the squatters were both law-abiding and were, with rare exceptions, employed in Johannesburg. Mpanza further played on the Council's fears by declaring his camp the first example of 'black self-government' in the urban areas.

James Sofasonke Mpanza being followed by a procession of women and children.

Shantytown dwellings were built with poles, sacks, and whatever other materials people could find.

To meet the challenge, the Council hastily devised a plan to provide temporary accommodation, and rows of breeze-block shelters of ash, sand and cement were erected in the new area of Jabavu. Roofed with corrugated asbestos and lacking fireplaces, chimneys and windows, these structures were 9 square metres, and stood 2.5 metres high at the back and 2 metres high at the front. In return for a bare minimum of services (bucket sanitation, and water and refuse removal), a monthly fee of 5 shillings (50 cents) was charged. The Council, however, demanded that squatters demolish their old shacks so that new arrivals could not take occupation and the land could eventually be cleared for a permanent housing scheme.

Mpanza was emphatic that not a single squatter should move to the new shelters, and urged Shantytown to stand united in its demand for permanent housing for all. He pointed out that expensive houses were being erected daily in the luxurious white suburbs and that the Council's shelters were an embarrassment to black people. But, by charging half of Mpanza's monthly fee for the shelters, the Council had created a split among the squatters. A Vigilance Committee formed within Shantytown to oppose Mpanza and his Sofasonke Party and, on 26 May 1944, they arranged for the first 200 families to move into the completed shelters erected by the Council. Despite the primitive nature of the dwellings, many families decided that they at least provided a legal home of their own and agreed to move. The Khanyeza and Leisa families were among the first to move. As Ethel Leisa recalls, they bore their new situation stoically:

Rooms were quite small, but those rooms were meant to accommodate a family. In the morning, when we got up, it was so difficult. For instance, the father of the family had to prepare to get to work while the children were still asleep. There was no bathroom; there was no other room. He had to get out of bed and bite the end of the blanket with his teeth to cover his front part and then put his legs into his trousers. There was not any other way of having privacy except to use that blanket.

'When we went to sleep,' Jane Khanyeza continues, 'there were so many of us. It was my brother, my father, my mother, my sister and me and the other children, the smaller children. We slept under the table. My mother and father got the bed.' Despite these cramped conditions, Jane has colourful memories of the life and spirit of the community. 'I had some friends, Sotho girls and Vendas, and others from all nations. I played with them, I taught myself Venda, Sotho, Tswana, Xhosa and Zulu. When we ate, we ate from a big dish. We just put porridge and meat there and ate with our hands.'

Violet Khanyeza has similar recollections:

You know when somebody came and said, "Help me with a piece of bread", we gave it to him. We didn't say, "No, I've got nothing." We were together. There was lots of brewing because there were lots of Basothos. Basothos like beer, kaffir beer. There were lots of Basothos performing famo [a Sotho dance]. They danced at night, they drunk and did everything.

The Council takes control

The alternative accommodation provided by the Council had successfully sabotaged Mpanza's committee and his power base began to crumble. The Council also began to investigate conditions in Shantytown – and the large sum of money in the Sofasonke bank account. Confident that they had enough evidence to discredit Mpanza, the JCC declared that Shantytown was to fall under its strict control and said that they would 'not tolerate any usurping of its powers by any body of natives'. (*The Sunday Times*, 28 May 1944)

On 28 August 1944, the Council thus withdrew official recognition of Mpanza's committee and assumed control of Shantytown. On 17 November, the government passed new legislation to prevent squatting and enable a magistrate to remove people who unlawfully occupied land or a building. Large contingents of policemen arrived to tear down the shacks and move the squatters to the shelters and, by March 1945, Shantytown had been reduced to 2 000 families, half the original number. The last of the families were removed from their shacks in October of that year, and Shantytown was no more. A population of 20 000 had been brought under Council control as registered tenants of the Orlando shelters.

However, although the Council had wrested control from Mpanza, the squatters had made appreciable gains. Shantytown had shocked the authorities and forced them to tackle the question of housing more seriously. The squatters' actions also gave a new sense of pride and self-respect to Africans. Shantytown was the first major mass-based community struggle in Orlando and, from that moment, acts of rebellion became part of township life. Moreover, the Council's victory was short-lived. They had not provided a real and long-lasting solution to the massive housing crisis and the same problems re-emerged.

The second wave

On 28 January 1946, a second exodus of squatters took place under Mpanza's leadership. This time, about 3 000 subtenants from Orlando forcibly occupied the half-completed and more spacious houses the Council was building in Orlando West.

Mpanza told a meeting of subtenants that the half-built structures were to be given to people from black areas the government wished to turn into 'whites only' suburbs and not to those living in appalling conditions within Orlando itself. He also pointed out that the Council planned to increase the rent for these houses which would place them beyond the reach of most ordinary people. Two cars bearing Council officials rushed to the scene, but both vehicles broke down in streams which had flooded. Helene Henderson, one of the officials, comments in an affidavit at the Central Arches Depot that Mpanza 'made use of the coincidental breakdown of my motor car and that of the Superintendent of Orlando, and the flooding of the motor car of the Non-European Affairs Department as further proof of his supernatural powers, claiming that it was he who brought this about'.

Squatters from Orlando occupy partly-built Council houses in Orlando West in 1946.

Nevertheless, the JCC remained more determined than ever to resist the squatter movement, and the feelings of the municipal officials became increasingly hostile towards Mpanza. Both they and the City Councillors came to view the movement as 'a concerted and engineered trial of strength'. Recalling those days, Wilhelm Carr, the Johannesburg City Council's Manager of Non-European Affairs, reflects this hardening attitude:

Following eviction from their original site, squatters cook a meal on makeshift stoves outside the Orlando Community Hall, to where they then moved in defiance of the Johannesburg City Council.

❝ *Mpanza was a criminal; he was a thug. He extorted money from every possible source he could. He was a man of very bad character. He fathered more illegitimate children in that part of the world than anybody before or since. He stole money. He was always drunk. He was an unmitigated pest. He had nothing, nothing, nothing, to do with the subsequent development of the area.* ❞

Convinced that 'an immediate and strong display of force will achieve the desired end', the Council twice secured eviction orders, only to see the squatters move just a few hundred metres away to a new site.

The Council finally persuaded the government to deport Mpanza to the farm on which he was born in Natal, but once again they found themselves frustrated by the determination of both Mpanza and his supporters. Mpanza successfully challenged his deportation order in the Supreme Court and was released from custody – halfway home on his train journey to Natal. Mpanza now took on super-human proportions. Upon his return, he paraded around Orlando in triumph. One onlooker is recorded in the Central Archives as recalling:

❝ *[Mpanza was given] an enormous reception and a procession... during the whole of the afternoon and part of the evening. In the course of the celebration, Mpanza was hailed as king. Afterwards Mpanza sat in state in a front room of his house and allowed an enormous crowd of his followers to file past and gaze upon him.* ❞

In the course of the next month, two events were destined to break the resolve of the Council. On 8 March, a 'riot' broke out at the third site to which the squatters had moved. Some of the women had tried to erect shelters as protection from the rainstorm and the police had torn them down. One death and several injuries resulted from this clash and the Council became concerned about the image it was projecting. Then, towards the end of the month, the Council's prediction that successful defiance by this group of squatters would prompt others on the waiting list for housing to do the same, came true. On 24 March, a group of subtenants from Pimville, under the leadership of Abel Ntoi, again occupied vacant land – and the Council's resistance crumbled. Following hasty consultations with the central government, it agreed to establish an emergency camp called Central Western Jabavu which would house the 991 families.

This, however, was not the end. In September 1946, yet another wave of land invasions shook the Council, spilling out of Pimville and other parts of the western and eastern areas of Johannesburg. Squatters soon congregated on a site to the west of Orlando, where their numbers swelled to over 30 000. On 28 January 1947, the Council finally conceded that the housing shortage was so serious, and the squatter population so huge, that it could no longer control it by force. A new emergency camp, called Moroka, was consequently proclaimed. About 10 000 sites were immediately made available to the new squatter camp residents, with another 10 000 contemplated for the near future. By June 1947, the move to Moroka was concluded.

Moroka soon became synonymous with South Africa's worst slums. Residents were expected to build their own makeshift shanties on cramped 6 metre by 6 metre plots, the communal, bucket-system toilets overflowed with excrement, and water outlets were so scarce – and so far away – that fights regularly broke out in the queues. The camp had clearly been constructed to limit costs, and to make squatter movement a less attractive option. The life span of the camp was intended to be no more than five years, during which its population would be moved to proper houses. Instead, the population of Moroka grew steadily to 58 800 in 1955 – 89 000, including Jabavu – and it was only dismantled 13 years after its initial proclamation. During these years, conditions continued to deteriorate. James Letsatsi, who lived in a shack in Moroka at the time, describes Moroka as 'the roughest place you've ever come across. It was dominated by thuggery. After 8 o'clock you can't go to the toilet because they have these communal toilets and if you go, the thugs will get you'. Before long, newspapers greeted each new squatter movement with the headline 'Another Moroka', while the original camp became widely referred to as 'Johannesburg's shame'.

'Johannesburg's shame'.

The establishment of the Orlando shelters, Jabavu and Moroka, decisively influenced patterns of black urbanisation in Johannesburg. To gain access to the camps, a man was required to be both employed in Johannesburg and 'be in family circumstances', so many migrant men now took the critical decision to bring their wives to live with them in the towns. Others abandoned their rural wives and married again without proper customary, civil or church procedures in what were commonly referred to as *vat en sit* arrangements.

In 1948, hard on the heels of the establishment of Moroka, an Afrikaner Nationalist government came to power and this was set to change the face of South African history for ever. The support the National Party gained from their electorate was largely the result of white fears regarding the rapid urbanisation taking place at the time and, consequently, the Nationalists campaigned vigorously for racially segregated cities. Once they came to power, the new government immediately set out to regulate the tide of uncontrolled black urbanisation. They imposed stricter pass laws which made it more difficult for black workers to travel to town; they cleared black freehold townships and other areas of black settlement in the inner city and peri-urban areas; and they established tighter control over the municipal locations which they intended to be the sole place of residence of urban Africans. This more vigorous policy, nevertheless, still took nearly a decade to implement fully.

From site-and-service to housing

By the time the Nationalist government came to power in 1948, there was a broad agreement between government and employers about the urgent need to solve the housing problem. Progress in this direction was, however, painfully slow. Although 7 000 new houses were constructed in the two or three years following the election of the new government, very little was accomplished in the years that followed.

The main problem facing both the City Council and the central government was the heavy financial losses incurred in conventional housing schemes. Most African families could not afford to pay the 'economic' rental which would allow the loans – required to finance both housing schemes and the interest on them – to be repaid. The balance between subeconomic rentals – which the Council was obliged to charge – and the real cost had thus to be carried by central government and the City Council. As a result, from 1949, loans from the National Housing and Planning Commission largely evaporated. By the end of that year, the housing backlog stood at 57 000 and the government now believed that the only way forward was to lease land to the Africans so that they could erect their own houses 'on an improved Moroka Emergency Camp' basis. In 1950, this was dubbed *Vukuzenzele*, meaning 'wake up and do it yourself'. (Thanks to S Parnell and D Hart for this material.)

The Vukuzenzele scheme, however, was stalled by disagreements between the City Council, the government and industry over stand sizes, servicing standards and financing and, by 1952, not a single new house had been built. The logjam was, however, about to be broken. Five years of research by the Council for Scientific and Industrial Research and the National Building Research Institute had produced standard designs for low-cost, four-roomed, 40-square-metre houses (the 51/6 plan) which were soon to spring up in identical rows all over the Witwatersrand. In 1951, the Bantu Building Workers Act was passed, permitting Africans to be trained as artisans in the building trade – provided they were confined to African areas. These tasks had previously been reserved for whites only, and this decision alone helped slash building costs by half. Finally, the Bantu Services Levy Act of 1952 imposed a weekly levy of 2/6d on employers for every African worker they employed, the proceeds of which were used to finance the provision of basic services, such as water, roads, sewerage, and street lighting, to new African townships.

Identical rows of drab, uniform, 40-square-metre houses sprang up all over the Witwatersrand.

Building Matchbox City

The central government was now in a position to impose its master plan on Johannesburg as well as on municipal authorities across the rest of South Africa – the site-and-service programme. From 1954, all homeless African families, as well as those resident in the Orlando shelters and Moroka, were required to move to sites measuring 12 metres by 22 metres and serviced by a bucket latrine on every plot, with a water outlet every 500 metres. Families were expected to build their own shanties until such time as proper housing – self-help or otherwise – could be provided. Once formal houses were built, rentals were to be charged on an 'economic' basis, thereby relieving the authorities of financial losses on future housing schemes. No further loans or housing schemes would be authorised by the central government unless Johannesburg and other municipalities agreed to these conditions.

The JCC quickly complied with these conditions and, in 1955, 10 000 serviced sites were opened up, allowing thousands of Moroka's residents to be removed. Mr Miller, a Johannesburg Town Councillor, declared of the new scheme: 'Once the Bantu find themselves on the large, properly serviced plots (seven times the size of the Moroka plots) and have more room to breathe and move about, some sort of order will emerge from chaos.' (*The Star*, September 1955)

By the end of 1956, the townships of Tladi, Zondi, Dhlamini, Chiawelo and Senoane had been laid out to provide 28 888 people with accommodation. In the following year, Jabulani, Phiri and Naledi followed. During the course of 1958, Moroka and nearly all Orlando shelters were finally cleared. But formal housing took a good deal longer to provide. Government loans enabled about 3 000 houses to be built in 1953–54, but this still fell far short of what was required to clear the housing backlog. The major breakthrough occurred when Mr Wilhelm Carr, JCC's Manager of Non-European Affairs, invited Sir Ernest Oppenheimer of the Anglo-American Corporation to visit Moroka. Carr describes the day of Oppenheimer's visit:

> *There were only the three of us; it was Boris, I and Sir Ernest. It was quite amusing. We went out in the morning in Sir Ernest's Rolls Royce. Now the roads were pretty well non-existent. And the Rolls, as you probably know, has a ground clearance of about that much. And the very first dip and this thing was grounded and couldn't go. So the rest of the day we rode around with my Ford. Everybody treated it like a joke. And we took the old boy to show him the Shantytown and he didn't say much; he was never a man who talked a great deal. But it was obvious that he was deeply moved by what he had seen.*

In the words of another councillor, Sir Ernest was 'aghast', and he arranged with his colleagues in the mining industry to loan the city R6 million to be repaid over 30 years. As a result, a massive housing programme was launched almost immediately. Between 1954 and the end of 1959, 24 000 additional houses were built in this area, of which 14 000 were constructed with the help of this mining loan.

Parallel to these activities, the township of Meadowlands was being built under the direct responsibility of the central government. In 1953, the government-appointed Mentz Committee ruled

"Lavatory Pail was their Passport to new life"

TO possess your own lavatory pail might not seem to be the ultimate in human ambition. Nevertheless, on yesterday's smiling, sunny Sunday, a pail and dustbin presented to each of 12 Bantu families by the superintendent at Jabavu Township, represented a passport to a new life and a new hope.

Pail in hand, the Bantu clambered on to a lorry that held all their possessions and were taken to their new stands on Johannesburg's first site-and-service scheme at Moroka North.

On each site they saw a "little house" that was for the exclusive use of their family. Proudly each family put the new pail into it.

Then they walked round the boundaries of their sites, exclaiming at the size.

The 40 ft. by 70 ft. stands seemed so vast after the pocket handkerchiefs of land, 20 ft. by 20 ft. or smaller, from which they had come.

These pioneers on site-and-service in the Johannesburg area came from a miserable unserviced squatter camp in the Moroka area oddly known as "New Look".

These nearly 200 families had been paying 23s. a month for the privilege of living on a bit of land without tap water and without a latrine.

—*The Star*, 18/7/55.

Article from The Star *newspaper, 1955.*

The different areas of Soweto.

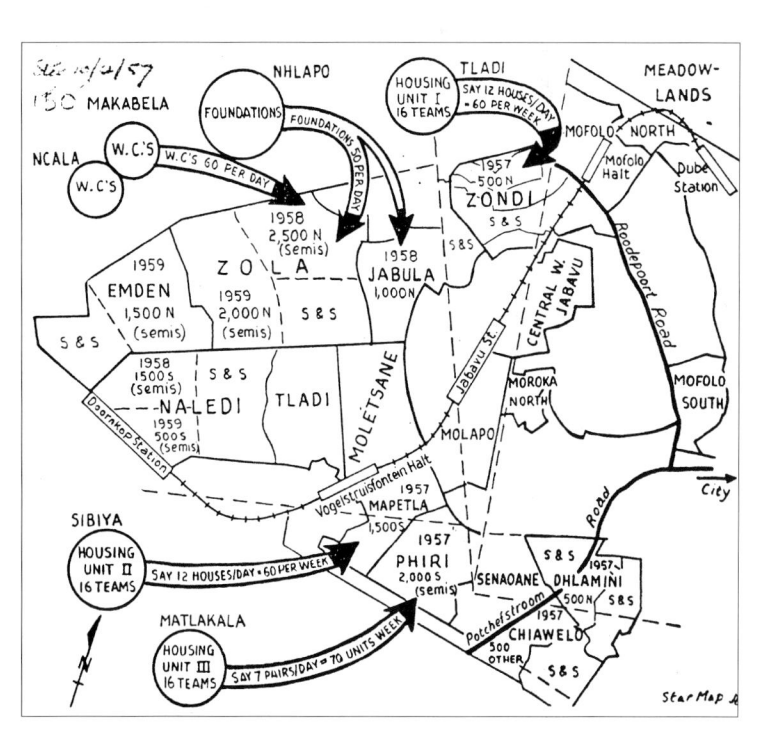

that all African residential areas in Johannesburg should in future be located in the vicinity of Orlando in the southwest. This meant that the African freehold townships west of Johannesburg (Sophiatown, Martindale, Newclare), as well as Western Native Township, were scheduled for removal. Between 1956 and the early 1960s, 23 695 houses were built in Meadowlands and Diepkloof to accommodate those evicted from these areas and, by 1960, the removals were more-or-less complete.

Different people responded to the new housing schemes in different ways. Many residents of the Western Areas were vehemently opposed to their removal, as were many residents of the Orlando shelters and Moroka, who were equally unhappy with the massive increase in rentals (from 5 shillings to 25 shillings a month for a serviced site in the case of the shelters) and the poor quality of the houses built by the municipality. Letsatsi Radebe, who moved from Moroka to Naledi, vividly remembers the quality of the municipal homes:

They built a house that is not plastered. Inside the house you'll find a big stone. They didn't care that this house is being built for a human being. The houses were built for animals. Most of the things, like plastering, have been done by people out of their own expenses.

For Ethel Leisa, on the other hand, a house was the summit of her ambition:

Before I got a house, it was like a dream. I used to come down every Sunday to look at these empty houses, and imagine that one day I would get a house and stay in Mzimhlope. There were double houses and single houses. In those days, it was tough. When you got a single house, you were a millionaire. It didn't belong to you, you were paying rent, but you felt well... Your children will be comfortable and you'll be comfortable and you'll be able to forget the past.

Seletial Maake had a similar response:

One day I got a letter from work saying I must go to the housing division. When I went, they said you got a house in Meadowlands; there is your number. I said, "What? A house in Meadowlands!" He said, "Yes." I said, "I'm not dreaming?" He said, "No. There's your number, go."

Policemen look at the rows of new houses in Meadowlands.

A substantial minority of Sowetans built their own homes. Before the Nationalist Party came to power in 1948, the Dube area of Soweto had been set aside as a place in which wealthier African families could obtain freehold title and build their own homes. But freehold tenure for Africans in Soweto was vetoed by the Nationalists shortly after they assumed office and 30-year leaseholds were granted instead. This obviously provided prospective African home owners and home builders with much less security, but some were prepared to accept half a loaf rather than none at all. In Dube and, for a time in other parts of Soweto, residents began to build houses for themselves, but these had to conform to one of the government's 30 officially sanctioned designs. By 1954, African residents had built 2 500 houses out of their own resources. Top-of-the-range houses cost £1 500 – compared to the paltry £250 for the NE 51/6 designs which had been built by the council and rented out to poorer Sowetans.

Dube soon became known as the most 'glamorous township' in Soweto. In fact, in years to come, Soweto's residents would describe Dube as the place of the 'excuse me's' – because the African intelligentsia who lived there were wealthier and were thought to speak overly polite English. They also identified the suburb as the place of 'highbugs', 'tycoons' and 'socialites'.

By the late 1950s, the spread of townships around Orlando housed nearly half a million people, but it remained a city without a name. The authorities simply referred to the area as the South Western Bantu Townships. Informally, the area came to be known as 'Matchbox City' because of the row upon row of identical, little brick boxes that dotted the landscape.

Then at last, in 1959, Mr Wilhelm Carr launched a competition to find a collective name for the Council's showpiece of slum clearance. He offered a £10 prize to the person who could come up with the best name. The response was quite enthusiastic. Goldella, Serena, Sothuni (a combination of the words 'Sotho' and 'Nguni', the two largest language groups in South Africa), Vergenoeg, Coon's Kraal, Sputnik, Black Birds Bunk, Creamland, Darkiesuburban, Dumuzweni (meaning 'famous the world round'), KwaMpanza, Khethollo ('segregation'), Kwantu, Thinavhuyo ('we have nowhere to go'), Oppenheimerville, Darkest Africa and Partheid Townships were just some of the thousands of entries which arrived each day at the offices of the City Council's Department of Non-European Affairs. Many suggestions were turned down because the committee felt that they favoured a particular 'tribe' or found them too complicated. Thari' Ntshu ('the black nation'), for example, was rejected because 'Europeans would find it too difficult to pronounce'.

After four years of heated arguments and deliberations, the naming committee arrived at a safe option – Soweto – an abbreviated version of 'South-Western Townships'. In April 1963, the *Rand Daily Mail* reported that 'South Africa's largest city within a city has at last got a name – SOWETO'. Carr commented that Soweto was 'short, easily pronounceable and does not favour one of the main language groups over that of another'.

It was this name which, 13 years later, was to reverberate around the world.

STAGES OF SOWETO'S DEVELOPMENT

1904	Klipspruit location is established on the site of present-day Pimville
1932	Orlando East
1944	Jabavu
1948	Moroka
1954	Mofolo
	Central Western Jabavu
1955	Meadowlands
	Dube
	Diepkloof
1956	Molapo
	Moletsane
	Tladi
	Dhlamini
	Chiawelo
	Zondi
	Phiri
	Mapetla
	Jabulani
	Naledi
1958	Emdeni
	Senoane
	Zola

It's short and easy to say, and the people are already using it

Africans like the name of Soweto

By MHLOLI

AFTER MANY MONTHS of brain-racking the Johannesburg City Council has at last decided to give the name SOWETO to the complex of African townships to the south-west of the city. The name appears to have met with the approval of the large majority of the Africans who live in it.

DIVIDE AND RULE

> **The most pressing single need of the Native community is more adequate housing. Only by provision of adequate shelter in properly planned native townships can full control over urban natives be regained because only then will it be possible to eliminate the surplus natives who do not seek or find an honest living in the cities.**
>
> Dr Werner Eiselen, Secretary for Native Affairs, 1951, in P Wilkinson, 'Providing "Adequate Shelter"'

In building site-and-service and other housing schemes in Soweto, the government's main aim was to assert its control. And this concern became even more central to their thinking after the Defiance Campaign was launched by the African National Congress in 1952, signalling the beginning of mass-based African resistance on a national scale in South Africa. The government's next priority was to secure this control at the minimum cost, and the result may still be seen in virtually every photograph taken of Soweto in the last 40 years: row upon row of identical dirt streets radiating from a central hub, line upon line of drab, cheap, uniform houses, a colourless mind-numbing monotony. It is almost as if the government felt that through regimentation and uniformity it could establish a firmer control that could not be challenged.

For external consumption, government officials tried to present Soweto in a more positive light. Government publications portrayed Soweto as an almost self-sufficient 'city within a city' with its 2 000 'Bantu-owned' shops, 81 sports fields, hostels and beer gardens. Official publications featured success stories such as that of Jeremiah Mofokeng, a 'once humble shepherd in Basutoland' who, by 1956, had accumulated business and other assets worth tens of thousands of pounds in Soweto's city of opportunity. 'Probably nowhere in the world,' claimed the June 1956 edition of *Bantu*, 'would the chances favour a man so much that he could start a prosperous chain of businesses out of £35 capital.'

The message projected to the South African public and the world at large was that Soweto was a place where energy and enterprise were rewarded, and yet the reality could not have been more different. Suffocating regulations stamped out virtually every sign of individual initiative and enterprise. Licences for shopkeepers were tightly restricted and shop owners were prohibited from stocking anything but a limited range of basic necessities. Herbalism and funeral undertaking were the most profitable business enterprises in Soweto, making disease and death its largest industry. Hawking and street vending were mostly prohibited and the daily labourers' pass, which, in earlier years, had allowed a section of the black urban population the freedom to be self-employed, was abolished in 1952. Additions to houses – even simple hen coops – were made either difficult or impossible. From the mid-1950s, in particular, uniformity and control seemed to override all else.

Two labourers en route to the goldfields.

Diversity

The monotonous physical environment of Soweto, however, stands in sharp contrast to the heterogeneous population it housed, for here, jammed into three- and four-roomed matchbox houses, was a population of almost infinite diversity. During the surge of industrial expansion which had taken place on the Witwatersrand since the mid-1930s, Johannesburg had become the main centre of job-seekers from far and wide. By 1948, as much as two thirds of Soweto's population was immigrant, having taken up residence in the Johannesburg/Soweto complex in the 20 years before. They had streamed in from every corner of South Africa on routes and journeys which were extraordinarily difficult and daunting.

A common thread in the lives of many African migrants to the Reef is a contract or a series of contracts on the mines. In the early years of the century, many tramped the weary miles to the mines on foot. Among the most gruelling and epic journeys were undertaken by labour migrants from Mozambique. Herman Mbulane, for example, left his wife and child in 1932 to set out for the Rand.

These studio portraits reveal the diversity of the population housed in Soweto.

Together with three friends, Herman walked through central Mozambique, through the Kruger National Park and other game parks until he reached the Rand. The route they followed was wild country and they were often worried by lions. At night, they slept in trees; during the days, they often had to scavenge to survive and even lion kills provided welcome sustenance. At times swollen rivers and swollen legs delayed them for days before they eventually arrived in Pretoria and then joined the ranks at the mines. After working a six-month contract, Herman escaped the party that was taking him to the train which would have transported him back to Mozambique. Instead, he made his way to the West Rand where he eventually found work as a school caretaker. There followed a job as a dishwasher and then a chef in a restaurant. At this point, his patient climb up the job ladder was halted when he was arrested for not having a proper pass. On his release, Herman sought sanctuary in the anonymity of the major freehold township of Newclare in the western suburbs of Johannesburg, where he fell victim to gang assaults from a second-generation urban youth and the theft of his possessions by the woman with whom he lived. Shortly after this, however, fortune began to smile on Herman. He met and married another South African woman, acquired a pass by underhand means and moved into the squatter settlement in Kliptown. After several successive changes of job and home, he finally secured a safe haven at the site-and-service scheme at Chiawelo, where he now lives.

Other migrant workers came by more roundabout routes. Many of those who arrived from the rural areas of the Northern and Eastern Transvaal (now the Northern Province and Mpumalanga, respectively) came via white farms, small-scale mining, and railway and municipal works, encountering a host of dangers on the way. Women often faced the most challenging journeys of all. Mmatumelo Mqiba was born in Teyateyaneng, Lesotho, in the early 1940s. Her family was desperately poor and, in her late teens, she was abducted by her husband-to-be – a fashion that was becoming increasingly common in Lesotho at the time. It was customary in such instances for the man to pay compensation to the wife's family, but on this occasion, Mmatumelo's husband did not. Instead, after fathering two children, he vanished to the Rand. Left destitute, Mmatumelo also migrated to the Rand where she joined women friends from Lesotho who found themselves in the same position and earned a living in the slums of Johannesburg and Benoni brewing beer and knitting.

The pressures of urban life gave rise to new social organisations and movements, especially among Africans. For many of those transported into the urban environment, the quest for order remained of paramount concern. Evangelical and Zionist churches attracted increasingly large congregations. Among their main attractions were faith healing in the high mortality urban environment and a new moral discipline which would bind families together, curb liquor consumption and provide a new spirit of community.

The 'Russians' on a train.

Burial societies were yet another way in which Sowetans came together and attempted to create a form of stability in an otherwise insecure and unstable world. These mutual aid societies – often known to Sowetans as 'neighbourhood societies' (*lekhotla la motsi* in Sotho and *ibandla lomzi* in Zulu) – provided their members with financial and other assistance when a death occurred in the family. This assistance was essential as funerals were large-scale, grand events in the township which followed lengthy and often costly rituals: an ox or goat was usually slaughtered and a huge feast provided to the mourners after the burial, and the costs of the casket and hearse were often exorbitant. Burial societies thus guarded against potential financial ruin and reinforced a strong community spirit.

More violent social movements also began to emerge. One of the most prominent was a Basotho immigrant gang. In 1947, increasing numbers of Basotho migrants working on the mines began to take jobs in the heavy engineering sector in the towns. At first, the immigrants formed two rival gangs, 'the Russians' and 'the Japanese'. As news began to filter through of the dropping of atom bombs on Hiroshima and Nagasaki in Japan, the name 'Japanese' was quietly dropped in favour of the common title of 'Russians', and so the two gangs merged. Letsatsi Radebe explains that the name became popular 'because many of the Basotho men went to war. After the war, they thought that they were the powerful people who had stopped the Germans. That's why they coined the name "Russians"'. Before long, the Russians again divided into two separate factions, the Matsieng and Ha-Molapo. The Matsieng and Ha-Molapo came from different regions of Lesotho and members of the different factions could be identified by the different blankets they wore.

Tsotsi, a member of a Russian gang in Soweto, explains that the Matsieng 'wore *Mafitori* blankets which were red with aeroplane emblems in front'. The Ha-Molapo wore a blanket called *Thapo ya Seiso* which was black with red stripes at the side. These blankets were expensive, however, and Tsotsi explains that the 'grey blankets were the ones which were mostly used in those days'. Radebe adds that it did not matter whether 'it was hot or cold. A Russian would have his blanket on', and Selatial Maake describes how 'their blankets always cover their mouths and nose. You only see their eyes. Some got their hats on, and you only see the eyes. You won't even recognise him under that blanket'.

Russians engaged in an extended sequence of fights – among themselves and with youth gangs, known as 'tsotsis'. Benoni, Newclare and Soweto were the main battlegrounds of these encounters – with up to 1 000 combatants – but they also spread across the length and breadth of the Rand. Some social commentators have ascribed these battles to the Russians' love of fighting. These warriors had been schooled in fighting as herd boys in the mountains of Lesotho and so, it was explained, their behaviour may be seen as a product of a rural socialisation. On another level, however, the Russians may have banded together to establish a measure of security and control in a forbidding urban world. They sought security against the attacks by tsotsis, of which all migrant and immigrant groups were particular targets. They sought some measure of control over housing and squatter camps at a time when residential space was in great demand and they especially sought control over the squads of Basotho women who were flocking to the Rand.

Discipline among the Russians was harsh and was applied equally violently to women. Tsotsi explains how 'if you are a Russian and loved a certain woman, you didn't propose. You just told her to come with you. And she will come and the others will know that she is yours. If someone from Matsieng stole my woman and refused to release her, I would take my gang and fight for her. If we won, we would take her and all other things, including blankets, and she would be with us forever'.

As Tsotsi's story illustrates, a woman who ran away from a Russian was treated with cruelty. 'This man who blows a whistle runs in the front and we would tell this woman that she had to catch him and we would beat her. I remember one year we fetched a woman from Lens [who had absconded with another man] and brought her here on foot. When she arrived here, she said, "I am tired and thirsty." The Russians pissed in a tin, a condensed milk tin, and they said, "Drink." She drank and then she died.'

The Soweto suburb of Naledi, where many of the Russians lived, was entirely dominated by the Basotho. Letsatsi Radebe explains that you wouldn't find tsotsis where the Russians lived: 'The tsotsis would go to other areas,' he said. 'The Russians were running the show. They would take protection money. They would come to me and say they were coming for money to protect me against hooligans. In Naledi, the people were afraid of the Russians.'

Many other new residents in Soweto gathered together in similar, but much less violent, social groups. Each had its own distinct values, customs, styles of dress and musical traditions, and each contributed in its own way to the variety of early Soweto.

Entrenching the divisions

South African policy-makers did not understand Soweto's diverse community, and imposed their own divisions on the population – with little regard for social reality. The officials divided the black urban population into the categories of tribal (migrant), semi-tribal (immigrant) and detribalised (urban). They believed their most serious problem was among the urbanised community and so they tried to prevent new additions to its ranks. White officialdom saw the immigrant section of the black urban population as being divided by traditional values and 'tribal affiliations' and tried to perpetuate these through ethnic zoning, mother tongue schooling and similar policies. The migrant group were excluded from permanent residence in the towns – unless they had worked 15 continuous years in the same urban area, or 10 continuous years for the same employer – and were compelled to live in bachelor hostel accommodation.

A fourth group was totally and permanently excluded from the towns. These were the labourers on white farms. White farmers had been one of the main constituencies that had brought the Nationalist Party to power in 1948. The new government was thus keen to protect the farmers' dwindling labour force. Nthato Motlana explains the predicament of black farm workers: 'If you were born on a farm, your identity document would define you as a farm-born black and that status could never change and you'd never be entitled, under any circumstances whatsoever, to come into an urban area to look for work. It was intended to assure the white farmer of cheap available labour at all times. Once you're in town, blacks were then classified under several categories.' The legal framework required to support the new structure of division and control was put in place with the passage of The Native Laws Amendment Act and the misleadingly named Abolition of Passes Act in 1952.

The despised but necessary pass.

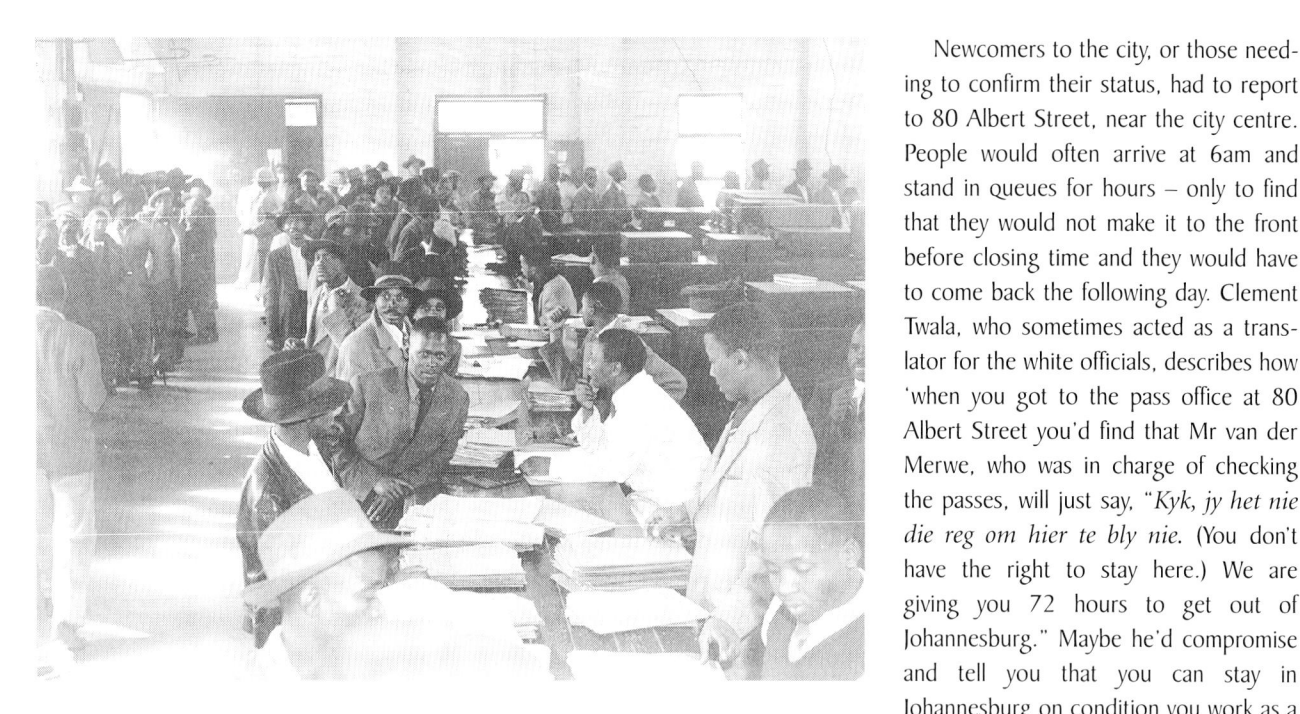

In order to clarify their legal status, black South Africans braved long queues at the pass office each day.

Newcomers to the city, or those needing to confirm their status, had to report to 80 Albert Street, near the city centre. People would often arrive at 6am and stand in queues for hours – only to find that they would not make it to the front before closing time and they would have to come back the following day. Clement Twala, who sometimes acted as a translator for the white officials, describes how 'when you got to the pass office at 80 Albert Street you'd find that Mr van der Merwe, who was in charge of checking the passes, will just say, "*Kyk, jy het nie die reg om hier te bly nie.* (You don't have the right to stay here.) We are giving you 72 hours to get out of Johannesburg." Maybe he'd compromise and tell you that you can stay in Johannesburg on condition you work as a domestic servant. Now you can imagine a person with a matric becoming a garden boy'.

Selatial Maake, who was living in Soweto at the time, recalls being refused a pass: 'I went there to the queue and they called me and they interviewed me. He was writing, he gave me the stamp and I was sure that I was ready. He said, "OK, take this paper and go to that table." Ooh, I was sure... I took the paper with a smile. I gave it to the white man sitting behind the desk. He said, "*Ja, jong... ja, ek verstaan. Ek wil jou nie glo nie.*" (Yes, man... I understand. I just don't want to believe you.) He just took the stamp, 72 hours to get out of Johannesburg...[I thought to myself] Oh, no... not again.'

More than 2 000 work seekers were turned away from the Johannesburg area every month. In 1956 Hendrik Verwoerd, the Minister of Native Affairs, triumphantly declared that 25 331 blacks had been turned away from the Witwatersrand.

After a person was 'endorsed out', the pass official would shout for an 'escort'. Clement Twala explains that the escort would 'come and take you right into a place called *ispaya* (the kraal). The kraal was just an open space where officials were processing people to be shipped back to their places of origin'. One day, Twala saw a person committing suicide because he had been 'endorsed out' but had nowhere else to go because he had given up his home in the rural area to come to the city.

In the past the Native work-seeker was prepared to leave his family in the rural areas and poured to the city to take up whatever employment was offering (sic). Today, due to the enforcement of influx control, he fears that if he returns to his home he may not be allowed to go back to the city. Therefore there is an increasing tendency for the immigrant work-seeker to be accompanied by his family.

Johannesburg Non-European Affairs Department, 1955

Hostel life

The tightening grip of the pass laws forced many migrant workers into making a fateful decision – to remain migrants or to raise a family in town. The large-scale provision of 'family' housing also persuaded many migrants to join the more permanently urbanised section of Johannesburg's African population. Many other migrants, despite growing job insecurity and the certainty that they would be restricted to the most arduous jobs, took the opposite decision. The result was that the large group of Africans that worked in Johannesburg who were neither entirely urban nor entirely rural – and who had not made a decision as to which lifestyle they would follow – were gradually thinned out. A much sharper line of division between township dwellers and migrants began to be defined.

The building of hostels further entrenched this division. Until the mid 1950s, many migrant workers lived on their employers' premises in the city. Zulu flat cleaners, for example, were accommodated in the rapidly multiplying number of apartment blocks in the city and its neighbouring suburbs. Other migrants lived as real or fictitious 'husbands' of female domestics in the servants' quarters of white households, or *ekitcheneng* ('in the kitchen'), as the migrants themselves termed it. Until then, the authorities had kept no effective check on their presence. It was only when the City Council re-organised its inspectorate in 1953 that it found 25 000 African men living on these premises. Thousands more single male migrants were able to rent shacks in the Western Areas and the freehold township of Alexandra in the east. These lifestyles and places of residence could serve as a bridge between migration and full urbanisation over which, in the past, many had crossed, but many more had in fact remained obstinately in the middle. Over the next four years, however, the government took stringent action to eliminate these accommodation options for migrants. In 1954–5, the Johannesburg City Council embarked on an energetic campaign to clear the male partners of female domestics from the white suburbs. In 1955–6, all subtenants were removed from the Western Areas, but the final blow came in 1956 when the government passed the Natives (Urban Areas) Amendment Act No. 12 of 1955, popularly known as the 'Locations in the Sky Act'. This legislation compelled flat cleaners who were living in the city to move to the new Dube hostel which was in the process of construction in Soweto. Many of those living in the Western Areas and the white suburbs were thus forced to move. And so the previously blurred line dividing migrant and urban became increasingly defined.

The pace of hostel construction consequently accelerated in the late 1950s and 1960s. Each hostel was reserved largely for a particular ethnic group. This was in line with National Party policy of entrenching 'tribal' differences. Dube Hostel, for example, was allocated to Nguni language speakers and virtually all of the occupants were Zulu. Nancefield Hostel, on the other hand, was reserved for Sotho-speakers. Living conditions in these hostels were grim. The Nationalist government rejected the JCC's plans for more comfortable accommodation and, instead, insisted on row upon row of crudely built barrack-like structures. Each bungalow accommodated 16 men who were given a bed without a mattress and a tiny locker for possessions.

The Act stipulated that the Zulu flat cleaners who were being forced to move into Dube Hostel be removed from the city within 12 months, but the hostels were not ready for occupation and the displaced cleaners faced some of the worst hostel conditions.

For the first few months, there was neither electricity nor cooking facilities. Most hostel dwellers remember the harshness of their lives. For Stephen Tshabalala, one of his worst experiences was the poor bathroom facilities: 'What I didn't like about the inside of the hostel was the arrangement of the toilets. We had six toilets in a row so you could see through. I would talk to a man next door and ask him for a toilet roll if I didn't have any. We would just converse while sitting there and doing our thing.'

Lesibana James Shika explains that he felt that he was being treated like an animal. He also resented the tight control exerted by the hostel superintendent and his staff:

Communal toilets in the hostels allowed no privacy.

> *We lived in a place that turned us into animals. What do I mean by animal? I mean that when your wife came to visit you, she had to wait at the gate. A policeman would come looking for your number. She would have to remain at the gate and that was where you were expected to talk to her and finish all your business. You returned to your bungalow alone. Now I think that kind of life was not very pleasant... This hostel also had its own nature. It oppressed us. They did not want us to do anything in the hostel. If you were found selling some vegetables or liquor, they would arrest you and take you to prison. We never knew when raids were going to happen. They would come in the middle of the night when you were sleeping and ask you for your permit. The thing about the hostel permit was that you must have paid your rent by the 7th of every month, failing which your belongings would be thrown out the very next day. When you came back from work, your pots, blankets and everything would be in the office. After paying, they would relocate you anywhere they liked. Sometimes, when you went to work in the morning, somebody pretended that he was sick only to steal your possessions during the day. When you came back from work, you'd find your place in a mess. You would also have to have a special pass to go out at night. We didn't live in this place because we liked it. We came here because we were forced to. We couldn't go anywhere else.*

Shika goes on to complain about the lack of respect among hostel dwellers:

> *In the township, you lived with respect for your neighbours and that built unity. Here, there was nothing like that. There was no respect and as a result there was no life. Life was not safe. A person came and blew their nose in front of you while you were eating. That is not respect...*

For Ellison Mohlabe, life in Mzimhlope Hostel was hell, probably because he was a lone Pedi in a predominantly Zulu room. 'You didn't live with your friends; you just lived with someone you had met for the first time. They don't know you, they don't care about you; you also don't care about them. So you just lived like animals.'

The cooking area in Dube Hostel.

It must be said, however, that Mohlabe's experience was not typical. For other migrants, hostel life was less alienating because they could immerse themselves among hostel networks of relatives and neighbours from their home villages. These neighbourhood groups imposed a personal discipline on migrants as well as providing a reasonably satisfying social life. They bear witness to the strength of the human spirit, and the capacity of people to humanise even the bleakest circumstances.

Andreas Njokwe remembers:

> *We were not allowed to visit the townships. Our elders warned us all against township girls who might turn us into absconders. The main worry was tsotsi youth who did not hesitate to stab migrants for their money. So, during our stay on the Rand, we did not meet girls. The activities which occupied our leisure time was singing Ingoma and Isicathamiya. We did this within the premises of the hostel.*

Shadrack Khumalo makes the same point:

❝ We were not allowed by the elders to propose living with township girls. They told us they would be infected with syphilis. The elders also controlled the way youngsters spent their money. The youngsters were expected to give their wages to the elders so that they could keep the money for them until such time that they were going to their parents in the countryside. There was absolute obedience to the elders. The youngsters also cooked for them. ❞

This rigid discipline, including the control exercised by elders over the wages of younger men, was common in the hostels. So too was a social life centred on *Isicathamiya* singing and traditional dancing. Samuel Ndebele remembers with some nostalgia:

❝ If there was a challenge from Dube or Imhlazani hostels, we would perform our traditional Zulu songs and dances. We would compete for a goat that would be taken by the winners. We would drink and drink, buying beer from the group that we visited. We would dance and dance until we went home. ❞

Migrants who were enmeshed in the culture of the hostels were disdainful of township life and placed a high value on rural ways. Augustine Ngobo 'never considered buying a house in the township because of the way I was brought up'. He valued the communal life of the country 'where you cannot starve while other people have food to eat. In the township, people are different. Instead of supporting you, they would rather laugh at you'. Shadrack Khumalo expresses similar sentiments. He preferred rural life 'because you can keep livestock as well as engage in farming'. Andreas Njokwe added that he did not like to find himself in a situation where he had to pay rent. He also 'did not like the kind of life led by township children, both boys and girls'. Hostels and the attitudes of the residents, therefore, reinforced and perpetuated this self-contained migrant culture and destroyed many of the bridges into urban life that had existed before.

The building of hostels in the settled urban communities in Soweto, however, aroused great controversy and opposition. Nthato Motlana recalls:

❝ Many, many meetings were held and people protested. I was part of that whole movement that said, "You cannot, in all conscience, build single-sex hostels in the midst of settled communities." They would be, we said, centres of crime. Young women would be raped and family stability would be disturbed. We campaigned vigorously for settled communities where men would be allowed to bring their wives from the country, to come and live with their families here. But Dr Verwoerd and his Mafia knew better than we all did and he built the hostels in the midst of these communities and, since then, our lives have never been the same. ❞

Nevertheless, despite these fears and prejudices, a good deal of friendly interaction also took place. Murphy Morobe recalls that 'we generally tended to associate with hostel dwellers around the weekend because many of the hostels had soccer grounds. Us young boys would also go and shower and use the hostel facilities. There weren't tensions'.

Similarly, the desire of many migrants to seal themselves off from what they perceived as the corrupting influence of urban women meant that they were not the sexual threat that many Soweto families had imagined. Linda Masemola, for example, occupied a house directly opposite the Mzimhlope Hostel. 'We were next to a hostel and I thought, well, they are going to give us men. That's why they say most of the women without men should come and stay in Mzimhlope. It didn't happen. I didn't have any proposal from the hostel people.'

In the long term, however, Dr Motlana and his neighbours were justified in their alarm. Ethnic grouping and the siting of hostels among the settled urban communities did, indeed, contain the seeds of disaster, and this would become abundantly clear in the 1970s and 80s.

Overcrowded conditions on trains led to the practice known as 'staff-riding'.

The Dube Riots

Ethnic conflict occurred soon after the Dube hostel was built, when youth gangs, or tsotsis, began to prey on Dube's hostel dwellers as they made their way to and from work. The tsotsi phenomenon had emerged in the 1940s and 1950s as a direct result of rapid large-scale urbanisation. Until the late 50s, more than half of Soweto's school-age population were unable to find places in school. In addition, most employers were reluctant to employ urban youth whom they believed to be lazy and undisciplined, so many of Soweto's youngsters turned to a life of crime and delinquency. Gangs – the XYs, the Spoilers and the Americans – proliferated and began to rob and harass Soweto's working population. A favoured tsotsi target were commuters, as these workers spent long hours travelling to and from work by train and walking to and from the train station. Few buses served the township and few black people owned cars so the trains were always packed to capacity. Many people were thus forced to travel, clinging to the outside of the carriages. This was commonly known as 'staff-riding', and it was under these circumstances that the tsotsis operated – with some ease.

The Friday afternoon and evening trains, in particular, became known as 'the death traps'. All commuters were likely victims but the newly arrived Zulu hostel dwellers, not yet familiar with township life, were easy prey. Stephen Tshabalala tells how 'these Zulus would go into the trains after they've had their pay packets and now there were tsotsis who were pickpockets in the trains. So they would pickpocket almost everybody, people who were not aware of what the tsotsis were doing'.

Lesibana James Shika, a Zulu hostel dweller who travelled daily on the trains, remembers the experience. 'Now, when you enter the door, everyone is squashed. You find tsotsis standing at the door as if they too are entering but instead they pickpocket you. Later you discover that your pockets are empty.' As the Zulu hostel dwellers came under repeated attack, their resentment and discontent grew. Linda Masemola remembers that 'they were tired of being pickpocketed at the stations'. They began to band together for protection – and reprisals – against their attackers. 'These Zulus got mad about this,' says Stephen Tshabalala, 'because they were losing money and they decided that there was only one thing they could do – they had to beat up these tsotsis. Now, how were the Zulus going to identify the tsotsis from the ordinary person? They realised that tsotsis wore caps. So they had a saying that said, *Shayikepisi kuphumutsotsi*. That means "hit the cap and the tsotsi will come out". So they got into the trains and started hitting the cap. What they forgot was that the Russians also wore caps and some of the Russians didn't carry blankets in the trains. They're just like tsotsis because their trousers were also small, they were 16–14 bottoms. So they looked very much like tsotsis and they wore takkies as well.'

The scene was now set for one of Soweto's worst ethnic conflicts – a clash between hostel dwellers, tsotsis and Russians. On the weekend of 14 and 15 September 1957, the conflict reached its climax in what later became known as the Dube Riots.

The riots were triggered when Zulu inmates from Dube Hostel attacked a funeral procession of Basotho. 'When we were above Inhlanzane station, we were accompanied by police,' describes one member of the procession. 'Many Zulus came from the direction of Meadowlands. The whites said, "Stop!", and the Zulus said, "Never!" They hit a police officer and, after he fell, another officer said, "Fire!" They used a machine gun and that's when the Zulus stopped. Many of them were dead, I couldn't even count them.'

The official report recounts a similar story. 'A large mob of Zulus armed with *knobkieries*, battle axes, cane knives and guns fired several shots at the crowd. On this, the police who were escorting the Basotho party were ordered to fire. Several bursts were fired from Sten guns, the hostile mob were dispersed and the funeral cortège proceeded on its way. Six Zulus were killed by the fire of the police.'

But the story would not end there. On the way back from the cemetery, the Basotho procession passed by the gates of Dube Hostel, and another three Zulus were shot dead by the police in the encounter that ensued. The fighting between Zulu hostel dwellers and Basuto Russians continued beyond the incident on this day, spreading to more general clashes between Zulu and Basotho residents in various areas of Soweto. Over 50 people were dead by the time the fighting eventually came to an end. Fanyana Mazibuko describes what he remembers of the first day of the riots:

I was walking to school when I realised that people were running around screaming and when I listened carefully, I heard the people saying, "the Zulus are coming". I was far from home and far from school, sort of in the middle, and I knew nobody in the immediate neighbourhood. And, as people were running around, I realised that the trenches that were being dug for the sewerage were the only place I could duck into, so I jumped into one of the pipes and I sat it out for most of the day, close to seven or eight hours. I heard gunshots and all sorts of screams. I could hear right almost on top of me people were fighting. When I decided to go out I thought everything had stopped, but what I saw was an ugly sight of men lying around with cement packets covering their bodies. At a distance, police were moving around looking at the corpses and I walked home sickened and confused... I didn't go to school that day.

Tensions later subsided and calm was restored. Stephen Tshabalala remembers:

But now when it stopped, they were friends again. There were no other reprisals whatsoever. It just stopped and they were all friends. We found the Russians drinking together with the Zulus in the hostel. It was beautiful again after that fight. In the morning, people would just get their towels and go to Dube Hostel and wash, laughing and joking, things like that.

Ethnic zoning

Ethnic zoning created additional lines of division between Soweto's permanent residents. Verwoerd justified the ruling by stating that 'those who belong together naturally want to live near one another, and the policy of ethnic grouping will lead to the development of an intensified community spirit'.

For Sowetans, the ruling meant that houses were allocated according to ethnic group, that traders could only purchase shops within their own ethnic area, and that children were forced to attend a school of their ethnic origin. Naledi, Mapetla, Tladi, Moletsane and Phiri were set aside for the Sotho- and Tswana-speaking people. Chiawelo was for the Tsonga- and Venda-speaking people and Dlamini, Senaoane, Zola, Zondi, Jabulani, Emdeni and White City were for the Zulu and Xhosa Nguni-speakers.

The white nationalist press supported the idea of segregation, saying that black people have an 'instinctive tendency' to want to live with their own group. One newspaper concluded that, 'the advantages of ethnic grouping are both psychological and factual and preserve for the Bantu that which we prize for ourselves in our own community: firm tradition, respect for natural leaders, preservation of mother tongue and mutual loyalties'.

The *Bantu World* strongly disagreed, however, insisting that 'the policy is a means of keeping the evil of tribalism alive and preventing Africans from welding themselves into one nation'.

The notion of ethnic grouping was also rejected by the Johannesburg City Council, although for rather different reasons than those held by township residents: 'The arbitrary separation of peoples on a racial basis is psychologically unsound and encourages the emergence of arrogance and militant racial consciousness which, in the case of primitive peoples, such as the South African Bantu, is always fraught with the very real danger of large-scale rioting and civil disorder.' The Council also pointed out that the policy ignored the fact that many of the inhabitants of the township were born and raised in Johannesburg and would know nothing of the tribal discipline the system was supposed to encourage.

The township residents had their own reasons for opposing the government's attempts to create distinct ethnic areas. The residents may have attached importance to their ethnic identities but they resented having their world ordered according to the government's perception of 'tribal loyalties'. They believed that the policy of ethnic grouping was simply the government's attempt to apply their maxim of 'divide and rule' within black communities. Rhoda Khumalo remembers: 'We were really upset because we had friends who were Zulus, we had friends who were Sothos but now we were going to be divided.' Ethel Leisa agrees:

> *We did not know that one was this and the other was that. We were happy. We were a unit. But now, uh-uh. I think the government discovered that when we were one group, we danced to the same music but if they divided us they were able to control us.*

Divisions did begin to develop as a result of the new policy. People who had previously lived together without a clear sense of tribal divisions, were now confronted with 'no go areas'. Susan Shabangu describes what happened among her group of school friends. 'Now we were divided as Zulus, Xhosas and Sothos in different schools. That created a lot of animosity while we were growing up in the sense that we would fight on the basis of languages. We'd say, "These are Xhosas, we've got nothing to do with them."' Sibongile Mkhabela, who grew up in Zola, elaborates on this point:

> *Zola is a Zulu area so, somehow, you were forced to unite on the basis of your language. A street away from my street is Naledi, a Sotho area. As long as I was walking in the streets of Zola, I was perfectly safe. But if I crossed the street into Naledi, then I'd have problems. As soon as I walked there I'd be a stranger to every kid and therefore a target. Parents were not involved. They'd say, "You go buy meat in Naledi," and they'd say it with a perfectly straight face. And you can't say no. You've got to go there. You'd collect a few of your friends; you were very anxious. You crossed the street, ran to the shop, bought meat, and ran back. You'd be lucky if you were not chased. Most of the time you were chased right into the shop. And the boys would wait for you outside the shop and you'd have to find a way of running back into Zola.*

Letsatsi Radebe tells how 'most of the people who were staying at Orlando were afraid to go down to Zola. The Zola area has got a Zulu name. They say *Mshayeazafe, Mshayeazafe* (Hit him until he dies)'.

Making ends meet

Influx control did, however, provide permanent or semi-permanent residence to a settled section of the African urban population, who were thus available to perform the semi-skilled and non-manual jobs in the new industrial economy. Employers invariably preferred to hire migrants for hard manual work. For skilled and semi-skilled work, however, they required a more literate and more stable labour force which, once trained, did not repeatedly leave employment to return home. Clement Twala, who lived in Soweto and worked as a clerk in the pass office, explains how this determined job opportunities of work seekers:

" *Section 10(1)(a) is supposed to be the best qualification. A 10(1)(a) is a person born in Johannesburg and has a birth certificate. It means you get the best jobs, like a clerk or a messenger. A white-collar job is for 10(1)(a). A section 10(1)(b) is a person who does not have a birth certificate but has enough proof that he is born and bred in Johannesburg. 10(1)(b) can also do a white-collar job... A 10(1)(c) is conditional employment. It means that this person comes from outside or has worked in Johannesburg for quite a number of years, but was not born in Johannesburg. Before you can get a white-collar job, you'll have to work as a domestic for quite a number of years. After 15 years, you can apply for a white-collar job. This conditional employment also affects your accommodation. If they find that you don't have a house in Soweto and you want to be on the waiting list, the authorities will say to you, "Look, according to Influx Control you're an outsider. You're not born and bred in Johannesburg. You must stick to the same employer for 15 years, then we'll be able to change your qualification to 10(1)(b); then you can apply for accommodation." *

As Twala suggests, 'white-collar' work was a key aspiration for many Sowetans. Also, because Johannesburg was the centre of the finance, business and service sectors of the South African economy, many more Sowetans were able to enter these categories of work and were far better off than, for example, those who lived in townships on the East Rand where most of the available work was in the surrounding factories. However, even in Johannesburg, fewer white-collar and non-manual jobs were available than there was demand.

Most Sowetans remained trapped in unskilled and sometimes semi-skilled manual jobs. Wages in these areas of employment were low and even declined between the late 1940s and the late 1950s. This was partly because African trade unions came under heavy attack in this period. The Minister of Labour, BJ Schoeman, frankly described his Bantu Labour Regulations Act of 1954 as a measure 'to bleed African trade unions dry'. An additional reason was the practice of hiring migrant labourers for work in factories at lower wages – which depressed the average wage level.

Poverty, then, was a very real and constant factor of the daily life of ordinary Sowetans. Most Sowetans suffered the hard grind of work from dawn to dusk. While husbands worked in the factories, wives worked as domestics or washerwomen, or had to engage in illegal activities such as brewing and selling liquor.

In the struggle to make ends meet, the people of Soweto began to develop or modify social institutions and networks of mutual sharing and support. In particular areas, this helped to create an extremely powerful community spirit.

The confined space of Soweto's houses contributed considerably to this sense of camaraderie, as much of the social life and social interaction took place when friends, couples, families abandoned their cramped matchboxes and took to the streets. By co-operating and sharing in neighbourhood

Much of the social interaction in Soweto took place outside the cramped confines of their matchbox houses.

groups, Sowetans were able to soften some of the harshness of life and develop a civic culture which would help block government strategies of control and division. In the 1950s, networks of mutual assistance developed to meet the challenges that faced families day to day. Rhoda Khumalo, who lived in Meadowlands, remembers how her neighbour helped her manage the competing demands of family and work:

> I started work at six in the morning and I had to leave home very early because we didn't have good transport. I was out of the house at 4.30am and arrived home very late. I used to ask my neighbour that, because my kids they were small, to open the house for them when they came back from school. And then my neighbour used to tell them, "Now it's time to clean. You must clean the house because your mum is at work." They also made the fire at half-past four so that I could come back and start cooking. Never mind that I came very late. They were small and couldn't cook so I had to cook for them.

Linda Masemola of Mzimhlope had a similar experience:

> With the help of both my neighbours I survived. If I didn't have any money, I just used to tell them, "Mama, I'm leaving and there's nothing for the children." But when I came back I would find that they've already put something on the stove. On weekends, when I got my wages on a Friday, I used to return their money. All my children used to have one shirt and then they used to wash in the evening, and then I used to wake up very early in the morning and iron their shirts for them. That's how I survived.

Ethel Leisa tells the same story. 'You could ask a person to cook some meat for you while you went to work. When you came back you would find it cooked. We were so friendly.'

People found ways to supplement their paltry salaries. Rhoda Khumalo tells how, in Meadowlands, 'my mum started to buy some vegetables, tomatoes and onions and all that. And then we put them in dishes and we would go around to sell them so as to survive and pay the rent'. On weekends, Linda Masemola also 'used to go to the grounds and sell porridge and meat for about 20 cents, two shillings'. Fanyana Mazibuko also remembers making extra income in his neighbourhood:

The kitchen in a Soweto dwelling.

> My aunt, with whom I lived, and other women in the area used to survive on selling homemade brew. From time to time, they would be raided by the police from Moroka police station and I was one of the little boys who used to sit outside the squatter camp to watch for the police. We gave a particular sound, a tarzan-like sound, to indicate to the old ladies that the police were on their way. And that kept the police frustrated because, every time they came, the brew would be returned to their holes just outside the township and if they found them these drums belonged to no one.

A wedding was a great opportunity for celebration in the township.

Weddings and parties were an opportunity for the neighbourhood to get together and celebrate: 'If we make weddings and parties, we allowed everybody to come and enjoy herself. We used to go there and look at the wedding and after that we got that meal. They didn't say, "No, you are not going to eat here because you were not invited." They just take us as brothers and sisters,' says Rhoda Khumalo.

Stokvels were voluntary associations or credit unions which raised money. The members of a *stokvel* – each with a name such as 'Cash Money', or 'One Day Makes No Harm' – would organise parties which sometimes lasted for two or three days. At these parties, the food, the drinks, the peanuts, the popcorn, everything was for sale. *Stokvels* were usually very well attended – most guests knew that they may be the ones organising the next *stokvel* and would then be dependent on the goodwill of their friends and neighbours to attend. Some exclusive *stokvels* were by invitation only, but they generated large sums of money for the township residents each month while also providing residents with entertainment and opportunities for social interaction.

Political resistance

The various laws and regulations of the 1950s which were aimed at dividing and controlling the black population were, in many ways, a response to the tide of black nationalism that had emerged during that decade. Mounting black defiance produced intensified efforts at repression and control and, at the same time, the repression simply served to heighten black resistance. The pass laws were undoubtedly the central grievance of the black urban population. Forced removals and unaffordable rents came a close second. During the 1950s, Sowetans mobilised themselves against all three.

Nthato Motlana remembers: 'You would leave Braamfontein station to find, hidden behind the building, a squad of cops, who would line up thousands of blacks and check their documents.'

Mass meetings became a feature of black urban life.

The campaign gained the most support in the Eastern Cape but Sowetans also joined the fight against the government's discriminatory practices. In Soweto, the pass law was singled out as the most important local grievance. John Nkadimeng, who later became an ANC, SACTU and SACP leader, was jailed for not having his pass and recalls what led him to join the defiance campaign:

❝ *I saw things in jail that I never expected to see there. It was terrible. I was absolutely angry. I was sick because I knew that I had not committed any crime. I knew that I had not done anything wrong! Except this bloody rubbish of the pass! And they took me to jail for such a long time and got me mixed up with terrible criminals! The campaign of the ANC against pass laws attracted me because I thought that was an evil law. I thought that the only thing I could do was to work to obliterate that law, to get rid of it, get it out of the way. So I joined the defiance campaign. We wanted to go out in the street to sing and walk about in town without any documents so that we can court arrest. The police spotted us during the day when we were singing and so we didn't really defy we just walked into the police van.* ❞

Elias Motsoaledi explains how he encouraged Sowetans to participate:

❝ *The best way of organising was a house-to-house campaign. I remember, in Mzimhlope, we did each and every house right from the top to the other side of the railway side, each and every house... There were mixed feelings towards the campaign. Some people would say, "Well, we can't do anything to a European; you are long defeated", and it is your duty to convince him of the necessity to fight back. And then some even chased you away. Sometimes you would argue with a man and the wife intervenes.* ❞

Motsoaledi also explains other ways in which activists tried to popularise their campaigns:

❝ *We took those who understood into a house and continued with political classes in order to give the movement its impetus; you must have real members not only paper members. People did not know the history of the ANC so we had to impart this knowledge to them. Secondly, they needed to know the day-to-day issues which affected them; to make him understand exactly why he was treated the way he was treated. I had so many people from all over Soweto who came to me for political classes. I remember trying to impart this knowledge to someone who was far older than I was. I outlined the difficulties and then he looked at me and said, "This is what I wanted to tell you, you can't tell me that." In other words, you struck the chord and gained the respect of these people because you were able to interpret their aspirations. You were able to articulate all their problems. Then they started to respect you.* ❞

In 1956, the struggle against passes intensified as the laws were extended to women. The government of the Orange Free State had tried to issue passes to women shortly after the formation of the Union of South Africa in 1910. They fiercely resisted this move and thousands of women were jailed for their opposition. After five years of continued resistance, the authorities finally relented – until 1956, when the Nationalist government reinstituted the campaign. The resistance from women was again intense, but this time the government would not back down. Nurses who were without passes were not permitted to be registered, and there were threats that their pensions would be withdrawn. These and other threats finally forced the black women of South Africa to carry the much-maligned pass books.

The Criminal Law Amendment Act of 1953, which imposed heavy penalties for civil disobedience, brought an end to the Defiance Campaign and it was followed by a lull in ANC political activity that would last almost two years. This suspension of activities, however, was broken by actions inspired by the Western Areas Removal Scheme, the Bantu Education Act, economic rentals, and the Congress of the People.

Although initially applicable only to black men, the pass laws were amended to include women in 1952. When these changes were implemented in 1956, women naturally protested.

By the 1940s, the Western Areas, with Sophiatown at its centre, had come to inspire contradictory emotions in white and black South Africans. For whites, and particularly for the Nationalist government, it symbolised all the evils of uncontrolled urbanisation. For blacks, it represented one of the few places where Africans could own land, and be free of the innumerable regulations that burdened everyday life in the municipal locations. During this period, the population of Sophiatown, Martindale, and Newclare multiplied rapidly. On these streets, Africans, coloureds, Chinese, Indians and the occasional white mingled easily and it became the cultural heartland of urbanised black Johannesburg.

Sophiatown was adjacent to the white working-class suburb of Westdene, whose residents had long agitated for its removal. A scheme to achieve this was drawn up in the 1940s, but was only acted upon after the Nationalist government came to power. In 1953, a Western Areas Resettlement Board was set up by the government, land was acquired in Meadowlands in Soweto and, a year later, the first houses were being built there to resettle the residents of Sophiatown. In an attempt to resist the scheme, the ANC held mass meetings, drew up a plan of passive resistance through a Reef-wide stayaway and called for volunteers.

Soweto — A History

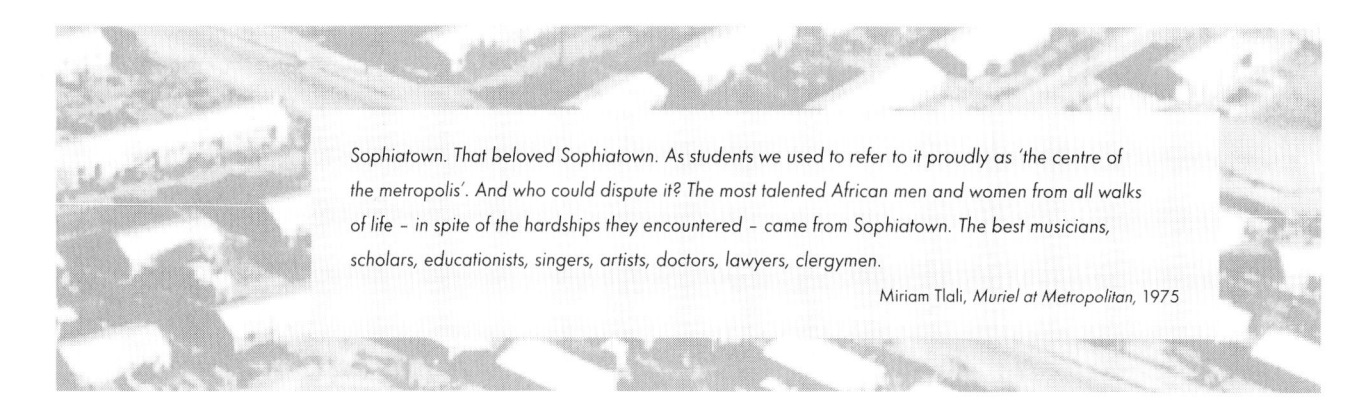

> *Sophiatown. That beloved Sophiatown. As students we used to refer to it proudly as 'the centre of the metropolis'. And who could dispute it? The most talented African men and women from all walks of life – in spite of the hardships they encountered – came from Sophiatown. The best musicians, scholars, educationists, singers, artists, doctors, lawyers, clergymen.*
>
> Miriam Tlali, *Muriel at Metropolitan*, 1975

The government, however, moved quickly to counter these plans, and the removals were advanced by four days and started on 10 February 1955. To carry out the plan, 2 000 armed police flooded the area on foot and in lorries. Aside from isolated acts by tsotsis, the resistance campaign crumbled. Sophiatown residents were removed in their thousands and left in the Meadowlands suburb of Soweto to brood in anger over the manner of their eviction.

In mid-1954, the decision had been announced that economic rental would be imposed on Soweto's residents and, by the time Sophiatown's residents began to arrive in Meadowlands, the boycott of economic rentals in the rest of Soweto was already in full swing. Mass meetings were called and James Mpanza, who opposed the call for boycotts, found himself jeered off the platform by a crowd of 5 000. As a result of the meeting, the Orlando Rent Protest Committee was set up with Soweto sportsman Xorile at its head. To consolidate support for the boycott, Xorile and his committee founded the 'Asinamali' (We have no money) Party which won a massive majority in the Orlando Advisory Board Elections at the end of that year. For the first time in a decade, Mpanza's Sofasonke Party was swept from office. ANC and Communist Party activists were leading members of Xorile's Committee and, according to Elias Motsoaledi, were responsible for much of the organisation and strategic planning of the campaign. At the initial mass meeting in August, at which the boycott was called, ANC activist J Molefe for the first time uttered the call for a wage of £1 a day. This was to become an important campaign issue for the ANC in the stayaways of 1957 and 1958. In the first of a series of legal actions, Xorile's Committee contested economic rents in court and, to the jubilation of Asinamali supporters, the court pronounced in Xorile's favour on 1 November 1954. A succession of court actions by Xorile and the Johannesburg anti-rental co-ordinating committee held economic rents at bay until their final appeal was rejected in December 1958. Thereafter, the boycott rapidly collapsed and the residents of Orlando and Moroka, who made up most of the boycotters, were faced with massive

The ANC organised a protest against the proposed dismantling of Sophiatown and the re-settling of its inhabitants.

rent arrears. Walter Sisulu's subsequent assessment of the campaign was that 'the people relied too heavily on legal victory and should have depended more on the organisation of the masses themselves. The main issue was the demand for a living wage, a minimum of £1 a day'. With the benefit of hindsight, we may agree but what is clear is that the ANC's prominent role in the boycott helped boost its following. At the end of 1956, the ANC swept the Advisory Board elections. In addition, as a result of the agitation, the City Council agreed to subsidise the statutory £15 limit on subeconomic rentals to the level of £20. Another landmark in Soweto's history was the Congress of the People, held at Kliptown between 26 and 27 June 1955. The Congress was the culmination of a two-year campaign aimed at drawing up a charter of demands on behalf of the disenfranchised black population. About 3 000 delegates from all race groups gathered in Kliptown Square to approve the Freedom Charter, which was to remain the ANC's basic policy document for 30 years.

A police truck in Sophiatown.

Popular discontent mounted steadily during 1958. In response, both the ANC and the Pan African Congress (PAC) which had split from the ANC in 1959, launched anti-pass campaigns. On 21 March 1960, the men, women and children of Sharpeville Township burnt their passes at a massive demonstration outside the new police station. Policemen fired their guns into the crowd of 5 000 and 69 people were killed as they fled from the police.

Mtutuzeli Matshoba recalls: 'My mother was a regular reader of newspapers though my father didn't have much schooling. My mother, who was a nurse, used to sit at table in the evening and they would discuss what was in the papers. As children, through curiosity, we would look at the pictures and ask what was happening. And one picture that remains very vivid in my mind is the picture of the Sharpeville shootings.'

Sharpeville and the State of Emergency that followed brought with them a decade of silence for black South Africans. The ANC and PAC were banned and thousands of political activists were jailed or went into exile. The trade unions had effectively been crushed. Sharpeville had marked the end of the era of resistance.

The aftermath of the Sharpeville shooting.

THE LOADED PAUSE

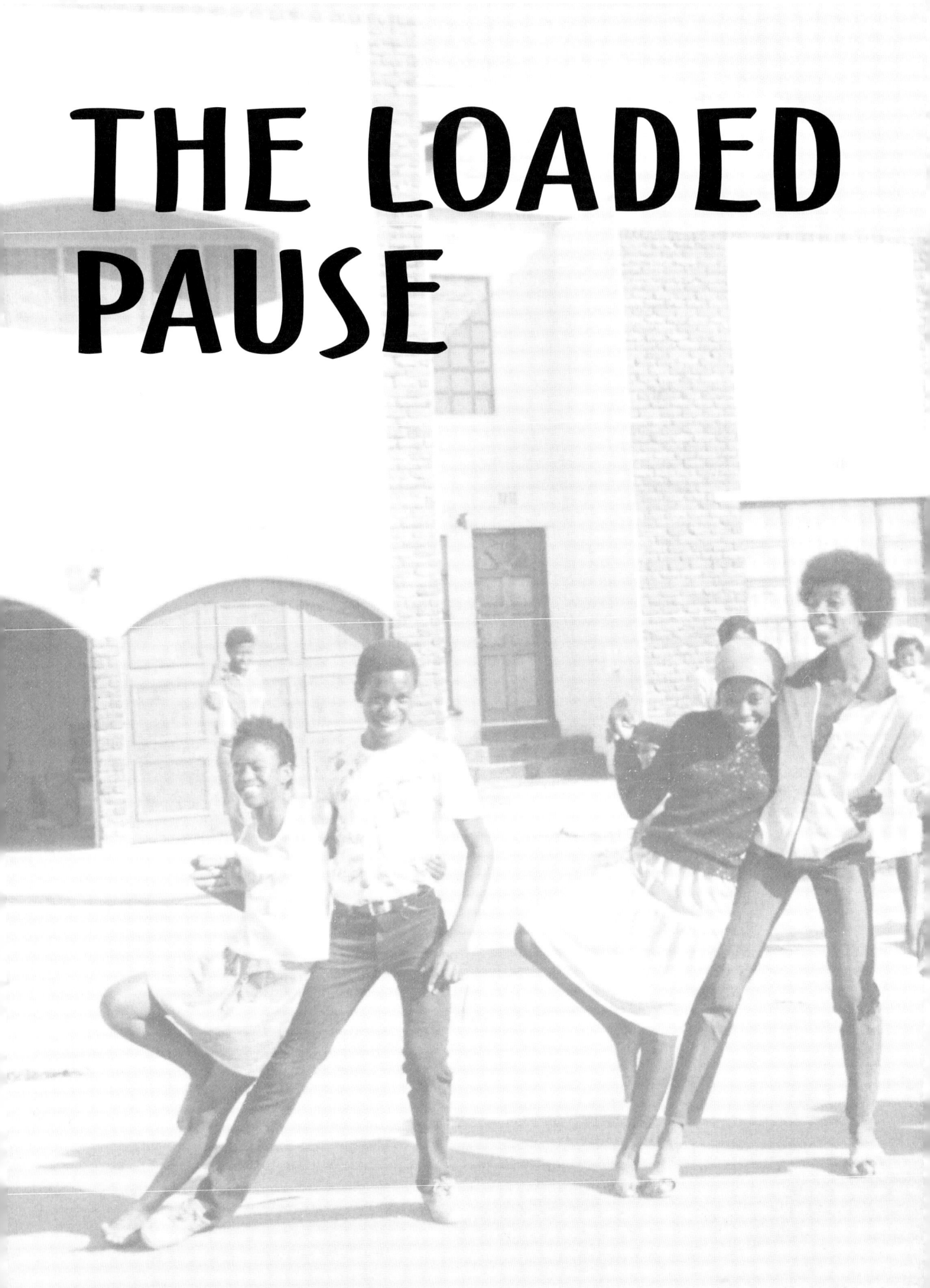

' *Soweto had been a beautiful place to live in... One only had to say Soweto and everyone listened... People from other townships copied our styles and ways. We were trendsetters... We were South Africa.* '

Nomavenda Mathiane, journalist, commentator, Sowetan

The Sharpeville massacre of 21 March 1960 changed the face of South Africa and, with it, the face of Soweto. The banning of the ANC and the introduction of a battery of repressive laws effectively outlawed non-violent political activity and resistance. The ANC, SACP and PAC responded by turning to the armed struggle. New laws which allowed for indefinite detention and the widespread use of torture, combined with the inexperience of the main liberation organisation in such activities, soon led either to the arrest and incarceration of large sections of the leadership or their flight overseas. By 1964, black political resistance in South Africa had been crushed. What followed was a decade of black political dormancy in Soweto and further afield. Nevertheless, these years proved to be a formative period in the development of Soweto, providing a pause during which a more stable, coherent and consolidated black urban culture could take shape.

The move to armed struggle

The first serious discussions regarding the move to armed struggle took place in prisons where some 20 000 activists were detained after the declaration of a state of emergency in 1960. ANC Secretary-General and Soweto resident, Walter Sisulu, recollects: 'What we were planning in gaol was the mobilisation of the entire country... Side by side there was a small group working on the question of the armed struggle.' The core group in these discussions were ANC executive and SACP central committee members drawn from Soweto and Johannesburg. 'Nelson, Duma Nokwe, myself, Joe Slovo, Rusty Bernstein,' Sisulu recalls.

The prisons began to release detainees in June 1960 but, for a while, strategies of civil disobedience rather than armed struggle remained at the centre of the ANC's thinking. On 31 March 1961 the ANC and its allies called for a three-day stayaway in support of a demand for a national convention to decide South Africa's future, failing which a campaign of mass non-violent action would follow. The government responded to the campaign with repressive measures, including nightly searches, arrests without charges, road blocks and a massive display of armoured vehicles and helicopters. Frustrated by the government's unyielding attitude, Mandela, Sisulu and others felt that violent resistance was now the only option. In Gerhart and Karis's *From Protest to Challenge*, Nelson Mandela observed: 'Unless responsible leadership were given to canalise and control the feelings of our people, there would be an outbreak of terrorism which would produce and intensify racial hostility between the races of the country.'

In June 1961, the ANC national executive approved a proposal put forward by Mandela and others for a sabotage campaign. On 16 December, a public holiday in South Africa marking the Voortrekker victory over an attack by Zulu warriors in Natal in 1838, the first blows were struck. The Soweto cell's first sabotage attempt came to a grisly end when the bomb malfunctioned and one of the group, Ed Dube, was killed.

Elias Motsoaledi, who was leading another sabotage attempt which had been synchronised to take place at the same time, remembers the moment vividly:

We used timing devices which were operated by glycerine. When the glycerine came into contact with chemicals, it would ignite. What happened was that these timing devices were not always tested so they leaked and resulted in many casualties. If the police forces were alert at the time, they could have arrested the lot of us because some of the bombs which were hidden in the bonnets of the cars started leaking while they were driving and exploded. I was fortunate because immediately after I heard the sound of a bomb going off in Dube Township, I was able to say, "No, this is untimely. Something must be wrong with the primers." I then said to my unit, "Leave this bomb here." I took the primer to the street lamp to examine it. It was fortunate because about 10 paces after I had left the bomb, it went off. So we scattered all over and ran away.

Over the next 18 months, 30 targets were attacked. During the same period, an underground railway was set up between Soweto and Botswana to ferry the recruits of Umkhonto we Sizwe (MK) – the armed wing of the ANC – for military training. Much of this operation was amateur in nature and, armed with new laws which permitted an almost unrestricted use of torture, the security forces closed in on both MK and the underground ANC. During 1962, many MK members were arrested and, on 12 July 1963, virtually the entire MK High Command was captured at a farm named Rivonia just outside Johannesburg. Walter Sisulu and Elias Motsoaledi were two of the ten people arrested that day. The backbone of internal resistance was broken.

Cape Times   13 July 1963

'A.N.C. HIDE-OUT' SMASHED

18 Held at Luxury Rand Home

News headline of Rivonia raid.

Boom time

The reaction of foreign capital and big business to the 1960 Sharpeville massacre had been panic, and money flooded out of the country. By the end of 1960, South Africa faced the worst balance of payments crisis since the Great Depression of 1932. But tough financial measures and the success of government repression soon saw confidence surging back. Companies such as Ford, Volkswagen, Colgate and Gillette either invested directly in South Africa for the first time or massively expanded the scale of their operations. Between 1965 and 1969, direct foreign investment increased by over 60 per cent and, buoyed up by this huge injection of capital, the South African economy grew by 9.3 per cent a year in the late 1960s. Cash registers jingled: boom time had arrived.

A small measure of this prosperity trickled down to black Sowetans. Wages for African workers in Johannesburg had steadily declined during the 1950s, but began to recover during the early years of the following decade. The Verwoerd government increased the minimum wage paid to Africans, and also repealed the legislation which prohibited African consumption of 'white alcohol' such as brandy and whisky. This restriction had been bitterly resented by township dwellers.

Writer Kid Casey colourfully describes this moment in an article, 'Confessions of an Illicit Boozer', published in *Drum* magazine: 'The powers-that-be decided to let the people guzzle. That is when we started buying booze over the counter. Well, the decree was one ill wind that knocked the enterprising old *gweva* out of business... The *gweva* had acted as a go-between for us non-voters and bottlestores.' In a different vein, Zulu migrant worker Shadrack Khumalo recollects somewhat ironically how, 'Verwoerd liberated us because people were allowed to drink freely and he ruled that people had to be paid at least R2 a day.'

During the early to mid-1960s, wage levels in Soweto continued to edge up. Increasing numbers moved into better-paid jobs as the workforce employed by manufacturing almost doubled between 1960 and 1970. The average number of wage earners per family also grew from 1.3 to 2.2 between 1956 and 1968 as wives found greater opportunities for employment and the children of immigrant families began to grow up and contribute to the family economy. The average wage gap between white and black workers narrowed across all sections between 1964 and 1974 – a clear index of the improved earnings of African workers, especially in the centre of industry on the Witwatersrand. If these were not quite years of prosperity for Sowetans, they were at least marked – for more stable households in Soweto – by the absence of the most extreme need.

Other aspects of life also marginally improved. By 1966, 87 500 formal houses had been constructed in Soweto and nearly all Sowetan children were able to secure access to a rudimentary – albeit inadequate – primary schooling. By May 1964, 85 000 children attended 133 schools in Soweto, most of them built over the previous decade.

Despite these few exceptions, however, many other areas of Sowetan life remained starved by the penny pinching and dogma of apartheid. No new secondary schools were built in Soweto after 1962 and less than 5 per cent of Sowetan children could find place in those that existed. There were no cinemas or shopping malls, few tarred roads, no electricity in private homes, and only a handful of understaffed police stations within the borders of the township. A substantial proportion of Soweto's population, particularly where no adult male breadwinner was present, continued to live below the breadline. In 1961 alone, 30 769 summonses were issued for unpaid rents.

Soweto style

Despite fierce influx control laws to prevent black people from settling permanently in the urban areas, Soweto's population grew steadily throughout the decade. Part of this increase was due to the presence of labour migrants who were housed in Soweto's multiplying hostel complexes. Most of it, however, consisted of the children of those who had first sought accommodation there in the 1940s and 1950s. Among this growing second-generation population of Sowetans, a new urban culture began to take shape. The outward signs of it could be seen in dress, fashion, leisure activities, domestic furnishings and social rituals, or else heard in urban dialects and musical styles.

By the early 1960s, if not before, Soweto was an extremely class- and status-conscious society. A survey carried out by Philip Mayer in 1964/5 in Soweto provides a fascinating glimpse into Sowetans' self-perceptions at the time. Most residents divided Soweto's population into three or four classes: a thin layer of professionals and businessmen who constituted a sharply defined elite; a middle-class of semi-skilled workers, drivers, policemen, clerks and so on who adopted a more urban western lifestyle with its associated middle-class trimmings and who made up about a quarter of the population; and the 'ordinary working people' many of whom were children or grandchildren of immigrants. The latter group could be further subdivided into the 'respectable poor' and the dissolute, often referred to as *abantu abaphakathi* (people who are in the middle).

> The presence of teachers, nurses, doctors, personnel managers and businessmen living side by side with working people and the poor has produced acutely felt status differences, much more specific than the distinction usually found in the working class areas (elsewhere in the world) between the respectable and the no-good.
>
> Philip Mayer, 'Soweto People and their Social Universe', 1977

A defining feature of the elite was their standard of education and proficiency in English. For many Sowetans, education held the key to self-advancement. As one middle-aged Sowetan clerk told Mayer's team: 'This is our daily prayer and dream – that our children will be the equals of everybody in South Africa. That is why we are educating them, since we realise that this is the only way.'

Education, however, was not seen as an unqualified advantage by all sectors of Sowetan society. The poor, or at least the 'respectable' majority, saw themselves as morally superior to the elite, retaining a degree of self-discipline which had been lost by the elite. Among this large middle to lower section of Sowetan society, the values of hard work and thriftiness continued to predominate – along with an egalitarianism and a willingness to share with others in times of adversity. The rich, by contrast, were seen as snobbish and lacking in *ubuntu* (humanity).

Among the youth, perceptions of status and style pervaded every aspect of daily life, from musical taste to dress and language. On Soweto's streets and in its schools, two urban dialects competed for domination. The one was imported into the Meadowlands area of Soweto from the recently demolished freehold townships around Sophiatown and was commonly known first as *Flaaitaal* and then more widely as *Tsotsitaal*. The name tsotsi, derived either from the 'zoot-suit' pants popularised by American movies or from the South Sotho word *ho tsotsa* meaning 'to rob', suggested urban slickness and sophistication. The other dialect had spontaneously evolved in the slightly older areas of Soweto, such as Orlando East and West. In the 1960s, it became known as *Iscamtho*, from the Zulu verb *ukuqamunda*, meaning 'to talk loudly or maintain a swift flow of language'. At first, *Iscamtho* was mainly spoken by the young men involved in criminal gangs in the area. The two dialects, however, differed considerably since the Meadowlands dialect drew heavily on Afrikaans while the Orlando dialect was based on the Zulu language. Meadowlands' youth derisively labelled youngsters from other areas of Soweto as *kalkoens* (Afrikaans for 'turkeys' after the way in which they supposedly talked). The Afrikaans-based dialect, therefore, gradually gave way to its Zulu-based rival in the 1970s which became a powerful part of black urban culture.

Youth fashion also made its mark on a developing Sowetan lifestyle which increasingly set trends for the rest of black urban South Africa. Hugh Masekela, the famous jazz musician, is quoted in *Drum*, June 1983:

By the early 1960s, Sowetans were extremely class and status conscious. 'Real' ladies, for example, dressed very stylishly.

❝ In those days, a man was known and recognised by the kind of label that was attached to his clothes. We used to spend hours cleaning our shoes, and then go to the cinemas, very early, just to show off. ❞

By the late 1960s, three distinct dress styles could be distinguished – that of the Hippies, the Ivies and the Pantsulas. The distinctive feature of the Hippies at that time was bell-bottomed trousers, and followers of the fashion went to great lengths to recreate the look. Seth Mazibuko remembers taking the bottom 'of trousers and adding cloth just to make your trousers into bellbottoms'.

Sibongile Mkhabela relates how the Ivies, on the other hand, 'would put their trousers right up to here and pump out their stomachs. They'd have their trousers coming up a bit so the sock must show. They'd be very dignified'. Murphy Morobe tells how one's trousers 'needed to go at least above the bellybutton, you know; then at least you make it into that category of the Ivy League in the township'.

Ivies also frequented particularly fashionable 'watering holes' and music spots. Seth Mazibuko recalls that 'the Ivies used to go to shebeens such as Banda. You'll get into Banda and they'll talk perfumes, you know... Aramis... and that's what made them sissies as far as the Pantsulas are concerned'.

The Pantsulas were distinguished by a rather more obvious working-class subculture. Steven Tshabalala describes the different style:

Those who wore caps with bald heads, those were the Pantsulas and the Pantsulas wore very expensive clothes. A Pantsula did not mind buying shoes worth R200, and a very expensive pair of trousers, a very expensive shirt. The Pantsulas wanted everything that is expensive. They entertained the girls very well. They would buy liquor but then, after the girls have drunk their liquor, they would just say, "Let's go." That's how they got their girls, you see.

Seth Mazibuko has other memories:

If you are Pantsula, when you get your wages on Friday, then you'd buy BVD – white underpants and white undershirt. You'd wake up early on a Saturday or Sunday and play your music at top volume and you'd get busy tending your garden in your new BVD underpants and shirt. The only time your garden was made was when you bought these from your wages... They'd put their trousers below their waist area and their BVD underpants would stick out.

The Pantsulas came to be identified by their cotton caps called 'sporties'.

Pantsulas also came to be identified by their cotton caps called 'sporties'. Even without their distinctive leisure clothes, you could spot the Pantsulas by the way they walked. Whitey Khanyeza points out that 'the Pantsulas had their own walking style. They even had their own way of talking. They had more of a lingo than any other gang. Many new words came in with the Pantsulas'.

But Sibongile Mkhabela explains that 'each male style had its lady counterpart. You had the tsotsis and the ladies who went along with them were called the *caberesh* – a very denigratory name. The *caberesh* later became the *emshoza* and the *emshoza* would later go along with the Pantsulas. It was the Ivy lady with the Ivy gentleman. They would all wear nice, dignified clothes. They would dress more sporty or smart casual. Then there would be the real ladies who would dress very formally. These were the trends'. Mkhabela also remembers the exceptionally high heels worn by young women, and the lengths they would go to to wear the fashionable hairstyles of the day:

It was the time when we girls used to relax our hair... straight, straight, straight. People actually used stones. They put a stone on the stove and put some Vaseline on your hair, and used the stone to stretch your hair. It was a terrible experience. There would be this stink of burning hair everywhere in the house. Can you imagine the smell? We used to look up to the girls who relaxed their hair as our role models. But what is interesting is, some time in the early 1970s, women would be scared to walk with that hair, especially in trains because there were the Zulu guys who would have their scissors ready and say, "We don't want cats. We want our women with their natural hair." So they would actually cut your hair.

Particular styles and tastes became popular and spread at least partly because of the boisterous and rejuvenated black press which had developed in Johannesburg in the 1950s and 1960s. Mass circulation black newspapers such as *Zonk*, *Golden City Post* and *Drum* all responded to and created an infinitely larger African readership than had ever existed before.

By the mid-1960s, 60 per cent of urban blacks could read – compared to 21 per cent in 1946 – largely due to Bantu Education. The new black press eagerly sought to capitalise on this new market and advertisers followed suit. By the mid-1960s, *Golden City Press* boasted a readership of over 200 000. In contrast to the staid *Bantu World* which preceded it, the black press celebrated black American, and subsequently black South African, role models rather than white. Famous singers such as Dolly Rathebe and other local personalities began to grace the covers and the pages featured indigenous South African interests. Advertisers also strove to create and break into a mass black urban market. Records, clothes, cosmetics (including, from the mid-1950s, lipstick) and furnishings were all advertised extensively in the black press. This helped forge a distinctive black urban taste and style, and contributed to the creation of a more uniform, shared black urban culture.

Typical shebeen scene in the comfort of a private home.

The shebeens or 'speakeasies' provided havens from the harsh realities of daily life. On virtually every street one or even two homes were turned into all-night, seven-days-a-week drinking houses. They were run by 'shebeen queens', usually single or divorced women courageous enough to defy the laws which forbade the sale of alcohol in the township outside the municipal beerhalls. Police frequently raided the shebeens, confiscating the liquor or pouring it out on the streets and arresting the shebeen-owner and her clients. But shebeen queens developed an uncanny ability to outwit the police and shebeens flourished. As Kid Casey writes in *Drum* (May 1977), 'Hell has no fury like an Aunt Peggy barred from getting the population a little giddy. A social service, even if she gets something in the process.'

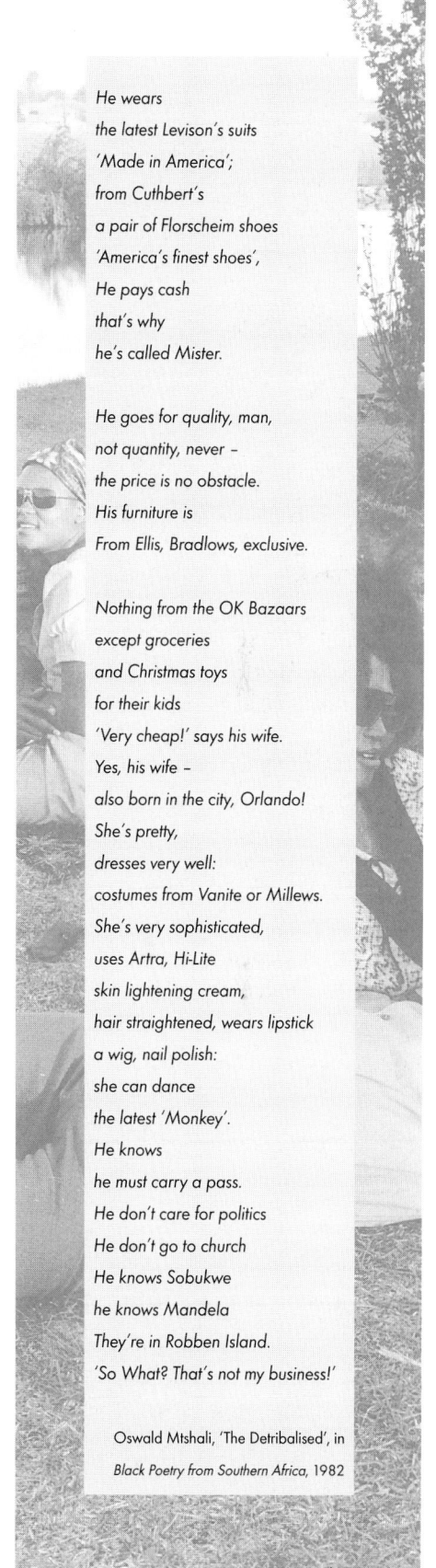

---

*He wears
the latest Levison's suits
'Made in America';
from Cuthbert's
a pair of Florscheim shoes
'America's finest shoes',
He pays cash
that's why
he's called Mister.*

*He goes for quality, man,
not quantity, never –
the price is no obstacle.
His furniture is
From Ellis, Bradlows, exclusive.*

*Nothing from the OK Bazaars
except groceries
and Christmas toys
for their kids
'Very cheap!' says his wife.
Yes, his wife –
also born in the city, Orlando!
She's pretty,
dresses very well:
costumes from Vanite or Millews.
She's very sophisticated,
uses Artra, Hi-Lite
skin lightening cream,
hair straightened, wears lipstick
a wig, nail polish:
she can dance
the latest 'Monkey'.
He knows
he must carry a pass.
He don't care for politics
He don't go to church
He knows Sobukwe
he knows Mandela
They're in Robben Island.
'So What? That's not my business!'*

Oswald Mtshali, 'The Detribalised', in *Black Poetry from Southern Africa*, 1982

Soweto — A History

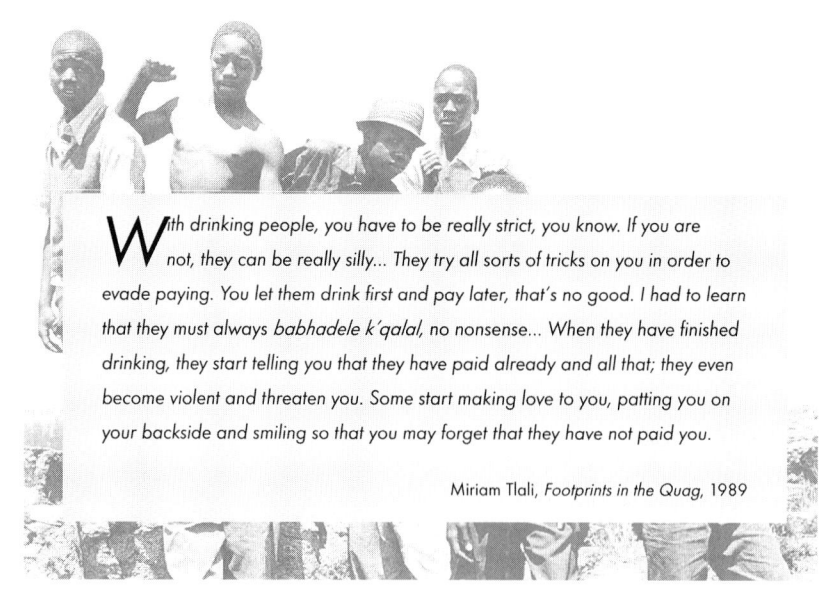

> With drinking people, you have to be really strict, you know. If you are not, they can be really silly... They try all sorts of tricks on you in order to evade paying. You let them drink first and pay later, that's no good. I had to learn that they must always *babhadele k'qalal*, no nonsense... When they have finished drinking, they start telling you that they have paid already and all that; they even become violent and threaten you. Some start making love to you, patting you on your backside and smiling so that you may forget that they have not paid you.
>
> Miriam Tlali, *Footprints in the Quag*, 1989

Drum magazine cover, featuring singer Dolly Rathebe.

The shebeens attracted a different clientele than the municipal beerhalls. Nelson Botile explains:

> **All the rank and file people would go to the beerhalls and fight there. Some people would not go to the beerhalls because of their status. When you go to a beerhall, people look down on you but at Mama's place [a shebeen], the old people would come and sit down nicely and drink nicely. You'd gauge yourself. If you belonged to a certain status, you'd say, "No, I don't belong to that class, I belong to that class, so I think I must go and drink with that class and so on..." Shebeens built status.**

Drinking in the intimacy of a private home made shebeens far more popular than the drab, uninviting rows of concrete benches and tables at the municipally owned beerhalls.

The shebeens themselves ranged from the upmarket and stylish to the more basic, lower-class shebeens which sold a potent brew called 'barberton' and other 'kill-me-quick' homemade concoctions such as 'mamba', made from brown bread, yeast and hops and other potent ingredients. These shebeens were frequented by people nicknamed '*lala vuka* drinkers' – those who would drink until they passed out and then start drinking again the moment they awoke. The more exclusive shebeens traded in wine, beer, champagne and spirits. As pointed out by Cliff Mashiloane, the shebeens also became the turf of different gangs:

> **When I was still a gangster, when we came back from town we liked going to shebeens. Each gang member would bring his girlfriend from town. We would discuss which place we were going to drink at. We used to go to the famous places which had big names where the big bosses, the "different titles", would hang out. We used to drink at Junior Spot and at Mafashions Place which we called "The Basement". We would drive to these famous places in our cars and when we got there, all the people would start saying, "the Hazels are here, the Hazels are here". Sometimes other gangs would hear that we are drinking in a particular shebeen. Maybe the Vikings would already be there and people in the street would think a fight was going to ensue. Sometimes the gang would split in two so that when other gangs attacked us when we were drunk, they would not find us in the same place.**

The late 1950s and early 1960s also saw the emergence of new standardised musical forms which quickly attracted a mass following among Soweto's population, particularly its large immigrant component.

The new style, whose first major exponents were Mahlatini and the Mahotela Queens, combined many existing urban sounds. Known as *mbaqanga* (bread) and *mzakazo* (radio) music, it was popularised by Radio Bantu, which officially started broadcasting in 1960 and which favoured *mbaqanga* neo-traditional style. The more educated and sophisticated second-generation black urbanites who had grown up in Sophiatown, Alexandra or Orlando were inclined to dismiss *mbaqanga* as a commercialised, unauthentic apartheid creation. Although this was true to some extent, *mbaqanga* nevertheless tapped many African musical talents and, at its best, produced its own authentic sounds.

By 1961, 124 000 regular radio listeners along the Reef testified to the huge popularity of this distinctive music style. Over the course of the 1960s and 1970s, *mbaqanga* made its own contribution to a new collective urban culture influencing and penetrating all other forms of musical performance, including jazz, rock and soul. Even today, it continues to enjoy immense popularity.

Advertisers created and captured a mass black urban market.

The managers of popular soccer teams were often drawn from the ranks of the more successful and colourful shebeen owners and were considered very stylish at the time.

All in a game

In the 1930s and 1940s, soccer teams had been small, local affairs based on neighbourhoods or factories. From the 1960s, however, soccer became semi-professional and much more commercialised. The growth of mass support for soccer provides one indicator of the development of a more common black urban identity. Orlando Pirates and Moroka Swallows were the pick of the African soccer teams in this period. The original nucleus of the Orlando Pirates team were the sons of families removed from Prospect Township near the centre of Johannesburg to Orlando East in the late 1930s, while the core of Swallows was drawn from children whose parents were evicted from Alexandra into Moroka in the late 1940s. From the late 1950s, both teams attracted mass support from Soweto's residents. In 1959, both *The World* and the *Golden City Post* greatly expanded their coverage of black soccer in recognition of its growing popularity.

Team players and team managers were awarded celebrity status.

> *We grew up chasing after girls; we grew up going to the swimming pool and even going to school together. Over time, this group graduated into a bunch of youngsters who began to look at themselves in terms of the territory within which they actually played and actually knew people. Even someone like myself who was brought up by my uncle, the priest, and was good mannered, couldn't escape being associated with one gang or the other.*

One of the most prominent gangs in Soweto, the Hazels, operated in Mzimhlope. Cliff Mashiloane, one of the gang's founding members, recalls that after the creation of the Hazels 'other areas in the township began to form their own groups. When they heard that there was a group called the Hazels in Mzimhlope, a group in Orlando started to call themselves the Vikings. And then another group arose in Phefeni called the Kwaitos, and there were the Dinotshi [bees] of Naledi and the Black Swines in Moletsane. Each gang used to have a uniform. The Hazels wore Khakis and tackies called "convoys". We also wore sporties and lumbers which had scotches inside and we used to wear them inside out'. These gangs were clearly not the innocent, neighbourly groups described by Murphy Morobe and others. They were often armed with dangerous weapons and presented a serious threat to the community.

One of the main targets of these gangs were the schoolgirls who had to cross gang borders in order to go to and from school. Sexual intimidation and, in fact, rape seemed to be commonplace among these young victims. Susan Shabangu recalls:

Gangsters armed with dangerous weapons posed a grave threat to the community.

> *If you had a relationship with these young boys who were sort of hanging around the corners, it was a problem for you. If they met you in the morning, it meant that you were not going to school the whole day.*

Ndoza, a member of the Damaras, exposes the ugly side of these encounters: 'We didn't treat schoolgirls badly. If you spoke to her nicely when you abducted her, she wouldn't say, "Someone has taken me by force." I don't know if they were scared of us or what.' Susan Shabangu, however, had experience of a number of such assaults:

> *I used to think that they are going to stab me if I refused. So it was just survival of the fittest and every day we'd be chased.*

On reflection, Ndoza explains:

> *It was not so bad. At that time the police were not as tough as they are now. Rape, well it was bad because five guys would sleep with one girl but at least they wouldn't kill her. They were just happy to have sex with her. They wouldn't slit her throat, no.*

Ndoza recalls that the gang spent a lot of their time 'fighting for women, the babies. You find perhaps that there is a girl that Mandla is "jolling" [having an affair] with and the other guy from the other gang also wants that girl. There wouldn't be any understanding between them...'

Gangs also made a habit of targeting trains. Cliff Mashiloane maintains that passengers were left alone:

❝ Despite the fact that the people were afraid of us, we did not harass people at random. Even in the trains, we did not fight with everybody. We only fought amongst ourselves as gangsters, fighting for girlfriends, things like that. We used to take the 9430, the Naledi train. There was this coach called Dumani [the last coach] and that was where the bosses met. We would compete for Dumani. Sometimes we would find that another gang had already taken the coach and we would have to fight to get it back so as to make way for our girlfriends to sit. Everyone would then make his girlfriend comfortable and then we would stand and drink liquor. The other gangs knew that if they came in, they would have to fight. One day I was on my way to the toilet because Dumani does not have a toilet. I met other gangsters in the passage. One of them suddenly attacked me and stabbed me and the knife went all the way through me. Luckily the train was now getting into New Canada station and I jumped off. There were always injured people getting off at New Canada. I was taken to hospital where I had to stay for three months. ❞

Although many women fell victim to intimidation and abuse at the hands of gang members, a number appreciated the privileges of being seen as the companion of a prominent gangster.

On other occasions, the passengers were not so fortunate. Before the advent of the taxi industry to Soweto, railway lines were the arteries of daily life in Soweto, pumping workers into the city to earn wages and then pumping them back at least slightly enriched by their earnings and purchases. Railway carriages and the vicinity of railways stations were, therefore, a vital part of the gangs' turf. It was here that they could lay their hands on money and the good things of life they so earnestly desired, and the pickings were particularly fruitful on Friday evenings after workers had been paid their weekly wages.

> The hand of the pickpocket does not probe and pluck so expertly as to be unnoticed by most of the people in the commotion, but even though they are aware of what is going on in their pockets they will keep mum for fear of the worst... The victim will stand stiff and straight until the thugs are through with him, whilst others will watch the episode frozen by the knowledge that their turn is either just past or still coming... There are days when delays involving trains on their way to the ghettoes in the evenings are attributable to the tsotsis' fiddling with the mechanical equipment. Passengers have no alternative but to alight between stations and search for buses or taxis to take them home. These hooligans see this as a golden opportunity for them to drag women and girls at knife-point into the open veld. They rape the expectant mothers-to-be. They even rape old women of their grannies' age on their way from their piece jobs where they eke out a living as washerwomen. *Sies!* They rape little schoolgirls who travel by train to various schools in the area.
>
> Berung Seluki, 'Dumani'
> in Mothobi Mutloase (ed.), *Forced Landing Africa South*

The Loaded Pause

Policing the townships

The South African Police (SAP) did little to curb the outrages carried out by the gangs of youths. In 1959 and 1960, the police had launched a series of campaigns against tsotsi gangs but this was simply because they seemed to be drawn into political demonstrations and violence. Once this threat receded in the early 1960s, both government and police paid the gangs little attention. Until the late 1960s, the entire Soweto complex had only four police stations, a number which was to prove entirely inadequate to combat serious crime. The Moroka police station, for example, serviced 17 Soweto townships alone. Unable and, it seems, unwilling to maintain a constant police presence in Soweto, the SAP concentrated their efforts on sporadic mass raids. Although these seemed to reduce crime for the brief period in which they occurred, the intention was simply to enforce apartheid laws such as influx control rather than concentrate on real crime. As long as the criminal activities rife in Soweto did not spread to the white areas, the government appeared to care little about the nightmare being endured within the township.

As a result, by 1960 the murder rate in Soweto was four times higher than in Chicago or New York. The incidence of juvenile crime escalated from 37.65 per thousand of Soweto's population in 1949 to 51.4 per thousand in 1965. In the mid-1960s, Soweto's residents were subject to a virtual reign of terror, particularly by night. Selatial Maake observed: 'The people in Meadowlands lived in fear. It was at least safe during the day but in the evening, when the sun set, "Don't go around".' And Meadowlands was probably the area least affected. Zola, among other suburbs, seems to have been a centre of murder, robbery, and rape, and was popularly known as Slagpaal (abattoir) and *Mshayeazafe* (hit him until he dies).

Sowetans responded to these problems by developing a distinct civic culture, and much of this centred on self-help and self-policing. Letatsi Radebe, a resident of Naledi, recalls that 'the neighbourhood suffered a lot from domination by thugs. There was thuggery in the trains and in the buses and people were not free and happy. Now that's why we decided that the only thing we could do now is to form Makgotla'.

Radebe, together with a few other residents, approached the Urban Bantu Council for assistance in forming Makgotla or 'people's courts'. A committee to organise the Makgotla was established and Radebe was appointed secretary. He worked to mobilise communities to create Makgotla across Soweto and, in the early 1970s, several Makgotla movements came into being. Their task was to judge and punish criminal offenders. Makgotla based much of its appeal on the precedent of African tradition. Radebe told residents:

The Makgotla hears a case and deliberates on the punishment to be meted out to the offender.

> Let us use our own tradition and culture because where African culture is involved you always find discipline and respect. We don't want to hear a thing about white man's law because it has brought the destruction of the black man, socially and otherwise. A black man is dead because of a white man's law.

Radebe went on to say that 'to control a black child is to thrash him. In order for a child to be a child, bring him up with a whip so that he should understand. If a man's daughter has been raped by a thug, he'll always come to us. We'll call the parents of the thug who has raped the girl. Then the boy will get 6 to 12 lashes and will pay the girl's family the costs of the doctor and hospital'.

Radebe explains that the purpose of the Makgotla was not only to stop crime: 'In Makgotla, we were dealing with cases of misunderstanding. If a man is not on good terms with his wife, he'll always come to Makgotla. If a man's got a problem with his children, he'll always report the case.'

Young Patrick Hlongwane, a youth who lived in Mzimhlope, offers his impressions of the Makgotla:

❝ *[The Makgotla was] an old-people kind of organisation which was about stopping all kinds of crimes that affected the community. Men from the Makgotla would search for the person who committed a crime. When they found him, they would bring that person to the Makgotla to question and discipline him according to the crime he had committed. When disciplining that person, they would let everyone decide on the number of whips they must give him. They would then pour water on to that person's body and start punishing him while everyone was watching.* ❞

Although many Sowetans supported the methods of the Makgotla, some strongly objected. Susan Shabangu reflects:

❝ *The objective when they started this thing, to curb crime in the township, was never met. The focus changed completely to domestic issues. You'd find them sjambokking women – elderly or married women – in public and that was a terrible thing. That is why, in the end, they were unpopular and tended to be a mockery. And I don't even know what happened to them in the long run.* ❞

The punishment imposed by the Makgotla was often harsh, but many residents of Soweto seemed to support and even embrace the activities of the Makgotla.

For fear that the practices of the Makgotla would get out of control, the police often attempted to suppress its activities. Nelson Botile recalls how the police said that 'if people want to raid the township, they must register and join the civil guards and go with the police to raid the township'. In the absence of any alternative forms of policing, however, the Makgotla would often revive.

Instead of pursuing the crime which tormented Sowetans every day, the police concentrated on offenses against apartheid laws, and this preoccupation led to their alienation from Soweto's residents. At the same time, the repression that followed the Sharpeville massacre had created a profound sense of apathy and powerlessness among many Sowetans. This is conveyed most graphically by Clement Twala who served as a police auxiliary (otherwise known as 'blackjacks') for the Johannesburg City Council. Blackjacks were poorly trained and poorly armed and were mostly charged with such duties as arresting householders in arrears with their rents. Twala recalls a number of such occasions where they would raid 30 people or more:

❝ *These people would move very peacefully without fighting back at all. We would move right behind them and they would never even dream of running away. We were never scared that these people would turn against us. We didn't carry guns. They feared punishment. It used to be a disgrace for any black person to be found defying the law then. I don't know why...* ❞

But, while Sowetans may have submitted in the face of arrest, they found other ways to beat the system. A typical feature of township life was paying bribes. People well down the waiting list for housing were able to move to the top by bribing municipal officials. Clement Twala explains:

> *The money was quite a lot. It usually ran into three figures. The person who didn't bribe – the innocent poor person – would wait for 10 years and not get a house because those who had money kept slipping the queue. That's why the waiting list kept growing.*

Lesibana James Shika, a resident of Mzimhlope Hostel, tells how a culture of bribery pervaded hostel life:

> *We used to live by begging and bribing the police. When they came to raid for liquor in the hostels, I used to give the police ten or twenty rands and then they would leave me alone. That was how we survived... If you did not give them something, then they would kick over your drums of liquor. That was how our oppression was. Each time you did something, you had to have money ready.*

High apartheid

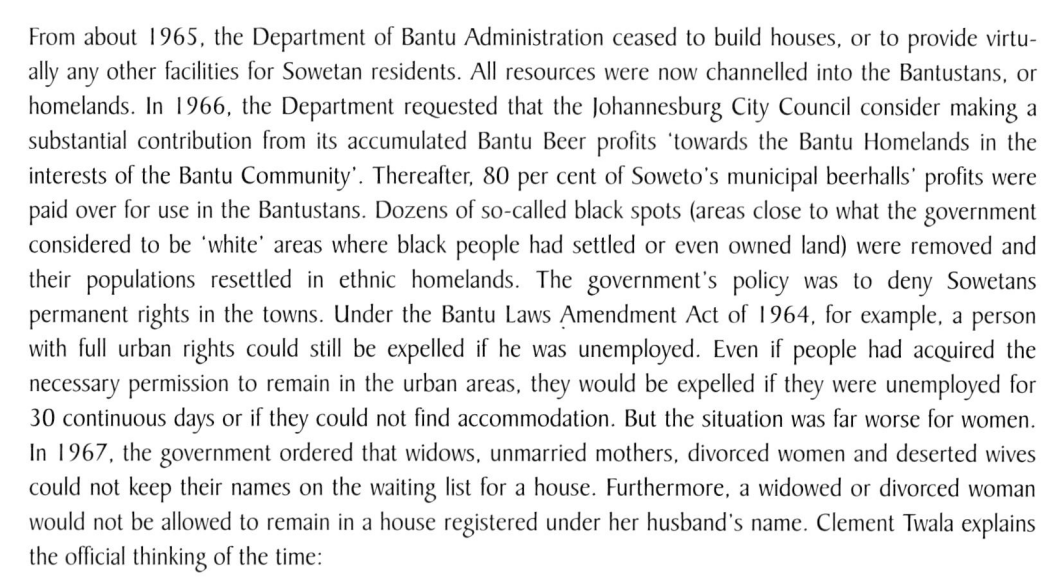

From about 1965, the Department of Bantu Administration ceased to build houses, or to provide virtually any other facilities for Sowetan residents. All resources were now channelled into the Bantustans, or homelands. In 1966, the Department requested that the Johannesburg City Council consider making a substantial contribution from its accumulated Bantu Beer profits 'towards the Bantu Homelands in the interests of the Bantu Community'. Thereafter, 80 per cent of Soweto's municipal beerhalls' profits were paid over for use in the Bantustans. Dozens of so-called black spots (areas close to what the government considered to be 'white' areas where black people had settled or even owned land) were removed and their populations resettled in ethnic homelands. The government's policy was to deny Sowetans permanent rights in the towns. Under the Bantu Laws Amendment Act of 1964, for example, a person with full urban rights could still be expelled if he was unemployed. Even if people had acquired the necessary permission to remain in the urban areas, they would be expelled if they were unemployed for 30 continuous days or if they could not find accommodation. But the situation was far worse for women. In 1967, the government ordered that widows, unmarried mothers, divorced women and deserted wives could not keep their names on the waiting list for a house. Furthermore, a widowed or divorced woman would not be allowed to remain in a house registered under her husband's name. Clement Twala explains the official thinking of the time:

> *Women were not allowed to become heads of families. If your husband dies, you'd have to get your son to be head of the family and, if he was too young, you had to get a close male relative to occupy the house. If a woman failed to get a man to take up tenancy, the house would be declared vacant and the woman had to go back to her place of origin or live as a lodger in other people's homes.*

Few home-owners, however, were willing to let rooms to women with families, and many women lived in the fear that they would be caught because they chose to live 'illegally'.

In 1966, Prime Minister Hendrik Verwoerd was assassinated in what was a second attempt on his life, and BJ Vorster was elected the country's new Prime Minister. Vorster's administration was equally committed to separate development and the homelands policy, and the onslaught on the status of urban blacks was resumed. A government decree in 1968 ended home leaseholdership rights in Soweto and other townships. Naturally, this dealt a crushing blow to the aspirations of township dwellers and aggravated the already growing sense of instability. Close to 10 000 homes in Soweto had been built or sold to people under the 30-year leasehold scheme which allowed a measure of security for residents who lived in these homes. This was especially true for those living in Dube, the only suburb in Soweto which had developed entirely on a home leaseholdership basis. Even these wealthier residents, known as the 'Dubenheimers', were now denied the right of home ownership.

After 1968, migrant workers were required to return to their original homes and enter into a new contract each year, which automatically prevented them acquiring permanent status after working 10 continuous years for one employer or living 15 continuous years in the same urban area. This, of course, denied them any rights they might consequently have 'earned' to permanent residence in the town.

The rights of traders and professionals in the township were also further restricted and, in 1969, the government issued specific orders to local authorities.

Traders in the township were prohibited from building or owning their own premises, and could not open more than one shop or do business 'for any purpose other than that of providing for the essential domestic requirements of the Bantu residents'. Black traders were also prohibited from trading outside of the townships, and trading companies or partnerships were outlawed. Letatsi Radebe describes how 'you had to apply for a licence from the Native Affairs Department in town. If you were very fortunate, you'd get a licence but you were given strict hours in which you could trade and, if you are found trading outside these hours, you were arrested and charged'.

Because of the severe restrictions on township traders, prices in Soweto were far higher than in the large supermarkets in Johannesburg.

The trading stores carried a very limited range of commodities such as groceries and toiletries, and the majority of Sowetans bought their food and clothing in the white city. It was estimated that Sowetans spent less than one-tenth of their money in the township, so the more liberal factions of the City Council protested, believing that the restriction on trading would erode the confidence and hopes of 'moderate Africans in Soweto'.

Vorster also set about tightening the apparatus of physical repression. The Terrorism Act of 1967 provided for indefinite detention without trial and BOSS, the infamous Bureau of State Security, was

> *Ensure that non-Europeans who render professional services (lawyers, doctors, etc.) are not granted office accommodation in Bantu residential areas. The Bantu should be persuaded to offer their services in the Bantu homelands. Professional services in urban Bantu residential areas should be rendered by whites. Those who already had such premises should be persuaded to move and establish themselves among their own people in the homelands.*
>
> Government directive to local authorities, 1969

A scene in a 'Mom and Pop' store.

established to safeguard the internal security of the country. The Department of Military Intelligence (DMI), which had been established in 1960, was given more extensive powers. Vorster told Parliament: 'I believe in the supremacy of the white man over his people in his own territory and I am prepared to maintain it by force.'

The era's most notorious piece of legislation, however, was the Bantu Homelands Citizen Act which passed into law in 1970. This Act compelled all black people to become citizens of the ethnic homeland corresponding to their own ethnic group – irrespective of whether they had ever set foot in those places or not. They would thus immediately be deprived of their South African citizenship.

In 1969 the Bantu Administration Department (BAD) began promoting its most bizarre proposal of all – the relocation of Soweto's 23 000 Zulu-speaking families to the proposed township of Waay Hoek on the outskirts of Ladysmith in Natal. The male breadwinners of these families were to be accommodated in Soweto's hostels during the week and would then commute the 400 kilometres to their families by high-speed train every weekend or 'whenever possible'. In 1971, a cowed Johannesburg City Council even agreed in principle to allocate R100 000 from its revenues for this purpose. The Council was concerned about the social problems which might arise from separating families but were, on the other hand, attracted by the scheme. According to the minutes of a meeting held on 13 January 1971 by the Management Committee of the Non-European Affairs Department, they believed that 'conditions may become so attractive in Ladysmith, that many of Johannesburg's Zulus would voluntarily move permanently from Soweto'. (Thanks to Prof. D Posel for this document.)

Soweto's population began to feel the constrictions and a more active spirit of resentment grew among its residents, particularly its youth.

Sibongile Mkhabela remembers how she 'used to resent that some men would walk into the house, bash the doors, walk in and say, "Get dressed, we are going." And they are talking to your father and your father does not say anything. He actually got dressed and got himself into that *kwela-kwela* van. You found your father acting like a boy, and for me, I personally used to resent that'.

Steven Tshabalala's circle of friends also resented the attitudes of their parents toward the demands of white people:

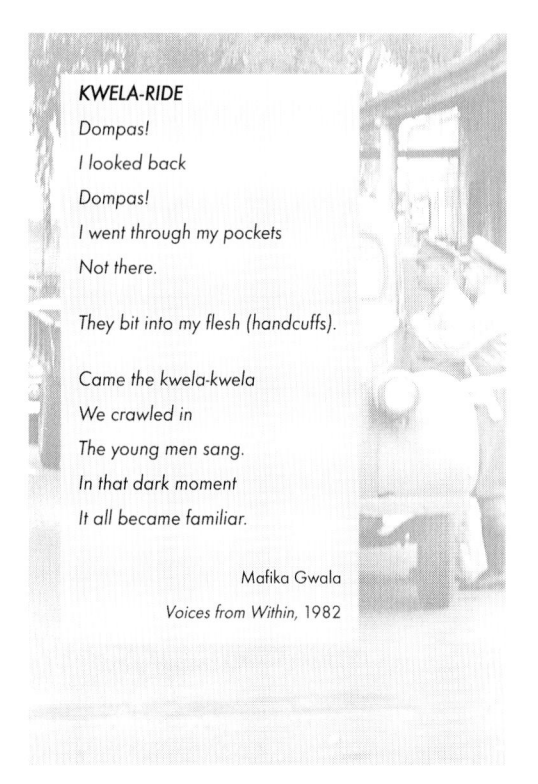

KWELA-RIDE

Dompas!

I looked back

Dompas!

I went through my pockets

Not there.

They bit into my flesh (handcuffs).

Came the kwela-kwela

We crawled in

The young men sang.

In that dark moment

It all became familiar.

Mafika Gwala
Voices from Within, 1982

❝ Our fathers were people who were what we called the "Yes, Baas" People. They believed that a white man was somehow a certain god, like the picture they saw of Jesus Christ. Most of the time you were told that you've got short hair and then your brains are short and everything that you say is very short. So you couldn't go anywhere as a black man. You just had to listen to what a white man was telling you. ❞

Black Consciousness

Beneath the economic growth and political calm that characterised the 1960s, a new, raw energy was bubbling. The very process of tightening and restructuring apartheid institutions had generated social forces that would lead to their destruction. In the late 1960s, the philosophy of Black Consciousness (BC) began to gain influence. Black Consciousness emphasised psychological reasons as the main barrier to black emancipation, and a generation which had known only the humiliations of 'grand apartheid' decided that the time had come to challenge the status quo. The main vehicle for the BC movement was the South African Students Organisation (SASO) launched at the University of the North in July 1969. SASO was formed after black students decided to break away from the multiracial but white-dominated National Union of South African Students (NUSAS).

SASO thus began to fill the political vacuum which had been left in black communities after the banning of the PAC and ANC. Influenced by the American Black Power movement, the organisation spoke a new language of political radicalism. SASO rejected passive acceptance of white superiority and domination and advocated a new black self-confidence and self-assertion. The organisation set out to win black communities to its cause and attracted thousands of followers eager to break out of the mould of their parents' resignation. In 1972, SASO – together with leaders from other African educational and religious bodies – came together to form the Black People's Convention (BPC), a political wing of the BC movement which aimed to mobilise South Africans around the BC ideology. The BPC wrote that they wanted to 'unite South African blacks into a black political movement which seeks to realise their emancipation from both psychological and physical oppression'. Steve Biko was the charismatic young spokesperson for the movement and his teachings came to be revered by many young black South Africans:

Black Consciousness seeks to instill the idea of self-determination, to restore feelings of pride and dignity to blacks after centuries of racist oppression. It is an attitude of mind and a way of life. It is the realisation that the most potent weapon in the hands of the oppressor is the mind of the oppressed.

Steve Biko's teachings were revered by his many supporters.

BC focused on problems of self-worth and identity. Biko denounced the black person who 'has lost his manhood' and who 'brightens up in sheepish obedience as he comes hurrying in response to his master's impatient call'. He emphasised the need for 'thinking black'. This message had enormous emotional power and acted as a beacon for many young blacks. It allowed them to challenge their legal status as second-class citizens, as 'non-whites', as well as the racial stereotypes with which they had grown up. Sibongile Mkhabela reflects on the prevailing attitude of many township dwellers towards white people: 'In those days the only white people you had contact with were the police who were harassing you or the doctor at the clinic who gave you an injection. So you had this image of whites. You thought of them as an extremely privileged class of people who could do anything, anywhere.'

Seth Mazibuko adds how his 'contact with whites was always the kind of contact where I saw myself as an inferior. This white was my boss, no matter how young or old he was. My grandmother was called a "girl" by her employers. The sight of a white person in the township used to scare me a great deal and I used to ask myself why was I so scared?'

Mazibuko goes on to say how 'the concept of Black Consciousness like "Be black and proud, close ranks and fight, Black man, you're on your own", built something in all of us. It was able to say to us, "Stand up. Resist!" BC became a way of life. It caught up with the youth of the time. It came to cure a person who'd been in this trance of fear'.

Murphy Morobe agreed that 'the strength of BC lay in getting people out of this psychological trauma of seeing themselves as victims and incapable of anything unless their master speaks'.

'BC preaches awareness among people,' said Soweto student, Khotso Seathlolo. 'You ask yourself: "Why am I not allowed to enter into that café with a White man, although I have the same appetite?"'

Murphy Morobe tells how BC influenced his own consciousness:

[I became] more conscious of the situation of black people in this country and this township. I was able to go into town; I was able to see the contrast, the differences and all that raised questions in my mind. Amongst us, we began to develop a keen sense for wanting to discover more ideas about struggles, not only in this country, but also about what happened in other areas.

There was always a list published of books that were banned and for us it meant that whatever the government banned must be something good and it was part of our adventure as youngsters to actually go out to actively look for those books. The 1970s were not long after the major student uprisings in Europe, France, and the Civil Rights movement and the Black Power movement in the United States. 1974 was, of course, the year of the Portuguese defeat in Mozambique and Angola and, when that happened, I think it had a major boost on us.

Sibongile Mkhabela adds:

Most of the literature that was around in those days emphasised Africanism, being black, being proud, knowing who you are. There was very little about non-racialism. We had guys who believed in non-racialism, but we would argue the whole night and I would say, "Are you going to tell me that somebody is going to enslave you and then free you? You must be crazy! You're asking me to take a bucket full of snakes and choose the nice ones. It's too much."

Gradually, the new language of defiance touched larger and larger sections of Soweto's youth. Teboho Mohapi remembers: 'They were talking about Verwoerd; they were talking about the education; they were talking about apartheid; they were talking about oppression. That was some of the new vocabulary that I gained.'

The popular press and township cultural events also played an important role in spreading the message of BC. What followed was little short of a literary revival in Soweto and poetry became especially popular. Teboho Mohapi tells how, 'Somebody would say, "Listen, I have a poem here." It would talk about being black and then you'd listen with interest.' Poems such as Mongane Serote's 'What's in this Black "Shit"?' were widely circulated:

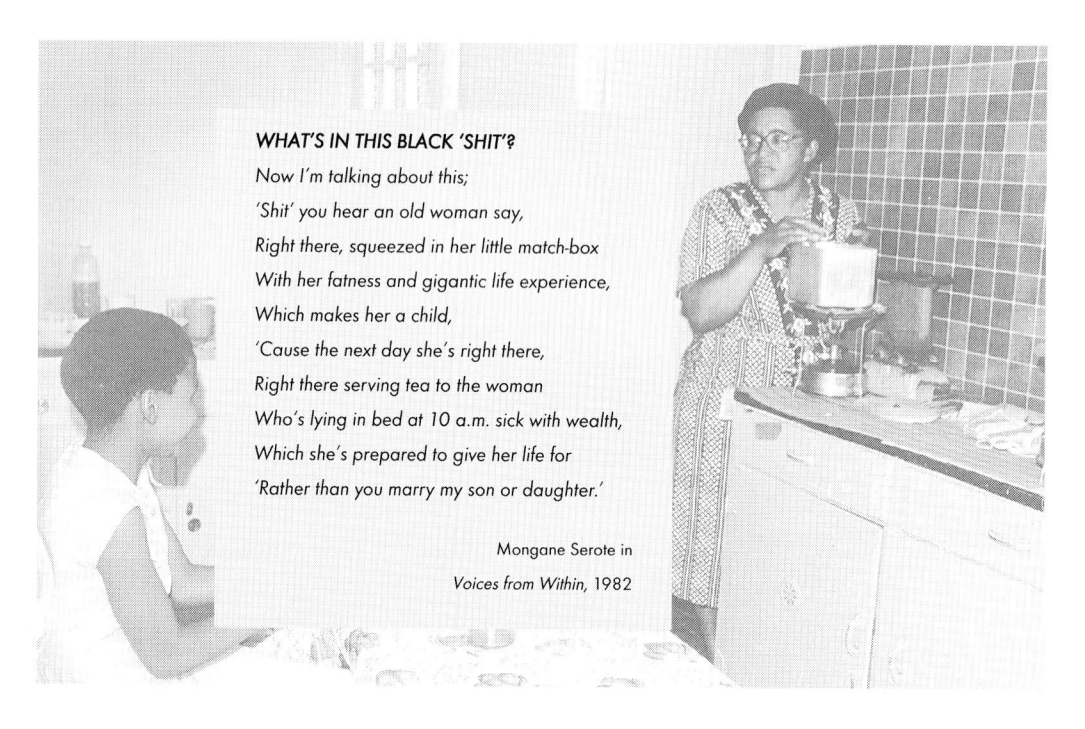

> **WHAT'S IN THIS BLACK 'SHIT'?**
> Now I'm talking about this;
> 'Shit' you hear an old woman say,
> Right there, squeezed in her little match-box
> With her fatness and gigantic life experience,
> Which makes her a child,
> 'Cause the next day she's right there,
> Right there serving tea to the woman
> Who's lying in bed at 10 a.m. sick with wealth,
> Which she's prepared to give her life for
> 'Rather than you marry my son or daughter.'
>
> Mongane Serote in
> *Voices from Within*, 1982

But it was the poet, Ingoapele Madingoane, who captured the heart of young Sowetans. Ingoapele became a regular feature at events in the township's community centres. His powerful voice, usually accompanied by the hypnotic rhythm of the drums, made his recitals highly emotional occasions. The poem 'Africa, My Beginning' was well known by township dwellers. Ingoapele described it as a tribute to 'those who have succeeded in liberating themselves and to those who are about to get their liberation'.

AFRICA MY BEGINNING

Azania here I come
from apartheid in tatters
in the land of sorrow
from the marathon bondage
the sharpeville massacre
the flames of soweto
i was born there
I will die there
in
africa my beginning
and africa my ending
lets do something
mbopha

Ingoapele Madingoane, 'Black trial'
in *Voices from Within* 1982

In this period of new intellectual creativity, black leaders spoke of 'going it alone' and weaning blacks from dependence on paternalistic white 'do-gooders'. All apartheid-created institutions such as Bantustans, and Urban Bantu councils were rejected. BC leaders urged the building of black organisations which would take their own distinct path. They also advocated black economic self-reliance through co-operatives, shops, farms or 'buy black' campaigns.

Pride in being black was also expressed in the dress and hairstyles of Africans in the township. Sibongile Mkhabela describes the sentiment of the time:

❝ It was the days of "Black is Beautiful" and you would sport big Afro hair and African attire, that sort of thing. It all went to emphasise that we are black people. If you are going to be involved in any kind of politics, you have got to appreciate who you are and not only appreciate it, but be very proud of who you are. ❞

Sibongile Mkhabela's father, like many of the older generation, warned against the naivete of the youth, saying 'Who do you think you are to fight the system? You can't win. Where is Mandela, where is Sobukwe? You definitely can never win against the system.' But Mkhabela explains that 'as a younger generation, we felt that this nonsense had to stop'.

The political calm that characterised Soweto in the 1960s and early 1970s can be seen as breathing space or pause, during which a new culture and a new generation emerged which would pose a more powerful and sustained challenge to apartheid than the generations that had gone before. That generation would realise itself in 1976.

The new African style expressed pride in being black.

THIS IS OUR DAY

❛ **The broad masses of Soweto are perfectly content, perfectly happy. Black–White relationships at present are as healthy as can be. There is no danger whatever of a blow-up in Soweto.** ❜

Manie Mulder, Chairperson of the West Rand Administration Board that governed the township, May 1976, Rand Daily Mail

On the cold winter's morning of 16 June 1976, thousands of black schoolchildren across Soweto took to the streets to protest against the forced use of Afrikaans in the classrooms. In an attempt to stop the march, the police fired teargas and live bullets into the student gathering. From that moment, the streets of Soweto erupted into chaos, and what started as a peaceful demonstration ended in a bloodbath. Enraged by the police brutality, large groups of young protesters, dressed in their black and white school uniforms, swarmed across the township, setting fire to government institutions as well as government-owned liquor stores and beerhalls. By the end of the week, violence had spread to other townships in the Transvaal (then known as the PWV – Pretoria-Witwatersrand-Vereeniging – area). The uprising in Soweto continued intermittently for the rest of the year and, after the events of 1976, Soweto became a household name across the United States of America and United Kingdom. The township would never be the same. Nor would the rest of South Africa.

Bantu education

The story of the uprising began more than 20 years before, with the National Party's introduction of Bantu Education in black schools in 1954. Bantu Education allowed many more children in Soweto to attend school than did the old missionary system of education, but the new system provided none of the facilities white scholars enjoyed. No school in Soweto had a science laboratory or a soccer field or a swimming pool; while white school pupils received free textbooks, black parents had to buy textbooks for their children.

As the number of students enrolling in schools grew much faster than allowed by the budget allocated to black education, educational standards entered a steep decline in the early 1960s. National pupil–teacher ratios increased from 46:1 in 1955 to 58:1 in 1967, and pupils had to take turns to use the overcrowded classrooms.

This meant that students received no more than two to three hours of schooling a day, and some lessons were taught to over 100 pupils at a time. As a result of poor government financing, there was a critical shortage of teachers and many of those teachers who were available were desperately under-qualified, with less than 10 per cent of African teachers holding a matriculation certificate in 1961.

Secondary schooling was even more disadvantaged than the primary level. No new secondary schools were built in Soweto between 1962 and 1971 because government policy dictated that all new provision for post-primary education should be directed almost exclusively towards the homelands.

Overcrowded classrooms had to be used on a shift basis.

The result was that secondary school classes were even more crowded than those in primary schools, and many teachers resorted to increasingly harsh methods to maintain control. Pupils bitterly resented this development, and matriculation pass rates slumped from 54 per cent in 1948 to 33 per cent in 1968.

However, instead of improving the abominable conditions of education in Soweto, the Department of Bantu Education (DBE) focused its efforts on compelling students to leave the township to attend the newly built schools in the homelands. It was only with the economic boom of the early 1970s that the situation began to change. Industry, at this point, was growing rapidly, creating an increased demand for skilled labour, and not enough white people were available to fill the jobs. Skilled black workers, on the other hand, could be employed at wages far lower than their white counterparts. Factory owners thus started to demand better education and training for the black urban workforce and, in 1972, the government reluctantly accepted that the Bantu Education system would have to improve if the needs of business were to be satisfied.

Within a remarkably short space of time, the DBE increased the number of secondary school enrolments in the township and, by mid-1974 there were 40 new schools in Soweto. Between 1972 and 1976, secondary school numbers in Soweto grew from 12 656 to 34 656 and, by 1976, one in five Soweto pupils was enrolled in secondary school. The official school population thus rocketed to 170 000, almost double the population of 90 000 at the end of the 1960s.

This huge expansion of secondary education in Soweto had a dramatic impact on youth culture. Previously, only a small minority of Soweto's youth had progressed beyond primary school, and the interval between leaving primary school and securing a job was often spent with youth gangs on the streets. Youth gangs were localised, territorial, hedonistic, and often lacked any clear political consciousness. The growth of secondary schooling, however, began to draw youths from the streets and from a wide range of neighbourhoods. As a result, a broader and more politically conscious youth identity began to develop. This was perceived by the gangs as a profound challenge to their position and, in the early 1970s, there were often savage conflicts between gangs and school pupils. The Hazels, The Dirty Dozens and many other youth gangs targeted pupils – especially schoolgirls – as they made their way to school. Pupils, however, responded with mass resistance and retaliation, and this further cemented a sense of pupil solidarity. In November 1974, for example, pupils and teachers from Phiri Higher Primary School retaliated against the attacks of the ZX5 gang by killing two and injuring five of their members.

GROWTH IN NUMBER OF AFRICAN PUPILS IN SECONDARY SCHOOL 1955–1975:	
1955	34 983
1960	47 598
1965	66 568
1970	122 489
1975	318 568

Department of Information, July 1976

After the onset of economic depression in South Africa in 1975, schools found themselves once again starved of funds. In that year, the government spent R644 on the education of every white child in South Africa while only R42 was spent on every African child. The situation in Soweto's classrooms was further aggravated by the DBE's decision to drop the Standard 6 year of primary school. Previously, only those who had obtained a first- or second-degree pass in Standard 6 were allowed to proceed to secondary school. By discontinuing the Standard 6 year, the majority of pupils were now able to proceed to Form 1. In 1976, 257 505 pupils enrolled in Form 1, which could accommodate only 38 000. Many of the Form 1 intake, therefore, had to remain at primary school. Junior secondary schools became chaotic, and one school even erected tents to provide temporary accommodation. Jon-Jon Mkhonza, a student at a Orlando West Junior Secondary School at the time, describes the situation in the classrooms:

❛ *It was so difficult because the teachers who were teaching us had in their mind just to punish us. They wouldn't enter a class without a sjambok. Whenever you don't have a textbook, you must go out. So we used to ask, "Okay, teacher, some parents are very poor. They can't even afford to give us money to eat. So, if a parent is going to get money to buy this child a book in November, you mean that child is only going to start attending your class in November?" The teacher would say, "Yes."* ❜

Under these conditions, learning was virtually impossible and the pass rate plunged to lower levels than ever before. Students, of course, grew angrier by the day.

> Aims and goals of a national student movement. To liberate the Black community as a whole i.e. physically and psychologically, the movement shall have:
> (a) to promote the spitit of self reliance amongst the students i.e. by writing Black poetry and organising relevant symposiums.
> (a) To promote the spirit of fraternity amongst the student i.e. by solving financial problems facing individuals especially among students within school premises.
> (c) To heighten the sense of awareness amongst the students i.e. by the publication of newsletters and reading of poetry,
> Newsletters should:
> (i) Criticise all racial segregated sport bodies.
> (ii) Criticise all government created bodies like bantustans, crc, saic,
> (iii) Criticise and discourage foreign investments.
> (iv) Bear clarity on the back ground of culture and education of the Blackman
> (d) Promote seminars.
> (e) Organise and comemorate eventful days such as Heroes Day.

Student organisation

The mounting discontent over classroom conditions, however, corresponded with the development of a political movement in Soweto's schools. The African Students' Movement (ASM), established in 1968 to voice student grievances and to challenge the conservative nature of church youth clubs in Soweto, took the lead. In the early 1970s, members of ASM encountered the philosophies of Black Consciousness (BC) and, in January 1972, the organisation pledged itself to build a national movement of high school students which would work alongside the South African Students' Organisation (SASO), the Black Consciousness organisation at black universities. As a result, ASM changed its name to the South African Students' Movement (SASM).

Leaders of the SASM initiated campaigns against Bantu Education in Soweto's schools but they faced many difficulties. The DBE issued stern warnings to principals and teachers against allowing any kind of political activity, and departmental inspectors regularly visited schools to ensure that this warning was observed. Police also repeatedly harassed, banned and imprisoned the leaders of both SASO and SASM and, as a result, high school pupils were afraid to participate in overtly political events. 'People who were politically inclined didn't last long,' recounts Teboho Mohapi of Morris Isaacson High School. 'Once it had become conspicuous that you were politically involved, you were nabbed by the system and your family would be harassed. Your principal would be in danger as well. So most principals protected themselves by not allowing student political activities in their schools. This delayed political awareness.'

Murphy Morobe, also a student at Morris Isaacson and a prominent member of SASM, describes the ways SASM found to outwit the authorities and to create political awareness among fellow students:

> *I remember trying to organise a meeting when many people were on the run, with the police all out to detain people. We all pretended to be swimmers and we had the meeting at the swimming pool in Orlando dressed only in bikinis and swimming trunks. I must say it wasn't the most comfortable way to have a serious meeting but it was out of the sight of the authorities!*

School debating societies were another important forum. SASM introduced provocative political topics and a growing number of students attended the inter-school debating tournaments. In this way, contact between high schools was established and, in order to reach students and avoid police surveillance, SASM members started participating in church youth clubs. Teboho Mohapi remembers how, 'between sports or before the usual event, someone would talk to the students, saying things like, *Mayibuye, amandla awethu* [Come back, Africa. Power to the people]. It wouldn't look like a political meeting but someone would give us reports of, for example, a teacher being picked up and detained because he's political'.

It was through meetings such as these that Mohapi became politically involved: 'People who belonged to SASM... started to invite me to underground meetings.' He adds how 'there were some supportive people who would provide SASM leaders with food and transport and the use of their houses for meetings... The whole thing was done secretly and I remember there was a sense of danger. We would sneak into a house one by one... I gained insights into organising students through those meetings'. Murphy Morobe stresses that 'there is no doubt in my mind that those small, secret meetings – where people took risks – contributed much to making sure the political flames kept flickering'.

SASM's efforts to promote political awareness were encouraged in early 1973 when SASO students staged walk-outs from black universities. Many of these 'drop-outs' became teachers in Soweto's schools. They were drawn particularly to Morris Isaacson and Orlando High because both schools had headmasters who tried to shelter activist teachers and students from the DBE. Armed with BC ideology, SASO activists inspired a new spirit of radicalism, and many students tell of the impact these teachers had on their lives.

Despite their successes, however, SASM encountered many obstacles. The organisation had very little money, and organisers based in Soweto had no access to facilities such as telephones and typewriters. (There were 39 public telephones in the township – one for every 25 900 people – and virtually no private phones.) Also, two leaders at SASM's main Soweto branch were found to be police informers and this demoralised many of the organisation's members even further. SASM also faced repeated attacks from tsotsi gangs such as the Makwaitos and the Bees operating in Soweto's schools. They regarded SASM as a threat to their territorial control and attempted to sabotage its activities. By the end of 1973, Murphy Morobe says 'the movement was almost in limbo and there were only a few of us who were still committed...'.

Nevertheless, 1974 was a turning point for SASM. It was then that Frelimo, the black liberation movement in Mozambique which had led the fight against Portuguese colonialism, won a remarkable victory in the country's first democratic elections. Frelimo's triumph brought the hope of change to young black South Africans and Frelimo's winning slogan of 'Power to the People' inspired increasing numbers of youth into action. 'Viva', generally understood as 'Long Live', became a prominent part of the political vocabulary of the township. WIth this renewed enthusiasm, however, students began to grow impatient with the older, more conservative BC leadership. Teboho Mohapi explains:

> *[SASM] had reached a point where it couldn't hide from students and we gradually became more and more conspicuous in the schools. When school knocked off for sports, a group would gather in the school hall and talk about student needs and it became known that those in the hall belonged to SASM. Towards the end of my Standard 8 year, we'd clearly gathered a large number of students at my school. Some of us started rotating from school to school to talk to the students. Corporal punishment was one of the basic projects of SASM... We'd also talk about Bantu Education as a poison that enslaved us. This was the gist of politicising students and influencing them. This was how we organised SASM into a fully fledged organisation.*

As SASM leaders began to gain confidence, they organised large-scale meetings and guest speakers addressed the students, their rousing speeches raising the political temperature at the schools. Sibongile Mkhabela, who joined SASM in 1975, remembers how 'the university guys who we respected a great deal, would come to address us and emphasise our consciousness as black people, our need to appreciate ourselves'. By the end of 1974, the strongest branches of SASM were at Morris Isaacson and Naledi, followed by Orlando High, Sekano Ntoana and Orlando West.

Although it is difficult to estimate precisely how many students were drawn into the ranks of the organisation, SASM events attracted large audiences and the movement undoubtedly helped to create a core of highly politicised and militant students. If nothing else, the spirit of the organisation was to inspire the events that followed.

The Afrikaans medium decree

It was in this highly volatile context that the Minister of Bantu Education and Development, MC Botha, announced the compulsory use of Afrikaans as a medium of instruction from Standard 5 onwards.

There were, however, other reasons for the Minister's insistence on the equal use of both official languages in the classroom. Television was

```
NORTHERN TRANSVAAL REGION
"REGIONAL CIRCULAR BANTU EDUCATION
NORTHERN TRANSVALL (NO. 4)
FILE 6.8.3 OF 17.10.1974
TO:  CIRCUIT INSPECTORS
     PRINCIPALS OF SCHOOLS: With Std V classes and Secondary Schools)
MEDIUM O FINSTRUCTION STD V - FORM V
1.   It hase been decided that for the sake of uniformity English and
     Afrikaans will be used as media of instruction in our schools on a
     50-50 basis as follows:
2.   STD V, FORM I AND II
     2.1 English medium: General Science
                         Practical Subjects (Homecraft-Needlework-
                                 Wood- and Metalwork-Art- Agricultural Science)
     2.2 Afrikaans medium: Mathematics Arithmatic
                           Social Studies
     2.3 Mother Tongue: Religious Instruction, Music, Physical Culture
     The prescribed medium for these subject must be used as from
     January 1995.
     In 1976 the secondary schools will continue using the same medium
     for these subjects.
3.   FORMS III, IV AND V
     All schools which have not as yet done so should introduce the
     50-50 basis as from the beginning of 1975. The same medium must be
     used for the subjects related to those mentioned in paragraph 2
     and for their alternatives.
3.   You are also referred to Departmental Circular No. 6 of 1974. The
     instructions contained in this circular must also be observed.
     The above arrangement has also been adopted by the Southern
     Transvaal Region.
     Your co-operation in this matter will be appreciated."
(Sgd.)    J.G. Erasmus
          REGIONAL DIRECTOR OF BANTU EDUCATION
          N. TRANSVAAL REGION
N.B. (a)  I have enclosed a photostat copy of Dept. Circular No. 6 of
          17.4.1974 for your information. The marking on the side is mine.
     (b)  S.Tvl Region = All schools in White areas in the S. Transvaal.
          N.Tvl Region =    "     "    "    "    "    "   N.Transvaal.
If there is any further assistance I can give you please do not hesitate
to ask for it.

Yours sincerely
R.N. GUGSHE
```

to be introduced in South Africa for the first time in 1976 and Afrikaans-speaking conservatives feared that it would strengthen the position and status of English in the country. They also believed that young blacks were becoming 'too self-assertive' and that forcing them to learn in Afrikaans would be a useful form of discipline. African teachers vehemently opposed the new policy.

The African Teachers Association (ATASA) thus launched a determined campaign against the policy, but the authorities remained uncompromising. 'No, I have not consulted the African people on the language issue and I'm not going to,' declared Punt Janson, the Deputy Minister of Bantu Education. 'An African might find that "the big boss" only spoke Afrikaans or only spoke English. It would be to his advantage to know both languages.' Other officials offered the same knee-jerk response. 'If students are not happy,' another added, 'they should stay away from school since attendance is not compulsory for Africans.' (Brooks and Brickhill, *Whirlwind Before the Storm*, 1980)

The DBE also claimed that, because the government paid for black education, they had the right to decide on the appropriate language of instruction. In reality, only white education was completely subsidised by the government. Black parents in Soweto had to pay R102 per year – an average monthly wage for Sowetans – to send two children to school. They also had to buy textbooks and school uniforms, and contribute to the costs of building schools.

The students fight back

From the start, black students were violently opposed to being taught in Afrikaans. Not only did they think of Afrikaans as the language of the oppressor, but they also encountered extreme difficulty in having to learn in two languages. Jon-Jon Mkhonza recalls:

There was one teacher by the name of Mr Modisane. He was teaching Afrikaans, History and Mathematics, so we told him that we didn't understand this language; couldn't he explain in English? He said, "No." So... I mean... we couldn't understand. Just imagine from March until... I think it was in May, we were still blank on those subjects.

Even teachers had great difficulty teaching in Afrikaans. 'The teacher himself couldn't cope with Afrikaans,' recounts Sibongile Mkhabela, a student at Naledi High. 'Half the time he taught in an African language, but we were supposed to write our examination in Afrikaans. It was totally chaotic and I actually failed my Standard 7 because I didn't understand what was happening in the class.'

'The kids were mad about this sort of thing,' remembers Dr Nthato Motlana, who drove children to school in his car. 'They would be sitting in my car, telling me what it was like to be a student in South Africa, to be taught History and Mathematics in Afrikaans by a black teacher who did not know Afrikaans himself and who had to consult a textbook to find out what a triangle or an angle was all about.'

As the weeks went by, students' anger mounted and Sam de Beer, the school inspector responsible for Soweto, was declared by the youth to be Public Enemy Number One. Seth Mazibuko clearly remembers the day Sam de Beer arrived at Orlando West Secondary School:

Sam de Beer took the platform and said, "This school is funded by the government and we decide the policies... and if you don't want to be in this school, there is the gate..." Two days after De Beer addressed us, History, Mathematics and Science textbooks written in Afrikaans were delivered to our school. Guess what happened. The students took those books, tore them up and burned them. We called it "braaivleis" [barbeque].

When schools reopened in 1976, however, many of the teachers refused to give instruction in Afrikaans but, despite this show of solidarity, students still believed that their teachers and principals were far too moderate. Students were also enraged with the attitude of their parents, many of whom expressed opinions similar to that of Steven Tshabalala: 'When my wife tried to tell me that my child had a problem with Afrikaans at school, I didn't care about that. I thought, no man, let her go to school. I am paying the school fees; she's got the gym dress, she's got the books, so why can't she go to school? She must learn. Let her go and learn.'

Susan Shabangu reflects the students' feelings at the time: 'When our parents accepted Bantu Education, they said "half a loaf is better than nothing". We were saying, we don't want any half loaf. We either have a full loaf or nothing at all. That became our slogan.'

'Our parents are prepared to suffer under the white man's rule,' another student wrote to *The World* newspaper. 'They have been living for years under these laws and they have become immune to them. But we strongly refuse to swallow an education that is designed to make us slaves in the country of our birth.'

The uprising

Although student activism was on the increase by 1976, the education authorities remained stubborn in their insistence on the ruling regarding Afrikaans. As the July examinations approached, Form 1 and 2 students from Orlando West Junior Secondary School, often referred to as Phefeni, staged a class boycott, and were joined by the students from seven other schools in Soweto. The DBE believed that these signs of resistance were caused by a small group of 'agitators' and relied on the police to sort them out. But, as Teboho Mohapi recalls, an incident at Naledi High School reveals that the SAP were unable to maintain complete control of the situation.

Students at Naledi wanted to confront the regional director of education, but when members of the Special Branch (SB) arrived at the school instead of the director, the students erupted in anger. The SB locked themselves in the principal's office and, even more incensed, the angry students overturned the police vehicles, stopping short of burning them. This was the first time the power of the students had been felt and was the first fruits of SASM's efforts to organise students in all the schools.

Inspired by this act of defiance, the students at Morris Isaacson hung a notice on their gates saying, 'No SBs allowed. Enter at risk of your skin.'

Sibongile Mkhabela, a leader of SASM at Naledi High, recalls that 'there was serious mobilisation in the schools and this was done mainly through SASM. SASM members were saying that this situation could not be allowed to continue. That was the build-up to the meeting on June 13th'.

Nearly 400 students attended the meeting in Orlando on Sunday, 13 June. It was there that Tsietsi Mashinini, 19-year-old leader of the SASM branch at Morris Isaacson, proposed a mass demonstration against Afrikaans on the following Wednesday. Mashinini was an extremely powerful speaker and his suggestion was greeted with cheers of support. An Action Committee was formed under the leadership of Mashinini and Seth Mazibuko, another charismatic Form 2 student who had led the initial class boycott at Orlando West Junior Secondary School. 'We thought that if we leave those classrooms and come as a big group and show the world that now it was tough out there in the classrooms,' recalls Seth Mazibuko, 'something would be done.'

'What was interesting about June 13th,' remarks Sibongile Mkhabela, 'was that students had a pact that parents should not be involved. They should not even be told about was going to happen on the 16th. Given the multitudes of students who were there, it was actually surprising to find that we all went home and kept quiet.' Murphy Morobe believes that parents were kept out because 'students had lost so much confidence in the adult population because of the ways things had happened over the years. We thought that if the news leaked out, we ran the risk of them deciding to stop it'.

On the cold and smoggy morning of Wednesday, 16 June, groups of excited students assembled at different points throughout the township. Teboho Mohapi's expectation 'was that it was going to be a very peaceful march and it was going to take everybody by surprise. We were talking about what a surprise it was going to be to our parents and teachers. They would just see us walking out of class and would try to stop us and then we would tell them "Wait, this is our day".'

At the appointed time, groups of students set off to meet at Orlando West Secondary School on Vilikazi Street. Morobe remembers the moment:

❝ *The plan was that the signal time for us to start acting and moving was the singing of* **Nkosi Sikelel' iAfrika** *in place of the usual Lord's Prayer in the morning assembly. When the principal at one school tried to stop his students, they said to him, "We have a duty to do", and then they marched out.* ❞

'I was filled with anxiety and of course excited, excited that ultimately our dream had come true. Now we were going to the streets,' recalls Teboho Mohapi. 'Now we were going to let our grievances be known through a public march.'

Columns of students converged on Orlando West from all over the township.

By 10.30am, over 5 000 students had gathered on Vilikazi Street and more were arriving every minute. Witnesses estimated that there were over 15 000 uniformed students between the ages of 10 and 20 marching that day. As the marchers threaded through the streets, they sang songs of defiance.

Asikhathali noma bes'bopha
(We don't give a damn, even if imprisoned)
Sizimisel 'inkululeko
(For freedom's our ultimate goal.)

The students also chanted *Amandla!* (Power), and *Inkululeko ngoku!* (Freedom in our lifetime). Their placards read 'Away with Afrikaans' and 'We are fed the crumbs of ignorance with Afrikaans as a poisonous spoon'. One placard suggested that 'If we must do Afrikaans, Vorster must do Zulu'.

Students raise their hands in solidarity with the protests.

'The spirit was the spirit of victory...' remembers Seth Mazubuko. 'For the first time, there was no more Sotho, Zulu, Xhosa, Moshangaan because, remember, the schools were divided into that. We were together and we were marching under one common cause; we didn't want a particular language that had separated us.'

Those parents who had not already left for work stood watching and wondering what was going on. Dr Motlana recollects that he was 'doing surgery at about 10 o'clock in the morning when, suddenly, there was this sound like a storm cloud gathering somewhere in the distance. And the storm was about to break around Dube. I asked my nurses, "What the hell is happening?" and they said to me, "Don't you know, Doctor? The students are demonstrating against black education today." So we all abandoned our rooms and let our patients go watch what was happening'.

'Our original plan,' explains Murphy Morobe, 'was just to get to Orlando West, pledge our solidarity, and sing *Nkosi Sikelel' iAfrika*. Then we thought we would have made our point and we would go back home. No one envisaged a process that would go beyond June 16th. Little did we expect the kind of reaction that we got from the police on that day.'

The students' placards made their feelings clear.

The police intervene

The Bureau of State Security (BOSS), created by Prime Minister BJ Vorster to take charge of all aspects of the country's security, was caught entirely off guard by the march. They hurriedly sent a squad of police vehicles to meet the swelling crowd and, as the officers emerged from their vehicles, they formed a wall in front of the throng of pupils singing 'Morena boloka sechaba Sa Heso', a line from what was to become the national anthem, meaning 'God bless our nation'. Jon-Jon Mkhonza was at the head of the march:

> **The police told us to disperse. But we refused, saying that, "No, we are not going to intimidate anybody, we are not going to loot, we are not going to do anything wrong. We are just going to march and demonstrate and sing and then go back home." They again said that we must disperse.**

Police dogs were then released. 'These vicious, well-trained dogs were grabbed by these little girls – and they were little girls – and destroyed,' an eyewitness recalls. For Murphy Morobe, that was 'when the police took up position on the hill above the school and started shooting teargas. All hell broke loose...'

Mkhonza recalls the panic as students were dazed and blinded by the teargas. 'Students were scattered, running up and down... coming back, running... coming back. It was some kind of game because they were running away, coming back, taking stones, throwing them at the police... It was chaos. Whenever the police shot teargas, we jumped the wall to the churchyard and then came back and started discussing again.'

As the teargas canisters exploded, people fled in all directions.

Soweto — A History

It was during this battle that journalists reported seeing a policeman draw his revolver and, without warning, fire directly into the crowd. Seconds later, several other policemen opened fire. 'That's when Hector Petersen was shot,' says Mkhonza, '...because he was crossing between the students and the police, trying to go home, and the police were shooting by then. So they shot Hector Petersen.'

Sam Nzima's photograph of an anguished young boy, cradling Hector Petersen's dead body with Hector's sister running alongside, transmitted the horror of the events in Soweto to South Africans and the world at large. The image fast became a symbol of the atrocities of the apartheid regime. The postmortem revealed that 13-year-old Hector was killed by a shot fired directly at him and not by a bullet 'ricocheting off the ground' as the police later claimed.

The students were now so enraged by the vicious actions of the police that they ignored the flying bullets and hurled rocks, stones and anything else they could find at the officers. The screams of children pierced the air, and the anger that was ignited at that moment could not be suppressed for many months to come.

For the leaders of the march, the situation had escalated beyond their control. 'In me there was this thing that now, good Lord, I have called these students out of their classrooms into the streets and here were now bullets and teargas and all those things. I didn't expect that to happen,' Seth Mazibuko recollects. Murphy Morobe agrees:

The photograph that shocked the world and symbolised the horrors of apartheid.

Many of the bottle stores were looted.

" **We were inadequately prepared to deal with the situation once those shots were fired. The only thing on our minds was to disperse everyone as soon as possible. We went back to the area to try to do that, but it was difficult. The first question people asked us was, "If you say we must go away, where must we go to? If these policemen come into Soweto, where must we go because this is where we stay." We were entirely out of our depth in terms of what to do.** "

Lacking a coherent strategy, groups of angry students began setting fire to the symbols of apartheid. 'Government buildings became an automatic target,' comments Teboho Mohapi. 'No one stood there and said, "This is our next target; this is what we're going to do." Some people were trying to say, "No!" Others were just saying "To hell with it".'

Municipal beerhalls and liquor stores, regarded as an evil by the students, were also set alight. Many liquor stores had been looted and the streets were littered with bottles and crates. Seth Mazibuko contends that students began to loot and burn because 'they were prevented from doing what they had planned to do, and some of them were shot and killed'.

PUTCO buses, which charged high fares to carry Sowetan passengers to Johannesburg, were yet another target of attack, as were the vehicles belonging to white businesses. Drivers watched helplessly as their vans were set alight or raided for their wares.

Seth Mazibuko saw students stop an oncoming truck, 'and they told the old man in there – who happened to be black – to take the money and use it for his children. They told him they wanted what was in the truck – yoghurt, milk, sour milk, buttermilk. "We are hungry, and we just want to eat," they said'. Another truck was stopped and opened and 'somebody was throwing things and saying, "Africa, you shall eat,"' adds Teboho Mohapi, 'and Africa ate'.

Hundreds of buses and other government vehicles were set alight.

As thick black smoke billowed up from all parts of Soweto, the police struggled to control the situation. Anti-riot vehicles, known as 'Hippos', streamed into Soweto in an effort to regain command. Members of the new Anti-Urban Terrorism Unit, dressed in camouflage uniform and armed with automatic rifles and machine guns erected roadblocks at all the entrances to Soweto and stopped white people from entering the township. The army and reinforcements from other urban centres were now placed on alert. Sibongile Mkhabela recalls:

> *For a township child, it was the first time we actually saw police in their full force. We were used to the small kwela-kwela vans but it was the first time we actually saw a hippo, that big ugly vehicle, or other military vehicles.*

Army helicopters dropped teargas on gatherings of students, and black policemen, who were not allowed to carry arms, were withdrawn from the actual fighting, as were Council 'blackjacks'. But the sight of scores of well-armed white policemen only served to stir the already seething anger of the students. More and more buildings and vehicles were set ablaze and, as the day progressed, some of the injured died at the gates of Baragwanath Hospital, its wards and floors were littered with bodies.

Although there were few attacks against individuals, two white officials from the West Rand Administration Board (WRAB) were beaten to death amidst cries of 'Black Power!' Melville Edelstein, WRAB's Chief Welfare Officer and, ironically, an ally of Soweto's youth, was killed inside the WRAB building. Teboho Mohapi tells how the other WRAB official 'was just about to pull a gun, and then his car was pick-axed. The windows were shattered and he was pulled out of his car and then later he died. He was put in a dustbin there'.

As the sun began to set, the police finally lost all control. Because there were no street lights in most of the township, policemen simply fired into the dark and were, in turn, pelted with stones and bottles by crowds of youths concealed by the night. Soldiers were placed on standby on the outskirts of the township. Patrick Shongwe remembers the sight that greeted workers returning home:

> *The whole sky filled with smoke. We didn't know what was happening. The train service was disrupted. We were asked to go home from work at 11 o'clock, but it was 9 o'clock at night before I could get into my house because the whole place was so dangerous. Police vans were driving this way and that and shooting at random. Municipal property and bottle stores were being broken down, smashed, looted and all of that.*

Soweto — A History

Students raise their fists in the power salute.

Despite the dangers on the streets and the tragedy that had befallen, the township was also embraced by an atmosphere of triumph and celebration. Steven Tshabalala tells how he and fellow workers 'encountered a group of students who had just hijacked a car. They were shouting "Power!" and held clenched fists in the air. They told us, "You must say Power", so we screamed "Power! Power!" right until we got home.

'Almost the whole township was drunk,' continues Steven Tshabalala, 'because now there was so much beer. Everybody was so generous. When you go past your enemy, he'd say, "Have a shot, man", and he'd give you a whole quart of brandy.'

Jane Khanyeza has similar memories. She got home to find 'all the people drunk in the street. When I got into the house, I found lots of beer. I didn't say anything, I was just drinking, happy because of what had happened'.

Jon-Jon Mkhonza remembers a scene that took place in the street in which he lived:

❝ Down the road from my house, a beerhall was destroyed and the youths found a safe which they struggled to open for hours. There was much jubilation once they opened it and everyone was grabbing money, helping themselves. Kids were running past my house clutching notes. ❞

The day after

In the early hours of 17 June, the extent of the damage from the battles of the previous day became evident. The charred remains of cars and trucks lay scattered across the roads, obstructing the passage of police patrols. Virtually every liquor store, beerhall and community centre lay in smouldering ruin. Dead bodies lay sprawled in the streets as patrols collected the corpses.

June 17: collecting the dead.

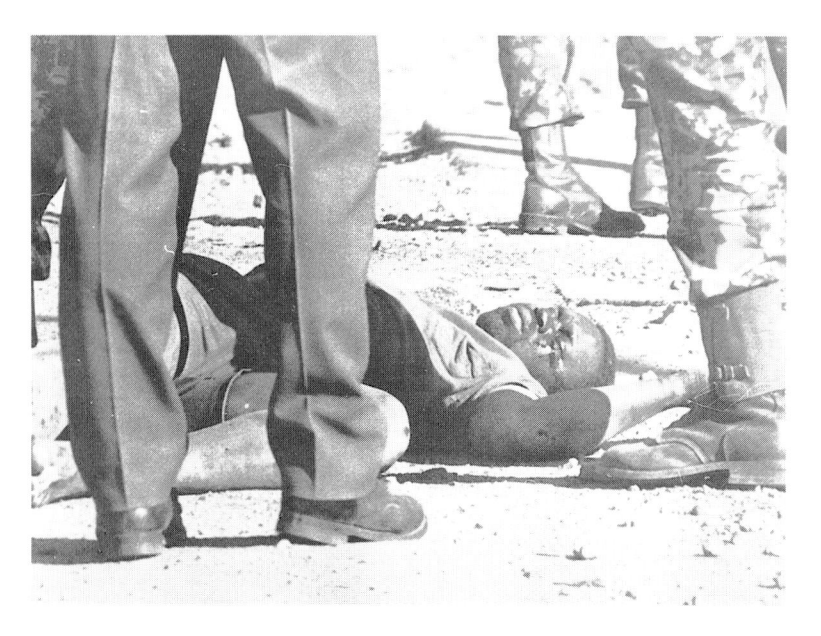

The official death toll was 23, but the real figure would prove to be much higher. Some reports estimated that over 200 people had died and many hundreds more were injured during the first day of hostilities.

By 8.15am, the fury at the sight of the carnage again brought the students onto the streets and skirmishes with the police were reported all over Soweto.

Asingeni! (We will not enter) was scrawled across the blackboards, doors and walls of all secondary schools. The resonant battle cry, *Amandla Ngawethu!* – Power to the People! – rang in the streets, and young non-school-going gang members entered the fray. It became a sport, referred to as *simbamba ama* targets (catching targets), for them to stop vans and delivery trucks from entering Soweto. Police patrolled the neighbourhoods and reportedly shot anyone who so much as raised a fist. As a result, even more casualties were reported on the second day of fighting. Nomavenda Mathiane, a well-known journalist who lived in the township, wrote of the chaos on that day:

❝ On June 17, I watched as bodies were dragged out of what had been a shopping centre on the Old Potch Road. I saw figures running out of the shop, some carrying goods. They ran across the veld like wild animals, dropping like bags as bullets hit them. I saw billows of smoke shoot up as white vehicles burned. I thought the world had come to an end. I saw leaders inside and outside Soweto plead for reason and I saw people detained and killed... ❞

Thousands of black workers stayed at home to watch over their families. In London, an early morning radio broadcast commented, 'It is clear now that Soweto will join Sharpeville in the calendar of apartheid.'

At the same time, news of the uprising reverberated through townships across South Africa. In solidarity with the citizens of Soweto, protests and meetings in the Transvaal and the rest of the country were arranged immediately. Placards proclaimed 'Don't start the revolution without us!', 'Soweto is our blood', and 'Amandla Soweto'. Buildings at the University of Zululand were set alight and, by the third day, Alexandra – a smaller township in the northern part of Johannesburg – was in flames and the white suburbs and industrial areas surrounding the township were in a state of panic. Students and residents of Alexandra fought back with every conceivable weapon, and the battle that followed has been described as even more violent than that in Soweto. But the official cover-up operation was by now well in place and a wall of silence blocked out further news in both the townships as well as other areas where the rebellion had flared. The authorities simply reported that 95 blacks had died in the Transvaal. Again, the accurate death toll was estimated to be much higher, probably well over 500. *The World* carried reports of the authorities carrying out secret burials of Soweto's victims under cover of darkness. The majority of the dead were younger than 23, and thousands of people were crippled or maimed. A later inquiry revealed that most of the deaths and injuries were caused by police bullets, often fired into the back of the victim. By the end of the third day of carnage, the Minister for Bantu Education had closed all schools in Soweto and Alexandra.

Reactions to the uprising

Local newspapers carried headlines of a 'political disaster' engulfing South Africa, and a story of the uprising, published in the popular black magazine *Drum*, was headlined 'A telegraphed punch'. In the language of boxing, this meant a clumsy blow that can be easily anticipated and thus avoided. Jimmy Kruger, the Minister of Justice and Police, however, told an emotionally charged gathering in Parliament that the government had 'not expected anything like this to happen' and could have done nothing to avoid the crisis. He simply blamed the 'riots' on 'agitators who were polarising the races in South Africa' and emphatically denied that the police provoked the violence:

❝ Many of the so-called grievances are far-fetched. I have not found any grievances that would indicate that the Bantu Administration has flopped on the job. My first task now is to rid South Africa of the thugs on the streets... The police conducted themselves with the greatest measure of patience in the face of the greatest measure of provocation. The police did everything in their power to bring the students under control and were eventually forced to fire warning shots over their heads. ❞

A police colonel who was at the scene, however, directly contradicted Kruger saying that, 'We fired into them – it's no use firing over their heads.' (*Rand Daily Mail*, 17 June 1976)

A young boy turns a dustbin lid into a means of defence.

(Below, bottom) Students hijacked buses to attend the mass burials organised throughout Soweto.

In the weeks which followed, Kruger blamed the 'international conspiracy of communism' for the spread of the resistance, and spoke of student leaflets filled with 'Marxist clichés' and showing young people with their fists in the air. 'Surely, this is a sign of the Communist Party?' he insisted. The only positive action Kruger took at the time was to appoint Transvaal Judge President Mr Justice Cillie as a one-person commission to investigate the causes of the uprising. The State Archives, however, recently released notes from the Cabinet meeting of 10 August 1976 in which a note, written by Kruger, states that the student movement 'must be broken and the police must maybe act a bit more drastically to bring about more deaths'.

Burying the victims

In the meantime, the Soweto community faced the debilitating task of identifying the dead and arranging for their burial. The government refused to publish the names of those who had died and hospitals were ordered to secrecy. Long queues of people stood for hours outside the mortuary to see if the bodies of their loved ones lay inside. Many students, on the other hand, simply 'disappeared'.

Although the government banned all public meetings, mass burials were organised across Soweto, and students even hijacked buses to attend. The highly charged atmosphere at the funerals rose from a combination of deep mourning and outrage. 'We are getting sick and tired of trying to tell the Prime Minister that the present South African way of life is unholy and oppressive,' Reverend Desmond Tutu, then Anglican Dean of Johannesburg, told a gathering, and other speakers urged the huge crowds to carry the struggle forward. Freedom songs replaced dirges and the dead were hailed as 'soldiers of Africa, heroes who have not died in vain'. Lefifi Tladi became a regular feature in the funeral programmes. Standing next to the fresh mounds of earth, the young poet emotionally recited the poem, 'Our Spears are immersed in blood', while the choir sang 'Hamba, hamba kahle' (Farewell, farewell).

'Parents, you should rejoice for having given birth to this type of child, a child who prefers to die from a bullet rather than swallow a poisonous education which relegates him and his parents to a position of perpetual subordination,' announced one of the leaflets distributed.

Thus, the uprising also stirred sections of Soweto's elder generation into action. Dr Motlana was amongst those who took the lead:

> As parents, we could not allow a situation in which our children were dying. I mean, they died by their thousands; we believe the figures given by the government were way off the mark. And, therefore, we could not allow that kind of thing to happen, to go unchecked. We had to be seen to be involved with our children in the ongoing struggle. And we decided there and then to form a committee which could talk to the children, talk to the authorities, form a bridge between the warring factions which were the police, the state and the children. It was called the Black Parents Association (BPA).

The BPA was officially launched on the 21 June 1976, and its broad membership included church leaders, social workers and teachers. Winnie Mandela was a central figure. The organisation initially co-ordinated the funeral arrangements of the victims and gathered funds for the afflicted families, but it later came to represent the black community as a whole. The government accused the BPA of controlling and manipulating the students, but this could hardly be considered the truth. The students, in fact, rejected any attempts by the BPA to make decisions for them and there were repeated clashes between the BPA and the more militant student body. 'Many students thought we should allow them to do their own thing,' recalls Dr Motlana of the first BPA meeting. 'They said that we, as parents, had failed over the years to address black disabilities, and who were we to try to control the students?' Certain student leaders did, however, accept the BPA as a mouthpiece, as Murphy Morobe attests: 'The basic attitude of the authorities was not to take us students seriously. The only way forward was to try to rope in adults and actually give them the briefing, give them the mandate to make representations to the Department and the Government.'

The involvement of the BPA signalled an end to the first phase of the struggle in which the youth had acted on their own. It heralded a new phase, in which the Soweto community was drawn into the fray.

OUR SPEARS ARE IMMERSED IN BLOOD

Our Spears are immersed in blood
We are on the warpath
Of Blood River
The distance is long
But the courage is thriced
We are the elephant
We are the warrior
Transformed to a guerrilla
The spirit of Sharpeville
Emerges from the present
Wearing a new mask
Soweto, Soweto, Soweto
History repeats itself
We are the elephant
We move the way of no return

A new phase

School holidays began at the end of June. Student activities came to a standstill but a mood of deep disquiet permeated the township. Damage to property ran into many millions of rands, and 22 PUTCO buses were destroyed, leaving few of the usual bus routes still in operation. Food deliveries had come to a halt and basic foodstuffs were scarce. Shops which still had supplies charged exorbitant prices.

At this point, the government attempted to reassert its control by tabling a number of reforms. Despite Prime Minister Vorster's claim that the 'language question played a smaller and smaller role in the riots' and that it was 'a hanger on which some people hung their hats', the DBE announced that schools would, in future, be allowed to choose their own medium of instruction. Ironically, the tragically high death toll achieved what 18 months of peaceful protest had not been able to accomplish.

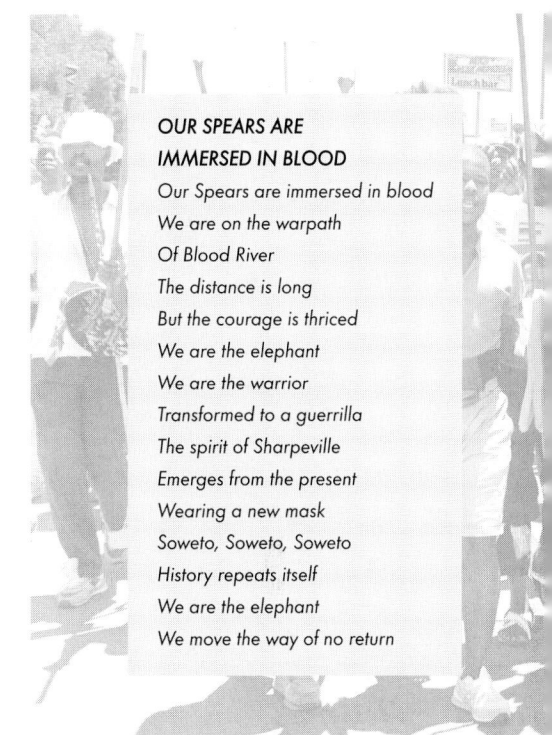

The government also finally abolished the 1968 law which banned traders from owning their own business premises and doctors, lawyers and other professionals from practising in the township. But what the government gave with one hand it took away with the other. A string of new repressive measures were enforced, and the police were granted the right to detain people without trial. Throughout July 1976, they detained hundreds of people in an attempt to identify the main 'agitators behind the riots'. Dr Motlana and Winnie Mandela from the BPA were among the first to be jailed.

The stories of many detainees reveal that the police simply wanted the prisoners to confirm the government's version of the events. Murphy Morobe was one of those interrogated:

The first thing they did was to tell me what actually happened and where I fitted into that. I had to fit into their scheme as to why June 16th happened, why the rest of the things happened, and what our role was in that. For them, we were just students who were being manipulated and used by forces elsewhere and were not responsible for what happened. Clearly, the government did not believe that the uprisings were a result of their policies, that the students were fed up with what had been happening. There had to be a plot.

Seth Mazibuko recounts a similar experience:

The police believed strongly that the ANC was behind the uprising. They believed that all the members of the Action Committee were ANC. We were not ANC at all, but they didn't buy the story that we were not. They would ask, for instance, who were the real people behind June 16th? They also wanted us to say that we planned the demonstration to kill the police, to burn the building belonging to the government and bring down the government, and we were doing this on instruction from the ANC in exile.

Damaged school buildings became an expression of students' hatred for Bantu Education.

Police often tortured the students in order to extract the information they required, and Sibongile Mkhabela recalls the experience:

They would put you in this very nasty interrogation room with lots of blood stains on the walls which scares you to death. I was standing in a cell like this wearing only my nightie. I was feeling extremely uncomfortable and very cold. I was not sure what was going to happen next. In walked four very big guys in their military uniform. They were so intimidating. They didn't say a word. They just kicked and slapped me and did whatever they wanted to do and they left me on the floor bleeding. They were followed by a security diplomat who came in speaking a nice Sotho. It was all designed to make you talk.

'You knew you would get electrocuted,' continues Murphy Morobe. 'You had a wet sack tied around your head and electrodes were put on your body and you were shocked.' After that, adds Dan Montsitsi, 'The security police would release you with blue eyes, swollen lips... in order to make an example to others of what would happen to them if they got involved.'

Following the imprisonment of hundreds of students, Minister of Justice, Jimmy Kruger, announced that the 'back of the unrest had been broken'. He had earlier warned that black schools in Soweto would remain closed 'until the blacks show a willingness to use schools for the right purposes', and now expressed confidence that schools would soon reopen. The rebellion, however, was far from over. Contrary to what the government may have believed, the reopening of schools provided the opportunity for leaders and students to regroup and reorganise. The 'poison' of Bantu Education and the entire system of apartheid now became the focus of attack.

Meanwhile, the events in Soweto provided a powerful inspiration to the rest of the country and, from August 1976, struggles broke out in townships in and around Cape Town. Thousands of young black and coloured students united for the first time. Coloured pupils carried placards reading, 'Freedom from oppression for our black brothers', and the resistance reached its climax when youths marched into Cape Town's city centre. This was the first time the struggle had directly spilt over into white areas. Soon afterward, rebellion flared up in many of the small towns in the Cape where there was little tradition of political protest. Students in the Bantustans also protested and many of the educational institutions in the rural areas were closed indefinitely.

This countrywide rebellion revived the fighting spirit of Soweto's students. New targets were attacked. The public library in Dube was destroyed, as were a number of clinics, black-owned shops, and houses belonging to African policemen. School buildings were burnt and, although children in Soweto almost certainly targeted the schools because of their hatred for Bantu Education, there was also speculation that the police had set fire to some of the schools in order to wreak havoc. In fact, throughout this period, complaints mounted about the behaviour of the riot police. Brigadier 'Rooi Rus' Swanepoel was nicknamed 'The Beast of Soweto' for his role in suppressing the rebellion of 16 June. 'We have heard numerous accounts,' read one memorandum to the Commissioner of the SAP, 'of principals and teachers which confirmed that, while children were unruly, gathered in crowds on school grounds and even outside, there was almost never violence or damage to property until the police arrived on the scene and their presence almost invariably provoked violence from the students. There is evidence of police blocking the doors of classrooms with children inside after they have thrown teargas into the rooms. Teachers who pleaded with the police were clubbed and arrested. We have heard eyewitness accounts of police kicking girls in their stomachs, beating them over their breasts.'

> One were the killings which I saw with my own eyes. I remember one instance when I was standing with a friend at a street corner. Opposite us, a little way down, were two young boys aged about eight and nine years, walking up the street. A police van with riot police drove down the street. They were pointing rifles at people, playing games – not shooting. As they passed the two young boys, they shot. The eight year old fell. We rushed across and he was still alive but there was blood all over. He died later because we couldn't find transport to get him to hospital in time. Now some of you may think what we have said here today are fairy tales, but they are real experiences which me and many others went through.

Eyewitness account of police brutality.

Extract from a memorandum issued by Tsietsi Mashinini, on behalf of the SSRC.

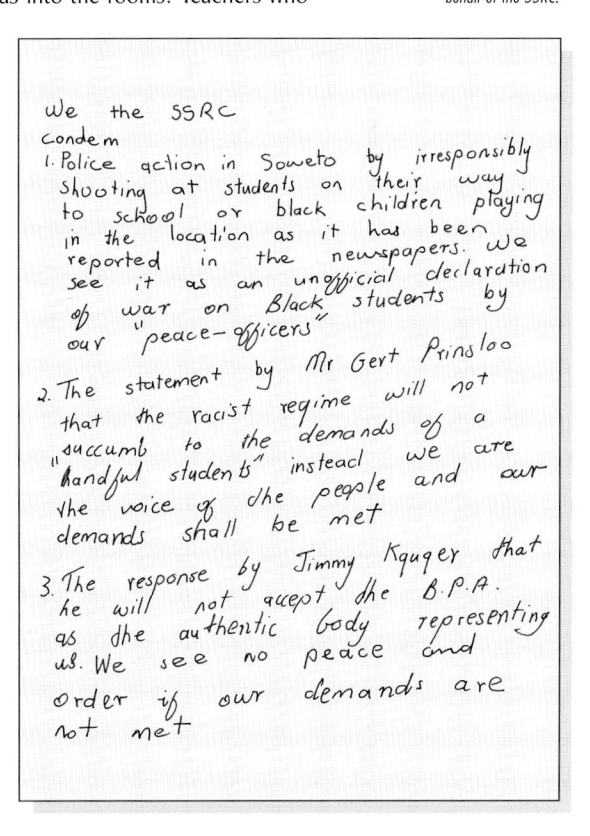

Children take the lead

The Action Committee, which had organised the initial march, was becoming increasingly concerned at the turmoil and lawlessness that was engulfing the township. They condemned police behaviour, but also spoke out against the burning of schools and the tsotsis and gangsters who had started taking advantage of the situation to assault and rob. The Committee called an emergency meeting of student leaders at Morris Isaacson on 2 August 1976. 'It was felt that more co-ordination was necessary,' says Sibongile Mkhabela. 'SASM set about it in this way: two representatives of each school in Soweto were nominated to an umbrella body. The Soweto Students Representative Council (SSRC), as it was called, set about mobilising the community.'

The SSRC adopted the slogan, 'The blood of martyrs will nurture the tree of liberation', and declared that its fight was no longer only against Bantu Education. Tsietsi Mashinini, who had acquired the status of a hero in the township for leading the march, was elected as chairman. He issued a memorandum on behalf of the SSRC.

> We the SSRC condem
> 1. Police action in Soweto by irresponsibly shooting at students on their way to school or black children playing in the location as it has been reported in the newspapers. We see it as an unofficial declaration of war on Black students by our "peace-officers"
> 2. The statement by Mr Gert Prinsloo that the racist regime will not "succumb to the demands of a handful students" instead we are the voice of the people and our demands shall be met
> 3. The response by Jimmy Kquger that he will not accept the B.P.A. as the authentic body representing us. We see no peace and order if our demands are not met

> TO ALL OUR PEOPLE IN SOWETO AND OTHER AFRICAN TOWNSHIPS
> "S T A N D   F A S T !"
>
> WE FEEL THAT IT IS HIGH TIME THAT OUR PEOPLE THROUGHOUT SOWETO AND OTHER AFRICAN TOWNSHIPS STOOD FAST AND PUT THEIR FEET DOWN AND BLUNTLY REFUSE TO BE MADE PUPPETS AND FOOLS OUT OF BY THE VANDALS AND THIEVES OF THE SOWETO STUDENTS REPRESENTATIVE COUNCIL AND OTHER ORGANISATIONS LIKE IT THAT SEEM DETERMINED TO PLUNGE THE BLACK RACE IN SOURTH AFRICAN INTO A NEW DARK AGE OF MISERY, DEATH AND DESTRUCTION.
>
> THE SOWETO STUDENTS REPRESENTATIVE COUNCIL CLAIMS TO BE A GROUP THAT FIGHTS FOR BLACK LIBERATION AND BETTER EDUCATION BUT ITS CLAIM IS PROVEN TO BE A LIE BY THE FACT THAT IT HAS PERSISTANTLY AND CRIMINALLY INTERFERED WITH THOSE OF OUR CHILDREN WHO WANWT TO STUDY, IT HAS RESOTED TO CMMUNIST TAC- TICS OF SLANDERING FELLOW BLAKC PEOPLE BY CALLING THEM "SELLOUTS" WITHOUT PROOF, OF ENCOURAGING THIS MOLESTATION OF TACHERS, OF CRIMINALLY EXTORTING MONEY FROM BLACK PEOPLE, OF BEAETING UP DEFENCELESS BLACK MEN AND WOMEN AND OF MUDERING FELLOW BLACK PEOPLE AND BURNING DOWN BLACK HOMES.
>
> WE DARE THE SOWETO STUDENTS REPRESENTATIVE COUNCIL, THE BLACK PEOPLE'S CONVENTION, THE BLACK PARENTS ASSOCIATION AND OTHER "BLACK POWER" ORGANI- SATIONS TO PUBLICLY DENY THAT THEY ARE PREACHING A DOCTINE WHICH WAS FOUND TO BE DANGEROUSLY NEGATIVE AND AS DIS CREDTIED AND ABANDONED BY THE
> AMERICAN NEGRO PEOPLE AMONGST WHOM "BLACK POWER" STARTED.
>
> WE ALSO DARE THEM TO PUBLICLY DENY THAT THEIR AIMS ARE SOLELY DESTRUC- TIVE AND NOT CREATIVE, THAT THEY DESTROY SIMPLY FOR THE PLEASUER OF DESTROY- ING AND ARE CAPABLE OF CREATING NOTHING. WE DARE THEM TO REBUILD JUST ONE SCHOOL AND JUST ONE CLINIC IN ORDER TO DISPROVE OUR ACCUSTION, WE DAARE THEM TO DO THIS OR ELSE DISBAND AND CEASE MAKING LIFE INTOLERABLE TO OUR PEOPLE.
>
> We further dare the Soweto Students Representative Council to pub licly deny that they hold the religion, ways and customs of Africa in contempt, that they are agents of Communism who teach our children that there is no God and that drug-taking, free-loving and homosexu ality are right and good. We dare them to deny that they are really lackeys and lickspittlings of the African National Congress which is a Communist organisation bent on creating disorder and death amongst our people in South Africa.
>
> They call themselves a "Black" organisation, but why have White leftists amongst them? They call themselves a "Black liberation" council, but why do they murder and ill-treat the very black people they claim to be the liberators of?
>
> COWARDS MASQUARADING AS HEROES! LIARS, CHEATS, MURDERERS AND DECEIVERS! DECEITFUL RATS WHO PLUNGE OUR CHILDREN INTO DEATH AND INJURY AND THEN RUN OUT OF THE COUNTRY TO SAVE THEIR OWN SKINS!
>
> SOWETO SHALL NO BLEED AGAIN ON ORDERS OF THESE DOGS! IGNORE THEIR IDIOTIC AND UN-AFRICAN OUTPOURINGS! STAND FIRM, BLACK PEOPLE! FIGHT BACK AND DO NOT BE INTIMIDATEAD ON THE SIXTEENTH OF JUNE.
>
> TO HELL WITH S.S.R.C!!

Pamphlet designed to undermine the SSRC.

In its first major campaign, the SSRC called for the release of all schoolchildren in detention.

At the same time, the SSRC repeatedly stressed its commitment to non-violence as expressed by Mashinini. They issued a press statement in *The Weekend World*, condemning anonymous pamphlets which urged people to use violence against whites and warned of 'stooges and plants in the township' who were inciting black people to 'irresponsible actions for the ends of the fascist regime'. The SSRC also condemned pamphlets which directly attempted to undermine the student body.

As a result, the SSRC formed 'squads' to discipline youth gangs and protect residents. Although more radical students dismissed the SSRC as 'moderates' because of their rejection of violence, for the most part the SSRC maintained the respect of the students and became the leading political force in the township. Many observers commented that school students now appeared to be leading the Soweto community, and the SSRC was referred to as a shadow government in Soweto.

The first major campaign of the SSRC was its call for the release of all schoolchildren in detention. They organised a march to security police headquarters at John Vorster Square on 4 August 1976 and called for workers and parents to stay at home for three days in solidarity with the SSRC's demands.

Observers believed that the ANC leadership in exile was behind the call for workers to become involved, and an ANC pamphlet was cited as proof: 'Because the protests [in June] were largely confined to the locations, damage to the economy, the heart of white power, was limited – the struggle must be taken into the cities, the factories, the mines.'

Another, more fiery ANC pamphlet declared, 'The War is on, so let us take it to the Whites right into town.' The SSRC, however, denied having any official links with the ANC. Student leaders report that they met with ANC members only on an informal basis and that the uprising had taken the ANC by surprise. The students were, however, drawing on the ANC's tradition of calling for work stayaways in protest against the government. An SSRC member confirmed this: 'We copied this stayaway campaign from the ANC.'

We don't ride

The SSRC embarked on a campaign to promote a stayaway but, on 4 August 1976, matters became violent. PUTCO buses were hijacked, trains were stoned and carriages were set alight. Cars were stopped and placards with slogans such as 'City-bound cars belong to betrayers who want to take a back seat during the struggle' were waved at the drivers, and part of the railway track to Soweto was dismantled. Police mounted a massive blockade to contain what a senior officer described as an 'extremely dangerous situation'. Police distributed their own pamphlets from helicopters, discouraging workers from striking.

The result was that about two-thirds of the black labour force failed to report to work at the height of the three-day period. The government and the press argued that 'agitators' and 'intimidators' were the sole cause of the high rate of absenteeism from the workplace. The students, on the other hand, proclaimed the first stay-at-home a major coup for the people of Soweto. In a pamphlet entitled 'Why we should remain united and not rest', the students wrote, 'We dealt the racist regime and factory-owners a heavy blow – they lost their profits.'

This success boosted the SSRC's confidence and they called for a second stayaway on 23–25 August 1976. Students concentrated their energies on mobilising workers. Door-to-door campaigns were undertaken and leaflets were again distributed, this time in larger quantities.

The first day of the boycott was remarkably quiet. There was less intimidation and conflict at the railway stations and large numbers of workers stayed at home. During the course of the day, however, it became clear that the migrant workers who lived in the hostels had refused to heed the 'Azikhwelwa' (We don't ride) call. As a result, they were taunted and stoned by students as they returned from work and, in retaliation, the hostel dwellers killed two students picketing near the Meadowlands Hostel. The following day, the hostel – housing over 10 000 men, and the largest in Soweto – was burnt. James Shika recalls what he saw when he returned to the hostel that day:

> When we came here we found that the whole place was a mess. The bar, beer lounge and the butcher were all destroyed. The corrugated iron walls were removed and the place was left naked. We did not know what had caused the whole thing. We had been to work; we had no idea of what started it all.

There was no evidence to show that the fire was started by the students, and many believe that it was an attempt by the police to break the student–worker alliance and to rouse the wrath of the hostel dwellers against the youth. And this is precisely what happened.

At 6.30pm on 24 August, a large group of hostel inmates gathered at Meadowlands Hostel carrying sticks, pangas, knobkieries and assegais. They proceeded to march on the residents of Meadowlands and Orlando West chanting, 'Where is your black power? Where is it?'

Linda Masemola, a resident of Meadowlands, remembers her daughter 'came in running and said, "Mama, the Zulus are attacking, the Iziqazas." She said Iziqazas [the name given to Zulu migrants]. She ran to the other side of the room and we closed the doors quickly. And we could hear them in the neighbourhood next door'.

Salathiel Maake describes how 'the Zulus came and kicked the door, molesting people, killing people, children'. Cliff Mashiolane adds: 'The Zulus attacked anyone they saw. When they came into your house, they looted whatever was available – baths, televisions, music centres. They took everything and even killed children. They did not discriminate.'

Ethel Leisa recounts how 'in one house, they killed three boys, brothers. In another house, the second house from the corner, they killed a man with his wife watching. Opposite my own house there was a dead body. I have never seen a thing like that in my life'.

STRIKE??

THE PEST IN OUR MIDST

THE PEST THAT KEEPS US FROM OUR WORK

THE PEST THAT KEEPS THE FOOD FROM OUR MOUTHS

THE MARCH TO "FREEDOM" IS A MARCH TO HUNGER AND TO A JOBLESS SOCIETY

ALL BLACK PEOPLE SUFFER UNDER THE BURDEN OF JOBLESS HOOLIGANS

A STRIKE WILL NOT HELP US – IT WILL ONLY MAKE IT HARDER TO FIND A JOB, AND FOOD, AND A HOME

A SACRIFICE NOW MAY BE A SACRIFICE OF THE FREEDOM OF UTURE GENERATIONS

IF YOU STRIKE YOU STRIKE A BLOW AT YOURSELF AND YOUR FAMILY

Propaganda pamphlets distributed by the police.

TO THE PEOPLE OF SOWETO

STAND FIRM!

RESIST THE SERVANTS OF DARKNESS WHO ARE BEING PAID BY COMMUNISTS TO SPREAD DEATH, CHAOS AND SUFFERING IN THE BLACK COMMUNITY!

DOWN WITH "BLACK POWER"!

TO HELL WITH THE S.S.R.C!

OUR CHILDREN SHALL LIVE – AND LEARN

Patrick Hlongwane, a young boy at the time, tells how he and his friends hid in fear:

> I hid inside the stove and closed the top and the wood blocked the stove. They went in and turned the house upside down and, when I met with my friends the next day, one told how he hid under the bed. Another said that he was in the roof. But in some other houses, they bashed down the ceiling. A lot of people were found in the roof and were killed.

Township dwellers fought back and a bloody war followed. 'Those hostel dwellers were subject to revenge by township people,' recalls Hlongwane. 'A lot of times they were stabbed with garden forks. And that was something that we saw with our own eyes. I haven't been able to forget that.'

Three days later, the death toll had risen to over 35 and over 350 had been injured. *The World* newspaper reported that 'anarchy is threatening to engulf townships in Soweto, with black fighting black residents'. Residents, carrying big paper carriers, suitcases and bundles of clothing on their heads, fled their ransacked houses to seek refuge with relatives.

The Urban Bantu Councils (UBC), angry about the attacks on their property, also helped the police mobilise the hostel dwellers. Winnie Mandela was told of a meeting of UBC members where it was 'agreed that youngsters who stopped workers from going to work should be killed, and the leaders of Dube and Inhlazane hostels who were present at the meeting had allegedly assented to carry out this function'. (*Rand Daily Mail* and *The World*, 16 August 1976)

Eyewitnesses reported that, throughout the brutal attacks, the police stood idly by. 'Whenever the Zulus fight,' claimed Salathiel Maake, 'there were no police to stop the Zulus. But when the residents went to fight back, the police were there already.'

Many residents testified that they saw the police escorting the hostel dwellers in 'hippos', and these accounts were confirmed by a *Rand Daily Mail* journalist who had hidden inside Mzimhlope Hostel. He saw a member of the Riot Squad, General Gert Prinsloo, telling the hostel dwellers, 'You are warned not to continue to damage the houses because they belong to WRAB. If you damage houses, you will force us to take action against you to prevent this. You have been ordered to kill only the troublemakers.' (*Rand Daily Mail*, 26 August 1976)

Armed hostel dwellers invade the township.

The journalist witnessed Prinsloo rewarding the hostel dwellers with a 'whole bakery van filled with bread. Packs of milk and mageu, so-called Bantu Beer, were also supplied and Prinsloo said, "Eat, so that when you kill you are full."'

But why were the hostel dwellers prepared to fight the township residents on behalf of the police and the UBC? Dinwa Nala, who lived in Meadowlands Hostel at the time, expresses a common view:

❛ We wanted to go to work; we didn't want to stay away from work. We were not loafers. I was working for my children, just as I am working now. I didn't want things to go bad. Even when my money was very low, my white boss would be the one to help me. I couldn't fight him. ❜

For most hostel dwellers, life in the city centred on work and earning a living.

Samuel Ndebele, another resident at the hostel, adds that he resented the behaviour of the youths:

❛ A group of kids prevented people from going to work. They said that we must strike. Really, in God's name, those kids fought with people and hit people. Buses didn't go, trains didn't go; the trains were empty. ❜

The other main complaint of the hostel dwellers was that the youth had not consulted them. One hostel dweller told *The World* on 26 August 1976:

❛ We did not want to fight our own people, but we have been forced into it. We want to say that if residents plan a stay-at-home protest we must be told. It will be better if we are approached before time so we can understand. ❜

The battle between the hostel-dwellers and the township continued over the next two weeks, spreading to other townships such as Naledi and Moletsane. Nothing, however, compared to the scale and intensity of the fighting in Meadowlands and Orlando West, where a group of students planned a counterattack on the hostels. Jon-Jon Mkhonza describes the students' actions:

❛ Three, four days later, we decided, no man, let's attack these people because, since this war started, these people are attacking us and we don't attack them. But now we had a problem because at the front there [of the hostels], there were police with hippos. So we asked ourselves, how are we going to attack this hostel? One guy said, "Let's use the river bank because nobody is watching there." We said, "That is a good idea because right at the end of the hostel is a small river, Klipriver." So we decided to organise about 30 guys with petrol bombs and weapons to attack the hostel. ❜

Residents fled to seek refuge elsewhere.

Salathiel Maake was one of the people requested by the students to join their task force:

> They even came to my place here. I said, "Who is it?" They said, "Come on, open up, we must go and fight the Zulus." I opened the door and I said, "I can't go and fight the Zulus. You must go and fight. You are young. You can still run." They said, "No, you must help because we are fighting for you." I said, "I am not going anywhere. If the Zulus come here and kill me, they will kill me here, with my family."

More than 70 people died in the war between residents and hostel dwellers, and many more were injured, with the possessions of both sides destroyed and damaged. By the middle of September 1976, large numbers of workers had fled the hostels in fear of their lives. Chief Gatsha Buthelezi flew up from KwaZulu in an attempt to restore the peace. He called for students and hostel dwellers to unite and asked Soweto for forgiveness. He also denounced the police, stating later that he had no doubt that 'certain members of the police fanned these flames of anger between these black people'.

Over the following weeks, students and hostel dwellers embarked on a process of reconciliation and, during the call for the third stayaway from 13 to 15 September 1976, student pamphlets emphasised the need for unity and addressed the hostel dwellers directly.

AZI KHWELWA!

Parents: Co-operate with us! Workers: Stay away from work! Hostels: Do not fight!

STAY AT HOME: Monday 13th, Tuesday 14th and Wednesday 15th September, '76.

NO VIOLENCE! NO BLOODSHED!

Extract from student pamphlet, urging unity in Soweto.

Migrant workers were said to have played an active role in winning support for the strike and the third of the stayaways was undoubtedly the most successful. *The World* consequently claimed that 'absolutely no attempt was made this morning to stop anyone going to work'. In Diepkloof, policemen apparently went from house to house, ordering people to report to work.

The stayaway led to the government taking even more drastic measures. Minister Kruger told Parliament that, 'The black man knows his place and if not, I'll show him his place.' The new Internal Security Act was thus passed, enabling the police to detain a person indefinitely, without any access to legal advice, family members or private medical care. The police immediately embarked on a new campaign of mass arrests. On a single day, security police detained over 290 people, and many more people were banned. Student leaders faced charges of sedition and terrorism, so thousands fled the country to Botswana, Lesotho, Swaziland and even Nigeria to escape the punitive conditions. Many, too, joined the liberation armies of the ANC and PAC.

The end of open confrontation

Brutal police repression, months of bitter struggles and the enormous number of casualties, however, began to take their toll on the people of Soweto. The stayaway in September 1976 was the climax of the uprising and, by October, open confrontations with the police ended. The SSRC still had an enormous influence in Soweto, but instead of open warfare on the streets, students now focused on more specific demands. They declared 1976 as a 'Year of Mourning' and, in a pamphlet addressed to 'All fathers & mothers, brothers & sisters, friends, all workers in all cities and towns & villages in the Republic of South Africa', they made a public appeal.

Liquor was a particularly important target for the students. 'Our daily experience,' wrote the SSRC, 'is that nothing good has ever come out of shebeens. Many of our black sisters have been raped and/or murdered by drunkards and thugs from shebeens. Shebeens have become houses of vice and immorality. We cannot tolerate to see our fathers' pay packets being emptied into shebeens... Shebeens must close down.'

The SSRC also organised a boycott of the end-of-year examinations. At most of Soweto's schools, the response to the boycott was mixed. Many students felt that Bantu Education was better than no education at all. At Orlando High, however, not one student turned up to write the matriculation examination. And, in the Cape, no students wrote examinations. The BPA, which had previously called on students to return to school, now supported the boycott because they believed that the detentions had to be stopped before normal schooling could resume. By September 1977, half of Soweto's 19 school boards and 600 teachers had resigned in protest against Bantu Education and in solidarity with the students. Thamsanqa Kambule who had been the principal of Orlando High for 20 years said that his conscience forced him to resign. After months of ongoing repression, the SSRC was finally banned in October 1977.

The consequences

The rebellion had far-reaching consequences. The most obvious of these was a change in the relationship between students and their parents. The youths' militancy and courage during the street offensives contrasted sharply with the submissive behaviour of their parents and deeply undermined the authority of the older generation. Parents had been forced to listen to the children who had taken the lead on political issues. 'The struggle is ours,' stated Khotso Seatlholo, chairperson of the SSRC at the time. 'The ball of liberation is in our hands. The black student will stand up fearlessly... against a political system which is stinking with immoral policies... We shall rise up and destroy a political ideology that is designed to keep us in a perpetual state of oppression and subserviency.'

> SOWETO STUDENTS REPRESENTATIVE COUNCIL
> ALL FATHERS & MOTHERS, BROTHERS & SISTERS, FRIENDS ALL WORKERS.
> IN ALL CITIES AND TOWNS & VILLAGES IN THE REPUBLIC OF SOUTH AFRICA.
>
> We appeal to you to align yourselves with the struggle for our own liberation. Be involved and united with us as it is your own son or daughter that we bury every weekenkd. Death has become a common thing in the townships. There is no peace. There shall be none until we are free.
> 1. Soweto and all black townships into a period of mourning for the dead. We are to pay respect to all students and adults mudered by Police.
> 2. We are to pledge solidatiry with those detained in Police cells and are suffering torture on our behalf.
> 3. We should show sympathy and support to all those workers who suffered reduction of wages and loss of their jobs because they obeyed our humble call to stay away from work a few days.
> 4. We should stand together and be united in demanding the release of the detainees.
> 5. We must be free.
>
> OUR CALL IS: ALL THE THINGS THAT WE ENJOY MUST BE SUSPENDED FOR THE SAKE OF OUR KIDS WHO DIED FROM POLICE BULLETS.
> - NO CHRISTMAS SHOPPING.
> - NO CHRISTMAS CARDS.
> - NO CHRISTMAS PRESENTS.
> - NO CHRISTMAS SPARTIES.
> - NO SHEBEEN DRINKING.
>
> Let us, your kids, for the first time, neither buy nor put on new clothes for Christmas or for New Year.
>
> The year 1976 shall go down into our historyas the YEAR OF MOURNING, the year that flowed with sweat and blood and tears for our liberation.
>
> We shall demonstrate this solidarity and sympathy with thos who lost their lives, relatives and those who lost they jobs and wages by:
> NO MORE GOING TO DO SHOPPING IN THE FOLLOWING:
> ALL CLOTHING SHOPS.
> ALL FURNITURE SHOPS.
> ALL BOTTLE STORES.
> ALL TOY SHOPS.
> ALL RECORD SHOPS, etc.
>
> We appeal to all Parents, Workers and Students and all Shebeen dealers to obey this call.
> We cannot find happiness in death
> We cannot CELEBRATE.

Public appeal issued by the SSRC.

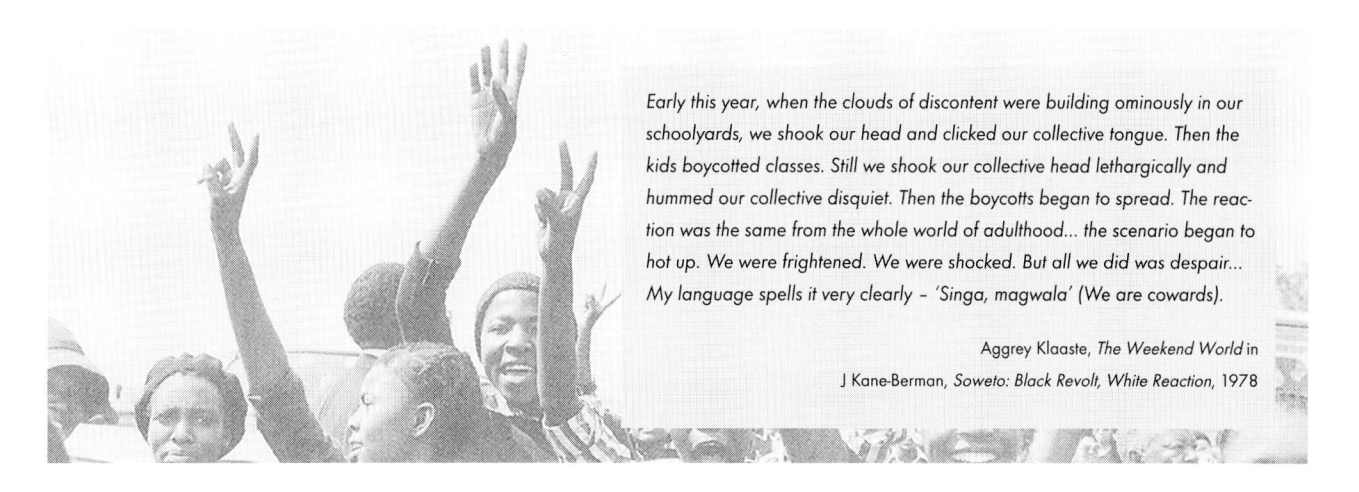

> Early this year, when the clouds of discontent were building ominously in our schoolyards, we shook our head and clicked our collective tongue. Then the kids boycotted classes. Still we shook our collective head lethargically and hummed our collective disquiet. Then the boycotts began to spread. The reaction was the same from the whole world of adulthood... the scenario began to hot up. We were frightened. We were shocked. But all we did was despair... My language spells it very clearly – 'Singa, magwala' (We are cowards).
>
> Aggrey Klaaste, *The Weekend World* in
> J Kane-Berman, *Soweto: Black Revolt, White Reaction*, 1978

The philosophical teachings of the Black Consciousness movement also changed the mindset of younger blacks in the township. A new spirit of determination and assertiveness had emerged and this was well illustrated in the poetry and writing at the time.

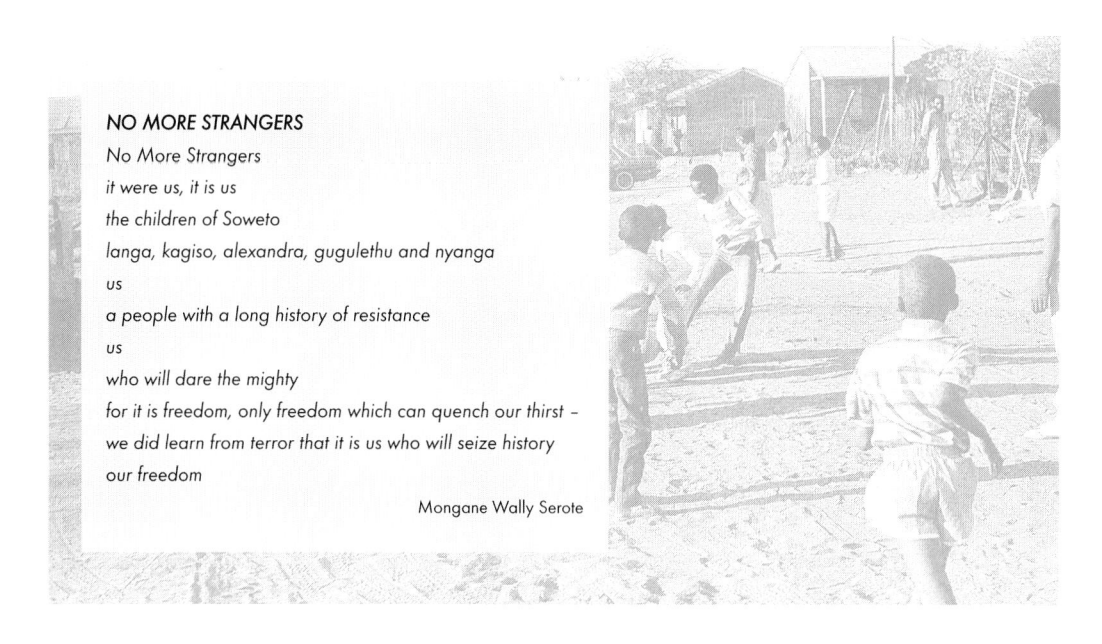

> **NO MORE STRANGERS**
> No More Strangers
> it were us, it is us
> the children of Soweto
> langa, kagiso, alexandra, gugulethu and nyanga
> us
> a people with a long history of resistance
> us
> who will dare the mighty
> for it is freedom, only freedom which can quench our thirst –
> we did learn from terror that it is us who will seize history
> our freedom
>
> Mongane Wally Serote

In his *Children of Soweto: A Trilogy*, Mbulelo Mzamane described the youngsters in the following terms:

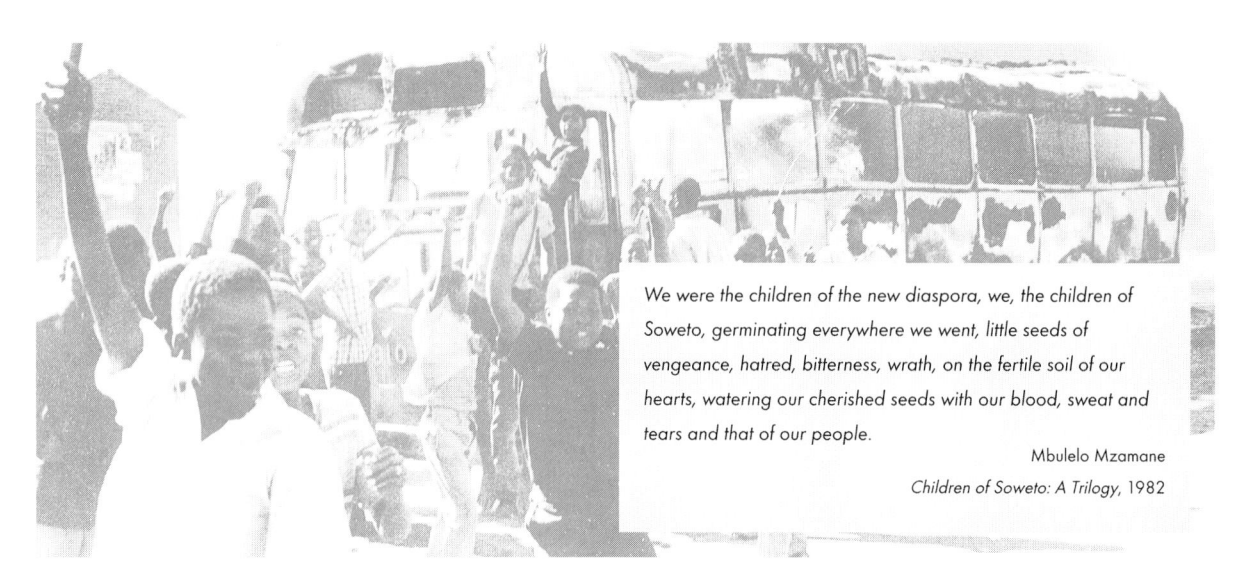

> We were the children of the new diaspora, we, the children of Soweto, germinating everywhere we went, little seeds of vengeance, hatred, bitterness, wrath, on the fertile soil of our hearts, watering our cherished seeds with our blood, sweat and tears and that of our people.
>
> Mbulelo Mzamane
> *Children of Soweto: A Trilogy*, 1982

Despite the courageous spirit of the children, the uprising had obvious limitations. The young leadership was inexperienced. Student demands swung wildly between the radical and the cosmetic, and their tactics were inconsistent. Although the four stayaways, led by the students, were the climax of mass participation in the revolts, black workers had acted mostly in solidarity with the initiatives of black youth, and worker organisation in Soweto was neither strengthened nor deepened. Most of the demands expressed during the uprising focused on Bantu Education and the release of detainees, but not on the conditions of the workers and black trade unions remained aloof.

For the political commentator, John Kane-Berman, 'June 1976, like Sharpeville 16 years before, was another turning point where South Africa did not turn.' (*Soweto: Black Revolt, White Reaction*, 1978)

In Soweto, black political organisation had effectively been silenced and the government remained largely in control. 1976 was, nonetheless, a watershed year and some important changes began to take place in Afrikaner thinking. Prime Minister BJ Vorster promised to investigate the 'shortcomings' of Separate Development, but continued to emphasise the principle that urban blacks must exercise their political rights in the homelands. He swore that the government would not be blackmailed by violence into granting black people the vote. Outside of the Bantustans, he proclaimed, 'the whites will rule and let there be no mistake about that'. In his 1977 new-year address, however, Vorster sounded less confident: 'The storm has not struck yet. We are only experiencing the whirlwinds that go before it.'

Unlike Sharpeville, Soweto was not the end but the beginning of a period of massive confrontation between the government and the black population. 16 June would never again be an ordinary day in South Africa. Nor would life for black South Africans follow its previous course. The stage had been set for the 1980s.

HATRED HATRED

White man! Call yourself a hate teacher
You! Have invented hate
Call yourself a racist
You have invented racialism

Whitey! You an imperialist
You came from doom
and you'll end in hell.

Why not call your self a murderer
How many Africans did you kill?
Since your white supremacy
You're war-mongers
extremists and opportunists.
Your Afrikanerdom
Vorsterism
Krugerism
is doomed

The black community
Has banned you
from their motherland
Including Africa as a whole.

Whitey! You an imperialist
You came from doom
and you'll end in hell.

Anonymous

AT WAR

> **I cannot foresee that the riots will ever happen again in Soweto. We have built the communications, we have established good relations with the people and I really cannot foresee that this will happen again.**
>
> *A South African policeman interviewed by BBC Television, 1977*

In the years immediately after the 1976 uprising, Soweto's fiery spirit of protest seemed to have burnt itself out. A number of political campaigns were mounted in the township but these did not exhibit the same levels of anger and militancy shown by trade unions, civic associations — commonly known as 'civics' — and student groups elsewhere in the country. Political inactivity in Soweto was especially evident in 1984–5, a period characterised by a slide towards ungovernability in many other townships. The 1976 uprising was nonetheless a great watershed which forever transformed Soweto's political and social landscape. Several important organisations were created after 1976 and, by 1986, Soweto had resumed its position of leadership in the national struggle. But why was Soweto initially left trailing behind? And what led to the resurgence of political resistance in the township?

The era of reform

The government's reform strategy was an important reason for Soweto's decline in political agitation in the late 1970s and early 1980s. After the 1976 upheaval, a new political alignment emerged in government. Reformers (*verligtes*) gained the upper hand over conservatives (*verkramptes*). John Vorster resigned as Prime Minister in September 1978 and Minister of Defence, PW Botha, became the new premier.

The forces promoting change, however, were an odd mix. They included Afrikaner businessmen, who saw reform as necessary to protect South Africa's capitalist economy; the military establishment, who believed that a relaxation of apartheid laws was a key to the country's security; and an assorted group of Afrikaner liberals. And, because of its volatile history, Soweto was earmarked for special attention.

PW Botha, who succeeded BJ Vorster as Prime Minister in 1978.

The new Botha administration thus began to transform apartheid. It granted rights to African trade unions and allowed important privileges for the urban African workforce, but it was the government's attempt to create a black middle class which impacted most on Soweto. 'The government hoped,' wrote Aggrey Klaaste, editor of *Sowetan*, 'that this class of black people would have too much to lose to help the masses in the struggle for liberation.' (Peter Magubane, *Soweto: Portraits of a City*, 1990) Central to the government's reform initiative was the reintroduction of 99-year leaseholds. Sowetans were once again allowed to buy, rather than rent, newly built houses as well as the older matchbox houses. They could also renovate their homes. The government embarked on an advertising campaign using the slogan 'Buy now, improve and feel secure'. Although few houses were bought initially, after new loans were made available to buyers, many houses were sold. And a new class of residents, concerned with the safety and value of their property, began to emerge.

Middle-class housing in Soweto, circa 1978.

The government's housing programme in Soweto also had a distinct middle-class bias. In 1978, there was a critical shortage of houses in the township, and it was estimated that 32 500 families needed homes. Most houses were severely overcrowded and poor living conditions were commonplace. Over the next six years the government and private sector built only 5 000 homes, most of which were built in the new middle-class areas of Diepkloof Extension (nicknamed 'Diepkloof Expensive' or 'Prestige Park' by the township residents), Orlando West ('Beverly Hills') and Selection Park. These new areas were, in the opinion of Thlokie Mofokeng, 'there to bluff outsiders that Soweto is not such a bad place after all. That is why the government decided to build smart houses rather than provide the majority of people with housing'.

But the affluent new suburbs accentuated divisions within the township. Says Jon-Jon Mkhonza:

Richard Maponya, one of Soweto's growing middle class.

❝ By forming Diepkloof Extension, the government succeeded in separating the people. In most cases those who moved to Diepkloof Extension saw themselves as better. People who went there could afford to buy R98 000 houses while those people who were left behind couldn't afford to even buy a bicycle. They no longer visited one another. They adopted the style of the suburbs. They have big dogs and they lock their gates. We are scared to go there. ❞

Velapi Mnguni adds that, 'If you look at the people who went out of Soweto, those were the people that we're relying on. That was the cream of Soweto, the people who were educated.'

Soweto's new class of citizens who drove around their upmarket suburbs in BMWs and Mercedes Benzs were referred to as 'Buppies' – black, upwardly mobile, urban professionals. One commentator remarked that the people living in the 'higher-income districts' of Mofolo, Rockville, Phefeni and Dube were considered 'arrogant by the rest of Soweto. They drove posh cars, were strongly Euro-American in their style of life, and were very much concerned with conspicuous consumption'. Thlokie Mofokeng asserts that 'they were no longer part of the Soweto community'.

Maud Motanyane, then editor of *Tribute* magazine aimed at a buppy audience, defends the rights of this class: 'There is no virtue in poverty. We do not apologise for encouraging our people to aspire to the best things in life.' (Peter Magubane, *Soweto: Portraits of a City*, 1990) Nevertheless, it was clear that many township residents resented the growing numbers of richer residents and continued to see them as *amahaiza* (snobs) who had forgotten their past.

But the government's housing policy was not the only reason for the fairly rapid expansion of a black elite in Soweto. Another was the changing patterns of employment towards the end of the 1970s. In the aftermath of the uprising, many American multinationals and other foreign companies operating in South Africa adopted the Sullivan Code which prohibited racial discrimination in hiring and promotion. Middle-class jobs for Africans multiplied – especially in Johannesburg, the country's primary business centre. Sowetans were able to take special advantage of the new employment opportunities because the township was closer to Johannesburg than others in the Pretoria-Witwatersrand-Vereeniging area (the PWV, now known as Gauteng). In general, jobs in Johannesburg paid better wages than the factories on the East Rand

Everybody talks about us being 'token blacks'. There is resentment. Looking back, I wish I hadn't moved to the middle-class area because of this credibility problem. I am seen differently from when I was living in a regular neighbourhood of Soweto.

Letter
Rand Daily Mail, 17 December 1982

and Vaal Triangle and because the residents of Soweto were able to enter into better paying, upwardly mobile jobs, the household incomes of Sowetans tended to be higher than these outlying areas.

Sowetans also enjoyed other privileges not shared by township residents elsewhere in the PWV, and this was largely due to the government's decision to pursue reform initiatives more actively in Soweto than in other black urban areas. Connie Mulder, Minister of Plural Relations and Development (previously, the Department of Bantu Administration), publicly promised to turn the township into 'the most beautiful black city in Africa'. In September 1979, Prime Minster PW Botha visited Soweto and announced the cancellation of the R11.5 million debt owed by the Soweto Community Council. No other African town ship was offered a similar concession and, when asked why Soweto was being singled out for preferential treatment, Deputy Minister George Morrison replied that the township was now 'a showpiece to the world'. The priority the government gave to Soweto's development was further reinforced when Louis Rive, one of the government's most able administrators, was made responsible for implementing a 10-year plan to electrify the township. Rive declared Soweto to be 'the mirror of South Africa's soul'. On the whole, the government worked on the principle that when Soweto sneezed, South Africa caught a cold and legislators took special care not to adopt measures which might provoke confrontation. When Soweto's Community Council tried to raise rents in 1980–1 and a rent boycott was mounted in response, the government cancelled the increases. Although this decision eliminated the prospect of protests in Soweto, the government's refusal to cancel proposed rent increases in other townships was, in fact, a major cause of the escalation of revolt in those areas in the early 1980s.

Changes in township life

The government's decision in the late 1970s to lift trade restrictions that had previously shackled black business in the township, also created new opportunities. Traders were no longer restricted to small stores which sold only basic daily requirements and, as a result, black businesses grew rapidly and even the appearance of Soweto began to change. New grocery shops, drycleaners, liquor stores, service stations and fast-food outlets were built throughout the township. A group of very wealthy businessmen emerged and, for the first time, black taxis were legalised. The number of minibuses on the road between Johannesburg and Soweto grew daily despite the fact that taxi fares were nearly double that of trains. Taxis were more convenient than the overcrowded train carriages and were much faster. They soon acquired the nickname of 'Zola Budd' – after the South African long-distance runner who broke the world marathon record. The South African Black Taxi Association became one of the largest business concerns in the township.

The 'informal sector' also expanded virtually overnight. On almost every street corner, someone was doing business. Fruit vendors hawked their fresh produce bought from the market in the early hours of the morning. Enterprising cooks sold grilled mealies and *boerewors* sausages cooked on braziers. Makeshift stalls of *spaza* shops stocked goods ranging from chewing gum, cigarettes and washing powder to skin lighteners and other cosmetics.

Hawkers on a street corner sell their wares.

Entrepreneurs were particularly attracted to bustling train stations and the rapidly growing taxi ranks. The throngs of passengers travelling to Johannesburg each day provided a roaring trade, especially during rush hour. The small-time businessmen erected their 'shops' every morning and dismantled them again every night. 'The possibility of selling a selection of food and other goods to passers-by gave many families in Soweto a chance to supplement their measly incomes,' comments Sylvia Dlomo.

The presence of these vendors also added to the liveliness of Soweto's streets where much of the township's social life continued to take place. The shouts of people hawking their wares now mixed with the music which blared from 'ghetto blasters' (portable music systems) and the chatter of young and old who gathered in their yards or on the pavements throughout the day. There were also changes in Soweto's nightlife during these years. Over 4 000 shebeens run from private homes continued to be the hangout for most Sowetans and Friday night was especially popular for the 'MaGents' – the stylish young men who would invariably be found 'in conference' in the shebeens.

In the early 1980s, the disco scene provided alternative entertainment to the shebeens. Mongezi Mnganyi points out that discos attracted a different clientele to that of shebeens:

There was no entrance fee to the shebeen but in the new clubs that started to appear you had to pay to enter. The liquor was much more expensive than in a shebeen. The people who went there could afford to pay the extra money. The dress code was also very strict. You couldn't just go there wearing T-shirts, tackies and jeans. You had to be more formal. It was now a matter of class and status. The owners of the club were also different. You wouldn't dare own a club if you were just an ordinary person. Most club owners had Mafia connections. You had to have channels to acquire a licence. You had to grease someone's hand.

Those Sowetans who frequented the new discos partied the night away to the sounds of Afro-rock, American funk and disco, and it was in these clubs that a man would seek his 'coal stove', someone to keep him warm. The Pelican Club – opposite Orlando Station and easily recognised because it is one of very few two-storey buildings in the township – was the most famous of Soweto's clubs. Club 707 in Orlando West was another favoured hangout, as was Club 2000 between Moletsane and Mapetla. After the release of the film *Saturday Night Fever*, the Bee Gees became all-time music favourites, but Soweto also produced some outstanding musical talents during these years. Ray Phiri, leader of the band Stimela, achieved international fame when he and his group provided the instrumental back-up for Paul Simon's *Graceland* album. His particular blend of Afro-rock, township *mbaqanga* and traditional African rhythms made him popular with a wide cross-over audience. Sipho 'Hotstix' Mabuse, another musical celebrity who emerged from the township, describes his own particular concoction of *kwela*, jazz and rock as 'Black Consciousness pop' and this musical blend had a strong influence on township music.

The newly crowned 'queen' is flanked by her princesses in one of the growing number of beauty contests staged in the 1980s.

The 1980s also saw the increasing popularity of beauty pageants and people crowded into community halls on weekends to watch local beauties being crowned with titles ranging from Miss Orlando Pirates to Miss Dube. The shows, known as BE (Black Elegance), were showcases for local musicians and dance groups who were given the chance to woo the audience before the contestants appeared on stage.

The relaxation of laws which governed the lives of urban blacks in the early 1980s changed township life throughout South Africa, but these changes were most pronounced in Soweto. They released new energies and created – for some people, at least – a new prosperity. But the new social structure also created divisions which would weaken the sense of community and contribute to the subdued political atmosphere in Soweto.

Organised politics in Soweto 1978-83

The relative calm in the township has also been attributed to the nature of political organisation dominant at the time. The great uprising of 1976–7 forever transformed important parts of Soweto's political culture and attitude and children who had once sung *Umame uyajabula, uma ngifike khaya* (Mama rejoices when I come home) in the streets, now sang *Umama uyajabula, uma ngishay bhunu* (Mama rejoices when I hit a Boer). Teenagers openly paraded their political affiliations by wearing T-shirts which endorsed political organisations. 'This far, no further', 'Vorster, your hands are dripping with blood' and 'Don't weep! Organise!' were some of the graffiti slogans prominently scrawled on street corners immediately after the uprising.

Regina Mundi church in Rockville, which holds the only black Madonna in the country, became the home of commemoration services for the victims of 1976. Speaker after speaker paid tribute to the brave young people who had faced the brute force of the apartheid regime. They also addressed the major grievances that still dominated township life. Despite government reforms, Soweto remained a dormitory city in which the majority of the residents struggled to eke out an existence. Housing remained entirely inadequate; there were not nearly enough recreational and shopping facilities; conditions in the schools remained appalling; and the economic slowdown of the early 1980s led to massive youth unemployment especially among the poorly qualified. Large crowds gathered at the church and, with fists thrust in the air, the songs of protest created a sense of both unity and rebellion amongst Sowetans.

The spirit of defiance in the township, however, was hampered during this period by the conflict between rival political groups and by poor organisation. By the mid-1970s, Soweto boasted the highest number of – and most articulate – Black Consciousness constituents of any area in South Africa. Following the uprising, however, they were increasingly challenged by ANC-aligned or 'Charterist' organisations and much energy was absorbed in the struggle between these two political factions.

Police surveillance outside Regina Mundi church.

The re-emergence of the ANC

The re-emergence of ANC-aligned organisations owed much to the course of events after the uprising. During the latter half of 1976 and 1977, thousands of young men and women fled Soweto to the neighbouring countries of Lesotho, Swaziland, Botswana as well as Tanzania and Angola. Some went to finish their schooling, but many others became eager recruits for the military training camps of Umkhonto we Sizwe (Spear of the Nation). Sibongile Mkhabela believes she understands the reasons behind the shift away from Black Consciousness in Soweto:

❝ When people went underground, most went into ANC camps. Few went into the Black Consciousness-dominated PAC camps because of problems in the PAC, such as shortages of money and resources. The ANC camps got a lot of members and that situation spilt over into the situation inside the country. ❞

From 1977 onwards, MK operatives launched an increasing number of attacks on key economic and strategic targets inside South Africa. The 'cadres', as they were known, were seen as 'liberators' by most black South Africans and 'terrorists' by the government and the white establishment. Moroka police station in Soweto was but one of many stations around the country that were firebombed. The sabotage campaign inspired confidence among township dwellers and the ANC enjoyed a resurgence of popularity.

There is Sasolburg, the Supreme Court, Warmbaths, Koeberg, Pitoli, going up in flames.
We are going there, the Umkhonto boys have arrived.
We are going there. Hayi, Hayi. We are going forward.
Don't be worried, the boys know their job.
Let Africa return.

Quoted in *Colonels and Cadres*, Jacklyn Cock, 1990

MK cadres secretly entered the township in growing numbers. 'The first time I saw people called "cadres",' recalls Pheteni Khumalo, 'they were on a mission. I was at a meeting, but we were not told that people like them would be coming. I was expecting to see a clumsy person from the bush who is hungry but I found that I met gentlemen who were on duty.'

The return of MK soldiers gave many Sowetans the opportunity to re-establish contact with exiled sons and daughters. Most families had not heard from their children and many believed that they had died in exile. The reunions which took place under the darkness of night were highly emotional occasions. Velapi Mnguni remembers the first time his brother, who had disappeared a few years before, visited him:

❝ I didn't know who was knocking on this night. My wife was very scared. Then she started whispering, "Velapi vula, tini Sakayethwa." That's my brother's name. I didn't believe it at first, but I went and opened the door and he came in. He stayed for only three minutes. He asked, "How is everybody? Is everybody still alive?" We said, "Yes." He said, "We are here in Dube and then I will be going again out." ❞

Sowetans also had contact with the ANC through Radio Freedom, the ANC's radio station broadcast from Lusaka. The station was banned but people risked arrest in order to listen. The jingle, 'This is Radio Freedom, the voice of the African National Congress, South Africa's tried-and-tested revolutionary movement' – accompanied by gunshot in the background – became well known to thousands of young Sowetans. 'Sometimes you heard the gunshots, *khwa-khwa*, over the radio. And then you'd hear a voice coming in, a poetic voice,' remembers Jon-Jon Mkhonza. 'Somebody speaks about Africa, how it was colonised and how must it be freed. We heard a lot of liberation songs. We used to sit around the radio. My mother used to get annoyed. She said, "I'm telling you, you will get into trouble and don't call me."'

For Velapi Mnguni, Radio Freedom provided valuable information:

> *We used to hear Oliver Tambo saying things that we didn't know were happening. Some of the things happened about a kilometre away from where I was staying, but I was not aware of it until I heard it on Radio Freedom and we found that it was true.*

The ANC's underground newsletter also began to circulate more widely in the township. The message it sent to Sowetans was clear: 'This is not the time to weep over our fallen heroes. It is time to hit back at the enemy with everything we have... Mobilise! Don't Mourn!'

The revival of the popularity of the African National Congress was marked by the founding of the Congress of South African Students (COSAS) at the end of 1979. COSAS adopted the ANC's policy document, the Freedom Charter, and its supporters were often referred to as 'Charterists'. The preamble of the Charter expressly welcomed white participation in the struggle.

> *We, the people of South Africa, black and white, together equals, countrymen and brothers adopt this Freedom Charter. And we pledge ourselves to strive together... until the democratic changes here set out have been won.*
>
> Preamble to the Freedom Charter

The nature of opposition politics

The Azanian Students' Movement (AZASM), established in 1978, was the Black Consciousness counterpart to COSAS. AZASM contended that white people could not be part of the political solution in South Africa and they consequently rejected the Freedom Charter. But, from 1979 onward, COSAS gained the upper hand in the schools and was an important force in building student organisation and mobilising opposition to Bantu education. COSAS's slogan 'Each One Teach One' became a popular student chant but, in the years to come, the fight between COSAS and AZASM for political and territorial control over Soweto was to degenerate into bitter conflict. Thlokie Mofokeng believes that this rivalry contributed to the rather weak state of student politics in Soweto, especially compared to other parts of the country: 'In other townships, especially the Western Cape, massive student boycotts in the 1980s brought schooling to a standstill. The same educational grievances existed in Soweto's schools but conflicts between COSAS and AZASM hampered the growth of student organisation and there was not much active student resistance.' Mongezi Mnganyi adds:

> *Parents played a big role in preventing student resistance. Whenever there was something that needed to be done at school, parents would be against it. The uprising was still fresh in their minds. Unlike in other townships, the older generation were tired of political upheaval. Some students were also reluctant to boycott classes again because they had missed many months of schooling during the uprising.*

Civic organisation in Soweto was also less effective than elsewhere. In 1979, the Committee of Ten – which had been formed by a group of prominent Sowetans after the 1976 uprising – was renamed and expanded to become the Soweto Civic Association (SCA). The SCA was initially aligned to the Black

Consciousness movement but later became Charterist in its orientation. Its manifesto stated that 'We, the people of Soweto, shall govern and decide on our own lives. We will formulate the Soweto Local Authority. It will be run by the people, for the people and of the people'. The SCA set out to create branches across the township and declared that they were 'committed to working at the grassroots for the removal of all disabilities that impoverish and dehumanise the residents of this ghetto'. They also fought the unpopular council system and tackled other local grievances such as high rents, housing shortages and high train and bus fares.

The SCA eventually played a key role in leading township politics but, in its early years, the civic organisation could not sustain support for its campaigns and failed to build a strong grassroots organisation. But the SCA recognised its own weaknesses and, reporting on the 1980–81 campaign against rent increases, it noted that 'we did not have the strength to sustain the campaign. Communication and report backs to the people did not take place and demoralisation began to set in...'. According to the minutes of a workshop held between 8 and 10 June 1984, they also made the point that the community saw the leadership 'as educated people who are apart from them. The civic leadership should be more mixed and there should be a place for the "ordinary man" in the street to serve the people'.

The obstacles to involving supporters in the day-to-day running and decision-making of the organisation undoubtedly hampered organisation, with the result that one branch after another collapsed and there was little activity between 1980 and 1983. In these years, the SCA leadership tended to rely on high-profile mass meetings as the only form of organisation and they were far less effective in spearheading the insurrections than those mounted by other townships. Thlokie Mofokeng comments that 'the civics in smaller townships were much better in building well-organised, community-based organisations that could guide political campaigns than the SCA'. Sprawling Soweto posed problems of an entirely different scale.

A new era

A turning point in Soweto's politics came after the formation of the United Democratic Front, known simply as the UDF. In August 1983, PW Botha invited coloureds and Indians to join the previously whites-only legislature through the new 'tricameral parliament'. However, not only was the African majority excluded from the new structure, but political equality evaded even the coloureds and Indians. Together, the Indian and coloured members of parliament had only 130 seats, while the white house held 178 seats. This meant that a decision taken in the white parliament could never be overturned by a combined vote of the Indian and coloured parliaments. The tricameral parliament, therefore, left white domination unchallenged.

For black South Africans, Botha's 'new deal' was seen as yet another government strategy of 'divide and rule', an attempt to undermine the unity between black, Indian and coloured people in their fight against the apartheid government. In response to the government's constitutional proposals, a diverse range of anti-apartheid organisations merged and formed the UDF, which set out to fight the constitution as well as the new laws on black administration. The UDF thus became the leading force in mobilising township dwellers in the struggle against apartheid.

Soweto — A History

At the launch of the UDF on 20 August 1983, tens of thousands of supporters stood up to applaud Allan Boesak's demand of 'All, here and now. We want all our rights, we want them here and we want them now'. The UDF committed itself to non-racialism and adopted the Freedom Charter as drawn up by the ANC at Kliptown in 1955. They adopted the simple and unifying slogan of 'UDF Unites – Apartheid Divides' and issued a declaration.

> We, the freedom loving people of South Africa, say with one voice to the whole world that we cherish the vision of a united, democratic South Africa based on the will of the people. We will strive for the unity of all people through united action against the evils of apartheid, economic and all other forms of exploitation.
>
> Declaration by the **United Democratic Front**

The mood at the first UDF meetings was jubilant.

The organisation was a catalyst in the development of politics in Soweto. Activist Khehla Shubane explains that 'it strengthened Soweto's local Charterist organisations by linking them with similar groups across the country through the federal structure that the UDF provided'.

This structure enhanced the capacity of organisations to mobilise support in Soweto. The SCA's affiliation with the UDF also strengthened the organisation as it was given guidance and was encouraged to focus more on local issues.

The UDF's formation, however, coincided with the severe economic recession which gripped South Africa in the early 1980s and which further exacerbated the poverty and poor living standards of many families in the townships. The government slashed township budgets and cut back on basic services such as refuse removal and conditions in Soweto, as in other townships, deteriorated daily. Litter piled up on the streets and no maintenance work was done on the roads or houses.

To make matters worse, more and more residents were unable to find work, and the number of families living in poverty doubled between 1978 and 1982. By 1984, the unemployment rate in Soweto stood at 53 per cent.

In the same period, growing numbers of young people were drawn into the rapidly expanding school system and nearly three times as many students were graduating from Soweto's high schools. The new graduates had no jobs to look forward to and their futures looked decidedly bleak.

Shock troops of the revolution

It was from these young, unemployed youths that the UDF drew its most energetic recruits. Youth congresses sprang up and affiliated to the UDF. The Soweto Youth Congress, SOYCO, was the second congress to be founded and its launch, in August 1983, generated high spirits. Chanting and singing youths applauded the formation of the first organisation for youth since political organisations were banned in October 1978. Zinzi Mandela, daughter of Nelson Mandela who had been in jail for 20 years, read a letter on behalf of COSAS: 'We salute the birth of Soweto Youth Congress... The future is in the hands of the youth.' SOYCO adopted the stirring slogan, 'Freedom in our Lifetime', and committed itself to 'organising and uniting the youth of Soweto in the struggle for a democratic South Africa'.

Along with COSAS, SOYCO worked in the schools to establish branches across the township and the young members of these two organisations soon became well known as 'the Comrades', a term which broadly meant 'friends in the struggle'. Seth Mazibuko explains that, during the 1970s, the term 'comrade' had been deliberately avoided 'because Black Consciousness people used to regard it as a Russian term and they were not inclined towards communism. The term started during the UDF era and it created a collective identity amongst youth who were engaged in resistance against apartheid'.

The comrades developed a distinct culture of their own and, although many women joined, most were young men who could be identified by their speech and clothes. Bold and colourful T-shirts displayed the political organisation or 'structure' to which they belonged and these became the comrades' trademark.

At the centre of this new culture was the jubilant, high-energy, militant dance routine known as the 'toyi-toyi', which was brought back to South Africa by MK recruits from the Zimbabwean guerrilla training camps in Angola. The Zimbabwean People's Revolutionary Army used the toyi-toyi as a warm-up exercise to boost fitness and morale and, accompanied by the 'freedom songs' which drew on images of war, it proved an instant success in townships across South Africa.

The young comrades glorified the symbols of armed struggle. They carried wooden AK47s (the rifles used by ANC soldiers), and wore the khaki uniform and black beret.

The high-energy toyi-toyi dance created a thrilling sense of unity and solidarity among Soweto's youth.

Motsamai Kobi, a young 14-year-old living in White City when he joined the ranks of the comrades, describes the popularity of the toyi-toyi dance:

❝ *Toyi-toyi happened everywhere, it happened anywhere... It kept the morale very high. It brought us hope and joy. When we raised our knees, they came as high as our chests. Then we realised that we are tomorrow's leaders. There was this song which we used to sing which says Siyaya Epitoli, meaning that we are going to Pretoria. That was the most famous and loved song within Soweto. It meant that we were going to occupy the Union building and remove whoever was in that building.* ❞

Lead: Mandela, Mandela
Chorus: Mandela says fight for freedom
Lead: Mandela says freedom now
Chorus: Mandela says freedom now
Lead: Now we say away with slavery
Chorus: In our land of Africa.

Lead: Rolihlahla
Chorus: Rolihlahla Mandela
Lead: Freedom is in your hands
Chorus: Freedom is in your hands
Lead: Show us the way to freedom
Chorus: In our land of Africa.

The toyi-toyi became the centrepiece of most gatherings and will be remembered as one of the defining features of life in the township in the 1980s, but a number of songs also became popular in the streets of Soweto, particularly those paying homage to Mandela or calling for his release from prison.

Politics became a way of life for the comrades. They saw themselves as soldiers dedicated to the struggle for the liberation of the people and many displayed an extraordinary courage in fighting against the system. Those who died became 'heroes and martyrs', and T-shirts were printed in their honour: *Hamba Kahle Comrade* (Go well, Comrade). Discipline was central to the comrades' way of life and they established a code of conduct which differentiated them from other youths. Mongezi Mnganyi speaks of the differences between ordinary youth and those who had committed themselves to 'the struggle':

❝ *The kind of things we did as comrades were very different from other people. We wouldn't mix with people who had criminal inclinations. We went around the location and, if we found people gambling, we would just whip them because gambling encouraged people to fight and stab each other. We thought that we can't waste our energies fighting amongst ourselves. We needed to be united and fight against one enemy. We'd also go around to shebeens, checking if there are any small kids under eighteen. We would chase those youngsters.* ❞

In these different ways, the comrades perceived themselves as moral guardians – the protectors and defenders of the community – and saw it as their task to ensure that people remained 'loyal to the cause'. Anyone who acted against the comrades was deemed an 'enemy of the people' and could be expected to be 'disciplined'. During the 1980s, it was thus the comrades who determined the pace of the political resistance.

Soweto's first UDF campaign

Towards the end of 1983, the SCA, SOYCO, COSAS and the Release Mandela Committee joined forces and embarked on their first UDF campaign in Soweto. They set out to organise a boycott of the elections for the new black local authorities (BLAs) – yet another attempt by the government to establish legitimate bodies to run the township. Dr Piet Koornhof, the minister responsible for the BLAs, claimed that they were a 'new deal' for urban blacks but, in the opinion of the SCA, they were no more than 'toothless puppets dancing to Pretoria's tune'. These bodies had to finance themselves and the SCA believed that the 'sell-out' black councillors would be forced into increasing rents and service charges in order to pay for the township's day-to-day costs. The residents would, once again, be the ones to suffer and 'pay for their own oppression' while the government bore no responsibility.

As a result, an Anti-Community Council Committee mobilised support from a wide range of Sowetans. It distributed leaflets supporting a boycott of the elections, and encouraged residents to resist the establishment of the new council.

On election day in November 1983, only 10 per cent of Soweto's registered voters turned out, the second lowest response in the Transvaal townships. Ephraim Tshabalala, a well-known business tycoon, was elected with just 1 115 votes in a township of well over a million people. Tshabalala had alienated township residents for many years. As early as 1965, he had declared that 'apartheid is a blessing to Africans' and later claimed that 'God created apartheid'.

The pace steps up

The anti-election campaigns in townships across the country were to signal the start of a long period of political upheaval. In August 1984, PW Botha called for another set of elections, this time for the Indian and coloured communities to vote for their representatives in the new tricameral parliament. These elections sparked off renewed protests in African communities and, added to their antagonism of Botha's fake reforms, was a growing anger over rent increases and what was seen as a hopeless situation in black schools. The most intense fighting took place in the townships of the Vaal Triangle, namely Sebokeng, Sharpeville, Boipatong and Evaton. Government buildings were destroyed, angry students barricaded the streets with burning tyres, and there were fierce battles with the police. This massive insurrection later came to be known as the Vaal Uprising.

Although Soweto was not at the centre of resistance at this point, the government treated it in the same way as the other more volatile townships and the army was sent in to quell the 'unrest'. Ironically, it was the soldiers' brutal tactics which strengthened the SCA, SOYCO and COSAS and heightened political protest in Soweto.

A lone protester makes his feelings clear.

Once again, it was the newly elected municipal councillors who became targets of the comrades' often brutal attacks. Petrol bombs were hurled into councillors' homes and councillors were also assaulted. Far fewer councillors were killed in Soweto, however, than in the Vaal and East Rand townships.

Despite the majority of township dwellers' obvious hatred of the council system, Letsatsi Radebe, a councillor at the time, defended their position: 'We thought that it was wiser to try to fight the domination of the government from within all the bodies that were here. We have done something as councillors in the local government-created institutions.'

Bennet Molokoane expressed the COSAS attitude: 'We had such structures and units to do away with councillors. Such people are not even civilians. They are enemy agents. In some instances, they had to be shot at; some of them lost their lives. And this is what our struggle demanded from our own side. We are not going to apologise for that.'

Sibongile Mkhabela, who had been a leader during the 1976 uprising and later became a member of AZAPO, was less happy to condone the actions taken against the councillors:

❦ *1984 is perhaps characterised by the murders of councillors. The comrades didn't want councillors. That was fine. But what was bad was that people were being killed. People died in the 1970s, but they died in the heat of things, like a policeman being killed whilst things were happening around him. There wasn't this malicious targeting of an individual in his house and his whole family would be put at stake. For me it actually killed a lot of things; I said, I don't believe in this.* ❧

Soweto — A History

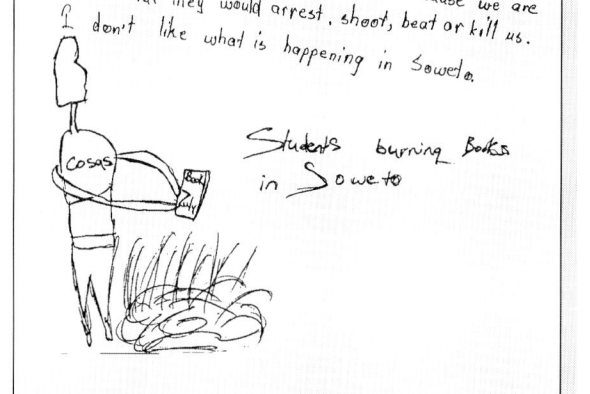

The young lions

It was the schools, however, which would prove to be the main target of the military. In mid-August 1985, the Minister of Law and Order, Louis le Grange, banned COSAS and vowed to detain every COSAS leader. He passed new emergency regulations which allowed police to arrest any pupil not in the classroom between 8am and 4pm. 'The police are cracking down. We will not allow 5 000 stupid students to disregard law and order in Soweto,' proclaimed Brigadier Jan Coetzee, the Chief of Police in Soweto. COSAS responded by stating that, 'the government is forcing students to take up illegal forms of struggle'. As a result, township schoolyards became increasingly dangerous places over the months that followed. Patrick Hlongwane considers his school days during this period:

Police raid a school.

❝ Police and soldiers were all over the schoolyard and, even if you have asked your teacher to go to the toilet during class hours, you can get beaten up because the soldiers didn't want to see you out of the class. We would only go out at breaks and then you would be able to go to the toilet. The police and soldiers didn't want to see a child of my age in the street. If they happened to find a child on the street during school hours, they would take him and put him in any of the schools and make him sit in a classroom until the class is out. ❞

This letter, published in Two Dogs and Freedom, *was written by a 13-year-old.*

At Musi High School in Pimville, a teacher and 10 pupils were injured when police opened fire with shotguns and rubber bullets for no apparent reason, and many similar incidents occurred in other schools throughout Soweto. Many pupils chose to stay at home to avoid the violence in the schoolyards, but security forces invaded homes each morning and forced children to go to class. Mongezi Mnganyi reports that children decided to stop wearing school uniform so as to avoid being identified: 'It was to our advantage to stop wearing uniforms because you could be easily abducted by the army, but if you are just casual they would not know if you were a school kid.' But nothing stood in the way of the SADF and the army began to carry out unexpected raids on schools and arrested children in large groups.

The behaviour of the SADF outraged the students and protest action and violent confrontations intensified as a result. 'If a student was arrested, we would fight for that person's release and there would be no schooling until that person was freed,' says Patrick Hlongwane. Mongezi Mnganyi continues: 'There was this slogan, "An injury to one is an injury to all." If one high school closed down, there would be sympathy boycotts and all schools closed down. We'd make sure no one would attend school. That caused chaos.' Despite the army's presence, however, demonstrations continued to be held outside the school gates.

In a few instances, these demonstrations led to the release of students, but many were detained for months on end. 'It was really terrible. I didn't think that I was a leader,' recalls Thloki Mofokeng who was detained for 11 months. 'I was held in solitary confinement for over three months, a situation which I never dreamed I'd be in. It was very depressing.'

In the space of just four months, over 1 400 people were detained in Soweto. The youngest was just seven years old, and the Detainee Parents Support Committee estimated that at least one fifth of detainees were under the age of 16. Anxious parents were often not informed of where their sons and daughters were being held, and many feared they would never be reunited because their children barely knew their own surnames or addresses. Parents' anxieties were further fuelled by the horrifying stories of detainees being severely abused in the police cells. Sicelo Dlomo, who was 15 years old when he was first detained and who was later shot dead by the police, endured a series of vicious interrogation sessions during his first detention. His testimony was conveyed in a film made by the Detainee Parents Support Committee after Sicelo was released from detention the first time.

> A South African Defence Force contingent raided the Thabo-Jabula Secondary School in Pimville, Soweto, yesterday and stood guard as police vans ferried hundreds of pupils from the premises to Moroka police station. Armed with R1 rifles and tearsmoke masks, one group stood guard outside the fence circling the school premises as another took charge of the pupils who were moved out of their classrooms into the police vans waiting in the yard.
>
> *Sowetan*, 14 August 1985

News report of a typical SADF raid on a school.

> *I was in an interrogation room when suddenly five figures rushed in. I was made to sit on a chair and I was handcuffed. Then I was told to take off my shirt. I refused and they just tore it. Then I asked them, "What's going on?" and they said that I must understand that I'm in an electric chair and if I'm not going to tell the truth, then they're going to torture me and kill me and leave me there to die. Suddenly, I felt the most terrible pain in my body as they electrocuted me. I lost consciousness and fainted.*

After his initial release, Dlomo's mother Sylvia Dlomo tells how, 'Sicelo was made to go to the police station every day because they wanted to make sure he was inside the country. If he didn't sign in, the police would come to the house and try to arrest him. It was a terrible burden on a young man's life.' In 1987, Sicelo was found dead in the veld, and his mother believes he was killed by the police.

A pamphlet distributed by the Bureau of Information blamed the death and detention of young children on the ANC. 'The abuse of children by the ANC and other revolutionaries is a crime against humanity – the need for the detention of children a saddening result of this horrendous abuse and crime. The so-called "child heroes" are terrorists guilty of the barbaric brutalisation of fellow human beings.'

Linda Masemola believes that the soldiers' savagery and the torture of young students led to the comrades' violence:

> *What changed our youth was that they were being victimised by the policemen. If these children go to school or even if they are just seated in a group, policemen would intervene and say they are busy with ANC matters... [This] really changed them. They were now aggressive.*

```
Dear Sir/Madam

You, like all peace loving people, must be very worried about the
unrest and violence in our country, and the effect it has on you
and your family.

Once again violent groups will want to sow the seeds of fear and
destruction. This is not the way you and I choose to build a new
South Africa.

In spite of them however, a new vision is growing among the peace
loving people of South Africa. A united vision of a new South Africa
which is built by Black and White together.

This is a time of standing together and we extend to you our support
in this time. We want you to know that we care about the security
and the future of you and your family.

Please take the necessary steps to protect your family and your
interests. The South African Police/Security Forces want to be of
assistance to you whenever you need protection. We will attend to
any problem that may arise with regard to the security of your family.
Your problems will be treated in a confidential and responsible man-
ner, so please do not hesitate to contact us at your nearest police
station. We need your help in order to provide effective protection.

We wish and you and your family a peaceful and prosperous future.

                                              MAJOR-GENERAL
DIVISIONAL COMMISSIONER : WITWATERSRAND
M VAN EYK
```

Pamphlet distributed by police to promote their image.

'I can say the police contributed more to our youth being violent,' agrees Lumkile, an activist from Diepkloof. 'Without provocation, our youth were shot; people were arrested and people were brutally assaulted. So the culture of violence started there.' (Monique Marks, 'Organisation, Identity and Violence', 1993)

Linda Masemola believes that parents in the township were also partly to blame for this culture of violence. 'Some parents used to be against the youth. Where were we driving them to? What did we expect them to do? They didn't know who to turn to.'

Velapi Mnguni felt that the relationship between the parents and their children began to suffer as a result of these severe strains:

Kids used to participate in structures from school like COSAS and SRCs, while the parents were not doing anything. Kids started to think that they know more about what was happening in South Africa. So parents started to lose control. They could not tell us anything. We were the people who told them what was happening.

```
FIGHT FOR YOUR RIGHTS! FIGHT AGAINST RENT
INCREASE! UNDEMOCRATIC INSTITUTIONS! FIGHT AGAINST
THE CRIMINAL RACIST MINORITY REGIME!
Now is the time to engage the enemy.
Join youth organisations, civic bodies, students organisations,
womens organisations, workers organisations etc.
Organise the unemployed, the church, and the community as a whole.
For structures where they are not there.
Workers organsations must form a Federation.
Organisations must join the mass popular Front.
Form underground structures.
Render yourselves ungovernable. Botha must go . . .
        FORWARD WITH THE YEAR OF THE YOUTH !!!
           FORWARD WITH THE YEAR OF THE CADRE !!!
                           Issued by underground unit of ANC.
```

In June 1985, the ANC adopted the notion of 'people's war' at the Kabwe Conference, and this encouraged new levels of violence among the comrades. The ANC committed itself to stepping up military action inside South Africa and training as many new members as possible – not only in training camps outside the country but also within the townships themselves.

As a result, MK cadres were sent to teach basic weapons handling and guerrilla tactics in black communities within the country. During his New Year's Day broadcast on Radio Freedom, Oliver Tambo also made a stirring speech calling on those in the struggle to 'render South Africa ungovernable'.

The comrades thus readily committed themselves to the programme of 'ungovernability'. 'Kill the boer' became a popular war chant and a new reckless heroism became evident. Nomavenda Mathiane, journalist and commentator, described violence as 'a blanket worn in the township'. Others, like Sibongile Mkhabela, were apprehensive of the consequences:

In the mid-80s, this comrade thing was coming up very strongly. Somebody called them the "Young Lions". I said, it is very difficult to train a young lion and, if you don't teach it, it may devour you after some time.

Liberation before education

While the young lions readily embarked on the ANC's strategy of a 'people's war', they received less and less direction from political organisations. The Soweto Students Congress (SOSCO), which was formed after COSAS was banned, was forced to operate in a semi-underground fashion. Most of the experienced leaders were behind bars, regular open meetings and report-back sessions were no longer possible, and the decisions were now taken by fewer, less experienced leaders. Neil Tobajne comments that 'the real leadership became spectators since they were in prison. They could not take full control of the situation. Activities were undertaken by other layers of leaders. Problematic campaigns started to develop...'. Student activists, for example, adopted the slogan 'Liberation before Education' and began to attack those who chose to attend school. Consequently, hundreds of restless young children roamed the streets of the township each day. Thloki Mofokeng, who was among those boycotting school in 1986, reflects on the strategy:

Most students boycotted school because they were sick and tired of the stupid teachers and stupid kind of education system in the schools. For some, it was a kind of escapism simply because they were not coping in the school. The boycott was very effective at rendering the country ungovernable. But it also had negative implications. The more there was no schooling, the more youth organisations lacked a coherent response to specific problems that were emerging. It became difficult to mobilise people because they were dispersed. It became difficult to assert organisational discipline.

The Soweto Civic Association attempted to intervene by organising a meeting of parents, students and teachers to discuss the education crisis. The Soweto Parents' Crisis Committee (SPCC) was then launched and it organised a nationwide conference to address the question of schooling. Delegates campaigned for the slogan of 'Education for Liberation' and urged pupils to return to school so that they could transform the education system from within. Nthato Motlana, who was at the meeting, explains the tensions that existed around the call to go back to school: 'We said that, as parents, we cannot allow our children to vegetate in the streets, but we had a problem with the children who thought that the parents – in asking students to go back to school – were, in fact, selling out. Finally, we did persuade them to go back to school.'

Thloki Mofokeng, who was a member of the SRC at his school at the time, offers his perspective: 'Personally I was very angry with the call. It felt like a retreat and it should not have been made by the parents. Most of our leaders were in detention. Why didn't the parents deal with the problem of releasing those children and then tell us to go to school? We did not want to go back to school and betray our comrades who were in detention.'

In the end, few students heeded the call to return to the classrooms and attendance in Soweto's schools remained low. Less than half the matric students wrote examinations at the end of 1985 and, by the end of 1986, 10 township schools closed their doors.

Funerals

Those students who remained on the streets continued to engage in protest action and the death toll continued to rise. In one of the most publicised incidents, Bongani Khumalo, the secretary of the Soweto branch of COSAS, was shot dead by the police a month after COSAS was banned. The Public Safety Act had placed severe restrictions on the funerals of 'unrest victims' during the State of Emergency, but people openly defied regulations which forbade them from displaying flags, banners and placards. Thousands flocked to the funerals of their student leader carrying the prohibited COSAS banners.

Masses of students attended the funeral of Bongani Khumalo, carrying the prohibited COSAS banners.

As a result, funerals became one of the most powerful expressions of political solidarity in Soweto. Packed buses and cars carried mourners to the graveside, and passing motorists were also stopped and forced to drive people to the cemetery. The spirit on these occasions was one of militancy and defiance. Comrades dressed in fake military uniforms thrust homemade wooden rifles into the air and chanted freedom

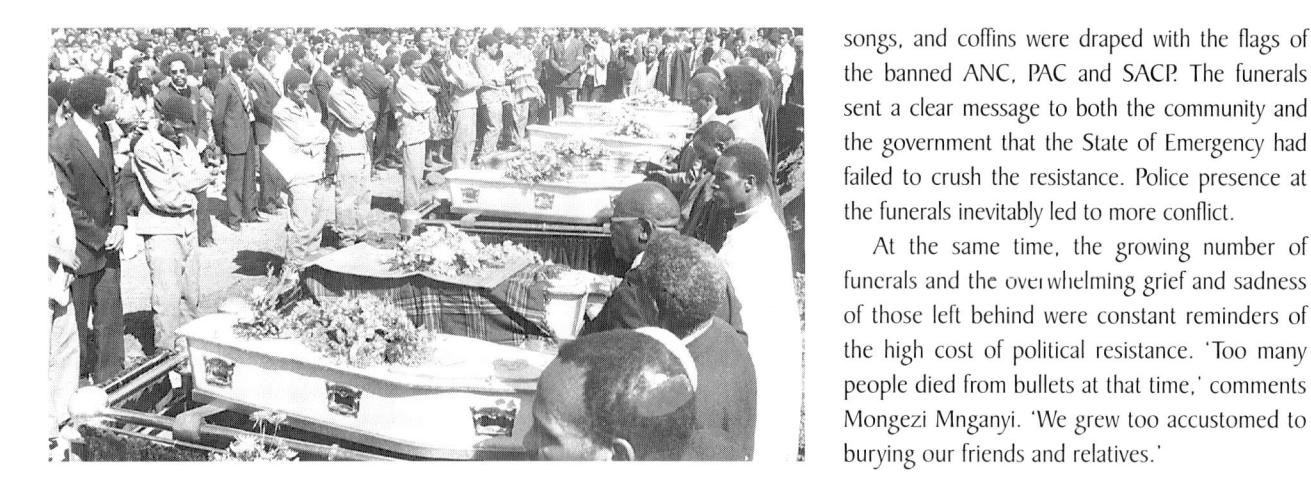

One of the many mass funerals that took place in the township during this period.

Comrades search consumers' bags in the centre of Johannesburg during the consumer boycott.

songs, and coffins were draped with the flags of the banned ANC, PAC and SACP. The funerals sent a clear message to both the community and the government that the State of Emergency had failed to crush the resistance. Police presence at the funerals inevitably led to more conflict.

At the same time, the growing number of funerals and the overwhelming grief and sadness of those left behind were constant reminders of the high cost of political resistance. 'Too many people died from bullets at that time,' comments Mongezi Mnganyi. 'We grew too accustomed to burying our friends and relatives.'

The people's war

The rising death toll in Soweto and the rest of the country encouraged activists to develop new, more covert forms of opposition. Consumer boycotts were one of the new tactics. These originated in the Eastern Cape where the UDF was strongest, and township residents were called to boycott white shops in town in order to extend the struggle from the black areas to the white city. Cries of *asithengi* (We do not buy) were accompanied by other demands, including the lifting of the emergency. The mass withdrawal of the buying power of black consumers forced many shops to close down while others barely survived the enormous drop in sales. Sections of the white local business community were shocked into action and, for the first time, they appealed to the government to make political concessions to the black community.

Naturally, the success of the boycott tactic in the Eastern Cape inspired similar actions in other townships. In Soweto, however, the boycott weapon seemed far less effective. Township shopkeepers were neither consulted nor given a chance to stock up sufficiently to cope with the increased trade, and many raised their prices to take advantage of their new position. But it was intimidation by the comrades that ultimately undermined the success of the campaign in the township. Youths attacked wholesalers' trucks delivering supplies and assaulted individuals who dared to shop in the white areas. Patrick Hlongwane describes the scene at Mzimhlope station:

I saw many things happening there. People were forced to throw down their goods which were bought in town. Even a sweet was not allowed inside your bag. If you had your own papers or anything personal that was okay, but not something like food. It was messy at the station, the platform was strewn with things like oil. If you had bad luck, you would be forced to eat some of the things, like washing powder, and some people ended up in hospital.

Motsamai Kobi was matter-of-fact in his assessment of the comrades' behaviour. 'If you had done wrong,' he states, 'and your case was put to the comrades, then you knew that you were going to get the necessary punishment or discipline that you deserved and you couldn't escape it.' Pheteni Khumalo, on the other hand, believed that her fellow comrades were ill-equipped to carry out these acts of punishment. 'Sometimes, we used to judge people wrongly because we were still young and we were not trained to judge.'

The leadership of the UDF recognised the dangers of a situation in which the comrades were simply left to impose their will on the community. One of the ways in which the senior leadership attempted to contain the radicalism of the younger generation was to establish street committees. The SCA took the lead in mobilising residents, and the township was divided into 29 branches, with each branch forming street committees. Rhoda Khumalo recalls the very first meeting in her street in Meadowlands:

> *The youth told us we must go to number so and so, there is a meeting there. I thought I must go because I wanted to know what is going on. I took my jersey and I went there. The youth addressed us and explained what a street committee is. They told the parents that street committees are to make sure that people of the same street know one another, that they help one another to stop crime and fights between families and neighbours and to fight against the police when they bring trouble.*

The CONSUMER BOYCOTT of all shops owned by WHITES & COLLABORATORS must continue!

Destructive rumours have been spread that the devastating consumer boycott of white-owned businesses is over. BUT we cannot and must not stop now ....

WHY?

- Our mothers and sisters are raped ...
- Seven, eight and nine-year old children in prisons go crying to sleep every night ...
- Parents, teachers and students – male & female – tortured every minute in prison ...
- Informers from our community are daily putting our 7-year-old children, our parents & students into prison ...
- The sanctity of our churches & mosques are regularly violated by police & troops ...
- Killer troops continue to terrorize our people in our townships

The perpetrators of these crimes need our money to maintain WHITE superiority (they call it law & order!)

SO THINK BEFORE YOU SPEND!!

Boycott all white shops and shops owned by collaborators!
An appeal to all oppressed people committed to the struggle:
ENFORCE THE CONSUMER BOYCOTT BY ALL MEANS POSSIBLE!!!
We owe this sacrifice to our parents, children, teachers, students and workers languishing in prison!

VICTORY IS CERTAIN!!!

Mtutuzeli Matshoba's impression of his first meeting was that it was 'quickly organised and well attended. I remember very well the opening speech by a 16-year-old. He spoke about matters such as the consumer boycott, as well as local issues such as burst pipes'.

For Nomavenda Mathiane, the committees 'were an opportunity for me and my neighbours to organise ourselves so we would not be alone and at the mercy of the comrades. It seemed ironic that it was the comrades that were inspiring this, but I started to get interested. We were participating in the running of our affairs – something new in the lives of most of us'. (Nomavenda Mathiane, *Beyond the Headlines*, 1990)

Steps were taken to ensure that the police did not know where and when the street committees met: 'During the street committee meetings, we had people who worked as our *impimpis* (informers). We would place them on each and every corner to watch who was coming and going. We would not allow a person to leave before the meeting finished. We did not trust such people because we knew that they were going to call the police,' explains Pheteni Khumalo.

Police presence in Soweto was pervasive.

As a result, the police struggled to locate meetings and street committees became a successful form of organisation during the emergency. They involved older residents in political activities and aided much-needed communication between the youth and their parents. Many committees earned the respect because they replaced despised local authorities and organised basic services. Jon-Jon Mkhonza offers his opinion:

❛ There were the bad street committees, and good street committees. But those that were bad were the ones where three or four people controlled the whole area. The good committees were those where everybody participated. By forcing the gangsters to disband, by raiding the dangerous areas during the night, and by preventing the youth from harassing the people, the community started to respect the street committees. ❜

Mkhonza adds that committees had a particularly beneficial effect on the comrades:

❛ There were those comrades who are genuine comrades and there were those comrades who were not clear and who were quick to act. They made many mistakes. Some of them even went to the extent of raping and robbing. Street committees educated the people to stop such acts. It was easy to educate the people at street level. ❜

In some areas of the township, street committees also functioned as people's courts. Pheteni Khumalo explains that, in Meadowlands, the people's court 'would move from one place to the other, because if it was to be at the same place we would have put the house owner in big trouble... because the courts were illegal'. In Moroka, on the other hand, a group of elderly residents who belonged to the local civic association established a permanent court at the Inkanyezi Youth Centre. The Moroka court dealt mainly with domestic disputes. In other areas, the courts controlled the hours of shebeens, searched customers for weapons and imposed curfews to prevent crime and violence on township streets. By offering these services, however, the courts challenged the government's authority. Bennet Molokoane believes that the street committees and peoples' courts had become 'the basic organs of people's power. We were starting now to govern ourselves'.

Indeed, by the end of 1985, the comrades believed that the people's war that they had launched had been successful in 'bringing the government to its knees' and that the Nationalist Party was indeed on the brink of collapse. Two separate events were to strengthen the comrades' belief that a revolutionary victory was around the corner: The first was the launch of the Congress of South African Trade Unions (COSATU) in Durban in November 1985. COSATU's formation settled an ongoing debate over the question of union involvement in political struggle. After hours of debate, COSATU came out in support of unions entering into permanent alliances with political organisations. At COSATU's opening congress, Cyril Ramaphosa of the National Union of Mineworkers declared that 'the struggle of workers on the shop floor cannot be separated from the wider political struggle for liberation in this country'. From then on, COSATU worked closely with the UDF and this affiliation greatly boosted the strength of the UDF.

The other pivotal event was State President Botha's announcement that the emergency was being lifted because it had failed to achieve its objective, and the majority of detainees were released. The Acting National Secretary of the UDF, Mohammed Valli, saw this as a UDF victory:

❛ We have devised ways and means of operating that enable us to withstand extreme repression. It is our people and extra-parliamentary movement which today dictate the nature and the pace of events in our country. ❜

In Soweto, as elsewhere in the country, the strength of organisation had indeed improved during the emergency. In the months that immediately followed the lifting of the State of Emergency, the SCA organised a series of successful marches and delegations to the Soweto municipal council to press for changes and they directly challenged the right of the Council to administer the township.

Street politics

The SCA's self-congratulation and that of its followers, however, proved to be premature. Just before the tenth anniversary of the Soweto rebellion, in what the township named the 'Year of Remembrance', PW Botha announced a second State of Emergency.

The State President stated that his action was necessary because 'the occurrence and increase in violence... is in my opinion of such a nature and extent that it seriously endangers the security of the public and the maintenance of public order... I am thus of the opinion that the ordinary laws of the land are inadequate to enable the Government to... maintain public order'.

This time, the State of Emergency covered the entire country and proved far harsher than the first. Over 100 political and community organisations were prohibited from holding meetings or public gatherings and all political publications – including stickers, pamphlets and posters – were banned. Political activity of virtually any sort was thus effectively silenced. Parliament ceased to have any real power over state policy and the politics of reform disappeared from the agenda. Botha now stated that 'there can be no reforms without security'.

In Soweto, a committee of soldiers and policemen took control of the day-to-day running of the township and, because of their concentrated efforts regarding safety and security, they became known as 'securocrats'. The press was effectively barred from reporting on the activities of the securocrats, and special government reports were the only information made available to the public. A deafening silence settled over political life in the township. Notices indicating that the newspaper was subject to censorship appeared daily in the *Sowetan* and blank spaces were now deliberately scattered throughout liberal newspapers as a way of bringing attention to the draconian restrictions faced by journalists.

Under cover of the press blackout, the securocrats attempted to re-impose 'law and order' on Soweto and undertook a series of upgrading programmes to improve the quality of life for residents in the belief that the appalling conditions in the township were a cause of the unrest. They began tarring roads, installing electricity and cleaning township streets but 'Operation Oilspot', as this programme was dubbed, had little impact in Soweto, although it did meet with more success in smaller townships such as Alexandra.

But what was far more noticeable to the people of Soweto was WHAM (Winning Hearts And Minds), an initiative which attempted to promote the image of the police and local government authorities. Residents were bombarded with pamphlets from the Bureau of Information which discredited black political organisations and warned the readers against political involvement.

The kitskonstabels *were the subject of much ridicule in the township.*

This type of propaganda continued, however, to be accompanied by blatant acts of repression. Soldiers occupied every available space in the township, from local sports fields to large stadiums. They worked with the newly armed, ill-trained black municipal police known as *kitskonstabels* (instant police), who were the subject of much ridicule in the township.

Despite their poor training, the *kitskonstabels* had the power to arrest and, together with the soldiers, they swept through the township detaining hundreds of people. The largest number of arrests occurred in Soweto, and most detainees were held under the notorious Section 29 of the Internal Security Act which allowed security police to hold a person indefinitely and subject them to interrogation. Comrades were thus forced underground to avoid the prison cells. Susan Shabangu describes how she survived in these difficult times:

As an activist, I could not sleep at my place. It was not an easy thing. Sometimes I would just go in and they would say the cops were looking for me. Then I had to go out. I couldn't even take clothing. When night fell, you didn't even know where you are going to sleep. I would go to my relatives and, as soon as they saw me, they would feel scared and say that I was bringing police because I was involved in politics. Being a woman on the run isn't an easy thing. It was difficult for my parents and family to accept because they believed that they had to protect me.

But political activists were not the only ones who were harassed by the police. Households in the township were often searched for no apparent reason. 'Things were frightening during the period of the State of Emergency,' recalls Pheteni Khumalo. 'The police had the right to enter your house without a permit. I remember when they came to my home. They broke the door and entered the house. Some threw food out of the fridge, some turned wardrobes upside down. Each of them was doing his own thing and you couldn't argue with them. If they liked, they'd take you to jail without being charged.'

Many detainees were held in solitary confinement for months on end, confined to their tiny cell for 23 hours a day without as much as a book to keep them company. The vast majority complained of torture and physical and sexual abuse at the hands of the security forces.

On release, detainees were usually forbidden to participate in any kind of political activity. The Detainee Parents Support Committee campaigned tirelessly against detentions, and made special appeals for shows of solidarity with detainees.

Nevertheless, detentions and police harassment were not the only way in which organisations were prevented from functioning during this period. Vigilante gangs, who were often believed to work with the police, openly attacked the comrades. 'The police hired gangsters because it was a better way of getting rid of comrades,' maintained Sylvia Dlomo. 'This kind of thing started in 1986. The police increased the gangsters' powers. They gave them cars and firearms and the police instructed the gangsters to burn down the houses of activists. My mother's house in Emdeni – where my son used to stay – was burnt down. Everything was damaged in the house – the TV, the dining-room suite, everything. My mother nearly died from that.'

Susan Shabangu tells the story of the Makabasas, a vicious gang in Orlando who targeted political activists in both Orlando and Diepkloof:

There were these gangsters in Orlando East called the Makabasa. They harassed people and raped young girls while, at the same time, they conflicted with the young activists in the township. They'd do all terrible things but you'd never see the police. You'd ask yourself where did they get their guns from and why were they not being arrested? Down the line, it was discovered that the police were using them to attack activists.

The UDF-supporting youth also claimed that the Makabasas were being used by AZAPO in the escalating political war between AZAPO and the UDF. Each of these organisations accused the other of wanting to wipe it from the political scene and both engaged in violent struggles for ideological and exclusive territorial control over as much of the township as possible. Youngsters throughout Soweto were thus forced to take sides, but the areas most affected were Dlamini, Tladi, Moletsane and Orlando East. AZAPO referred to UDF supporters as 'the Wararas', meaning people with no clear policy, while the members of the Azanian Students Movement – affiliated to AZAPO – were nicknamed 'the Zim-Zims'. In her article, 'The Deadly Duel of the Wararas and the Zim-Zims', Nomavenda Mathiane commented that the atmosphere in the mid-'80s was no longer like 1976. 'In those days,' she said, 'the activists had their guard up only against the police. Now, although... youth scuttle whenever the Mellow Yellow armoured police bus appears, the main conflict is between people who used to be friends and allies... The fight between the two is wreaking more devastation than the fight with the system.' (Nomavenda Mathiane, *South Africa: The Diary of Troubled Times*, 1989)

As a result, by the end of 1986, the war between different political groups within the township had caused more deaths than police action. The wave of killings horrified Soweto's residents, while the government gleefully spoke of the killings as 'black-on-black violence', implying that the security forces had no involvement in the bloodshed.

Revolutionary violence

The conflict between organisations, together with intense government repression, took a heavy toll on the township. It was virtually impossible for political structures to function and militant students and youth were left with no guidance whatsoever. Many turned to violence as the sole means of struggle and the practice of placing a burning tyre around a victim's neck – commonly referred to as 'the necklace' – became a popular form of 'revolutionary violence'.

Burning tyres were a regular sight in the townships during this period.

Although the necklace was occasionally used as a weapon in the war between the UDF and AZAPO, the most common victims were those branded as informers or 'sell-outs' by the comrades. Since the mid-1980s, police often used informers as a way of undermining political organisations. These *impimpis* were particularly disliked by the comrades because they were seen as betraying their own people.

Motsamai Kobi believes that the necklace was 'a useful weapon of struggle' because it 'lowered the number of informers and ensured that people were loyal'. Another activist also believed that necklacing was 'an effective strategy of preventing things from happening. People who committed grave crimes deserved necklacing. It prevented things from happening again'. (Monique Marks, 'Organisation, Identity and Violence', 1993) Mtutuzeli Matshoba, an older political activist, adds that 'the necklace came about as the deterrent of collaboration with the state and it became symbolic – the tyre, that fire, it represented people's anger'.

Not all comrades, however, were in favour of using the necklace against informers and many actively opposed this gruesome form of punishment. 'The necklace was a terrible thing. I wanted to believe that it was not the comrades that were involved in carrying out those acts of terror,' comments Thlokie Mofokeng. Those who were directly involved in necklacing were often severely traumatised by their experience. 'If you necklace a human being it's so terrible...' recalls one youth. 'You just sleep badly because you think of what is happening there and you'll never eat.' (Monique Marks, 'Organisation, Identity and Violence', 1993) The youths' behaviour generated strong disapproval amongst Sowetans and the broader public alike. For Sibongile Makhabela, the mid-1980s saw 'the total destruction of values amongst the youth. I don't know what we're going to do with the kids we're bringing up because they're likely to be psychological wrecks,' she commented.

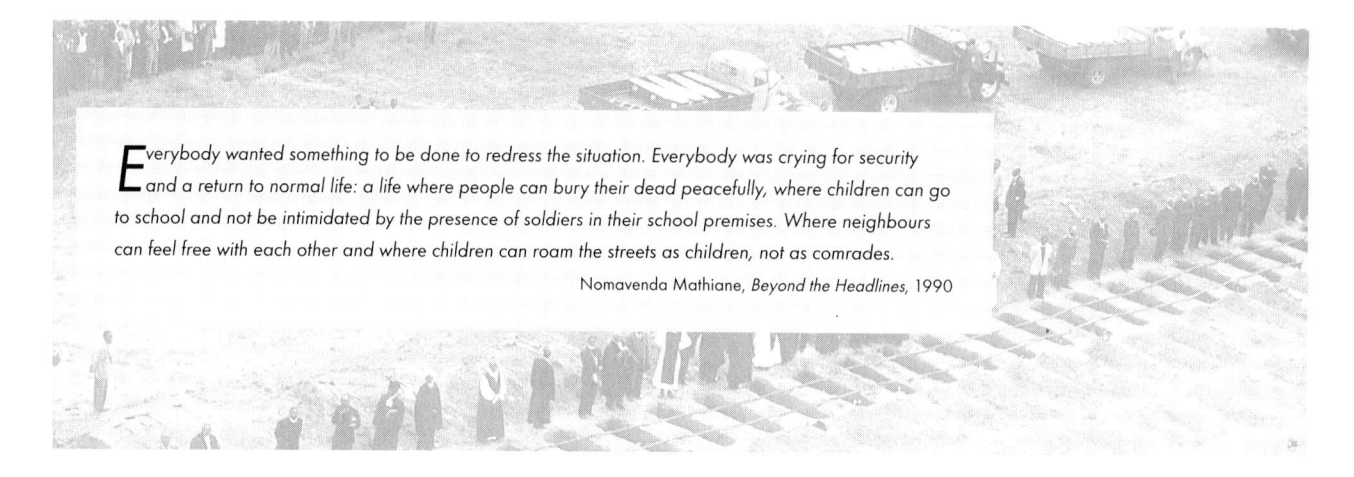

Everybody wanted something to be done to redress the situation. Everybody was crying for security and a return to normal life: a life where people can bury their dead peacefully, where children can go to school and not be intimidated by the presence of soldiers in their school premises. Where neighbours can feel free with each other and where children can roam the streets as children, not as comrades.

Nomavenda Mathiane, *Beyond the Headlines*, 1990

Soweto's resurgence

Two separate initiatives served to contain the spontaneous behaviour of the youth and reinforced a sense of discipline among the comrades. The first was the formation of the South African Youth Congress (SAYCO) which was launched secretly at the University of the Western Cape early in 1987. SAYCO united youth congresses around the country under the rousing slogan, 'Freedom or Death, Victory is Certain.' The new organisation was headed by Peter Mokaba, a young militant who spoke a radical language which appealed to the youth. Many students were drawn back to organisation and were guided towards more disciplined strategies by SAYCO's commitment to non-violent methods of struggle, as well as their motto 'From mobilisation to organisation'.

Street politics were no longer seen as a sufficient form of resistance. SAYCO also strongly advocated working-class leadership and, towards the end of the 1980s, there was a noticeable shift towards union- rather than student-led campaigns.

Ultimately, however, it was the SCA's call for a boycott of rents and municipal service charges which revived political spirits in Soweto. The boycott ensured that the township asserted itself as a major centre of resistance in the country. Rent boycotts had become a powerful form of protest in townships across the Transvaal when the government increased rents in 1984 and, after the second State of Emergency, over 50 townships boycotted rents. In Soweto the boycott was triggered by a new 'electricity levy' imposed by the councils. The levy was apparently to pay for the electrical system which had been installed in the township in the early 1980s, but it doubled a household's service charges overnight and placed a huge financial strain on residents.

A boycott was first called in May 1986 by the Mzimhlope branch of the SCA. 'We are no longer prepared to finance our own oppression,' proclaimed one speaker. 'We won't pay rent. We won't pay the salaries of our enemies, the puppet councillors, and their police.' The boycott call spread quickly throughout the township through the well-established system of street committees.

Two-thirds of Soweto's households supported the boycott from its outset and previously passive residents were drawn into local political structures. For Velapi Mnguni, the rent boycott 'was one of the things that made the people of Soweto realise what the struggle was all about'.

The boycott enjoyed widespread support for a number of reasons. In a survey which asked individual residents why they were not paying rent, 60,9 per cent said it was because the rental and service charges were too high given the appalling services and living conditions. R400 million had been pumped into upgrading the township over the past 10 years, but a doctor who surveyed Soweto in the mid-1980s still concluded that the level of services were a hazard to 'the physical, social and mental health of the community'. Most houses, for example, still had no inside water connections. An additional 14,3 per cent of residents said they supported the boycott because they did not have enough money and they welcomed the extra income each month. Those residents who could afford to pay their rents believed that the boycott was a powerful form of protest against the deeply unpopular and unrepresentative local authority.

The Soweto Council – which normally collected R9 million in rent and service charges – now found itself with less than R3 million at the end of each month. As a result, the Council adopted a hard-line position and refused to negotiate with the SCA or to acknowledge that there were any legitimate causes of the boycott. Councillor Letsatsi Radebe told residents, 'If you don't pay the rent, you're out. That's our policy and that's our stand', while Soweto's Deputy-Mayor Jwara declared that, 'people in general are keen to pay, but they fear victimisation from instigators – being necklaced or having their homes burnt by comrades'. The Council consequently opened an office in Johannesburg to allow for the 'safe payment' of rent and also made arrangement for rents to be paid by post. Very little rent trickled in, however, and while the essential services in the township came to a standstill and litter piled up in the streets, the authorities again turned to force as their solution.

The government provided the Council with a large contingent of newly trained municipal policemen whose first task was to serve hundreds of eviction notices which ordered residents to pay their rent within seven days or vacate their premises.

WE WON'T PAY RENT FROM 1 JUNE!

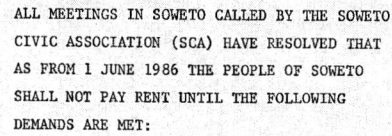

ALL MEETINGS IN SOWETO CALLED BY THE SOWETO CIVIC ASSOCIATION (SCA) HAVE RESOLVED THAT AS FROM 1 JUNE 1986 THE PEOPLE OF SOWETO SHALL NOT PAY RENT UNTIL THE FOLLOWING DEMANDS ARE MET:

1. That all councillors should resign
2. That pensioners should not pay rent
3. That refuse be collected and sewerage pipes be fixed on a regular basis
4. That we need street lights in our township
5. That the soldiers must leave the townships
6. That because of low wages our people cannot afford high rents

NO to high rents!
NO to high electricity and water bills!
WE WANT HOUSES WE CAN AFFORD!

Pamphlet issued by the SCA calling for a rent boycott.

Police inspect the ruins of a house during the rent boycott.

Most households simply ignored their eviction notices. Evictions thus began in earnest and the behaviour of the council police sent shockwaves throughout the community. Velapi Mnguni describes a common scene: 'They'd come with armoured cars – I don't know how many police and helicopters there were – to evict one house. I think that was a strategy to put fear in people who participated in the rent boycott.'

The council police also earned a reputation of being 'gun-happy' because they shot without warning, and the SCA reacted to the violence by declaring that 'An eviction of one is an eviction of all'. Together with SOYCO and the street committees, the SCA devised ways of protecting residents. Large numbers of people could be mobilised at a moment's notice to either resist the police or reinstate the family in their home after the police had left. These methods of protection encouraged households to support the boycott and both the SCA and the street committees were greatly strengthened because of the positive role the township's residents perceived them to be playing. The SCA's newsletter declared, 'People's Unity Stops Evictions.'

The widespread resistance infuriated the authorities and Letsatsi Radebe personally led an armed group to abduct and assault youths in Naledi who had been protecting householders from evictions. But this incident proved a minor transgression compared to the bloodshed which was to follow in White City. White City – given its name because of the concrete-roofed 'elephant houses' which were originally painted white – is the most densely populated suburb in Soweto and housed the lowest income group. On average, more than four families shared a yard in this crime-ridden area.

The 'White City War' began on the night of 27 August. The police burst in on a meeting that had been called to discuss the issue of evictions. A few people in the crowd were chanting, 'We are not fighting', and were reported to be holding up their hands in peace. Without warning, the police opened fire, killing 21 people and injuring 98. Following the carnage, the Council beat a hasty retreat and their housing director, Del Kevan, stated that it was now 'too provocative to carry out evictions when there is such trouble in the townships'. Most councillors fled Soweto and moved to white Johannesburg where they were supported by the City Council in their state of 'exile'.

By 1988, the police violence during evictions had served to unite much of Soweto – 95 per cent of the township supported the rent boycott, and the Soweto Council was now in debt for R274 million. In the municipal election of that year, the Sofasonke Party (SP) promised to stop evictions and to negotiate an end to the boycott. The SP won the elections and although only 12 per cent of the registered voters went to the polls, the SCA agreed to enter into talks with the new Council. The Soweto People's Delegation (SPD) was formed for this purpose. It was made up of a group of prominent Sowetans who had the full support of the SCA.

The demands of the Soweto People's Delegation were far more radical than when the boycott first began. The call for the resignation of councillors and an end to the State of Emergency was now complemented by a new set of conditions.

The last of the demands was the most important. In 1987, approximately 96 per cent of all formally employed people in Soweto worked in Johannesburg and over 70 per cent of their earnings was spent in Johannesburg. For years Soweto had contributed to Johannesburg's economy but, because of the township's status as a separate city, the Johannesburg Council was not obliged to contribute to Soweto's upkeep. Moreover, Soweto's own economic development had been severely stunted by the various apartheid laws which curtailed black entrepreneurship. The demand for a single city, therefore, transformed the rent boycott from a local campaign into a call for the end of racially segregated cities.

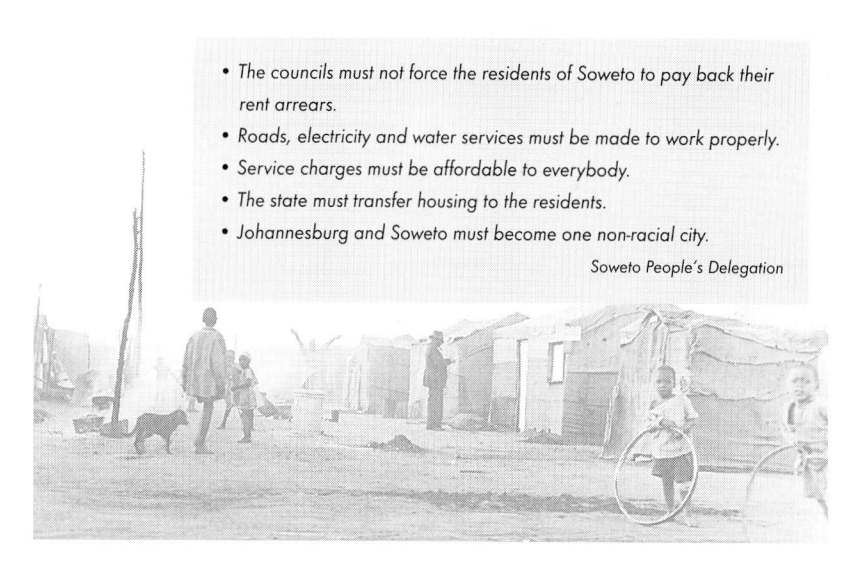

- The councils must not force the residents of Soweto to pay back their rent arrears.
- Roads, electricity and water services must be made to work properly.
- Service charges must be affordable to everybody.
- The state must transfer housing to the residents.
- Johannesburg and Soweto must become one non-racial city.

Soweto People's Delegation

After months of negotiations, the historic Soweto Accord was signed. In it, the Transvaal Provincial Administration (TPA) agreed to all the demands of the SPD. The R515 million debt owed to Council was written off and the foundation was laid for Soweto and Johannesburg to become a single entity. The four-year boycott had ended in triumph for Sowetans. For the first time, the government had listened to the demands of a black community. For Bennet Molokoane, the young comrades were responsible for this success:

Workers stage a protest against 'Whites only' regulations.

❝ It is us who have put South Africa on the correct road to freedom. It is also us who have managed to keep the struggle going so that we could weaken the black local authorities that no longer seemed accountable to us. There were signs – all over South Africa – that if there was no positive response, if there was to be no negotiations with genuine representatives and leaders of our people, the country would become a wasted land. ❞

Bennet's assessment was partly accurate. The popularity of the rent boycott did indeed owe much to the work of the comrades. Soweto once again occupied its former place of prominence in the struggle against apartheid, and the 1980s ended with a new surge of resistance in the country. In 1989, all organisations affiliated to the UDF declared themselves 'unbanned' and SOSCO was one of the first to do so.

The Mass Democratic Movement, made up of the UDF, COSATU and other organisations opposed to apartheid, embarked on new acts of resistance, the most successful of which was the Defiance Campaign. Like the 1950s campaign, activists set out to defy apartheid legislation.

Black people arrived for treatment at 'white' hospitals and travelled on transport which had been reserved for 'whites only'. Apartheid was unravelling at the seams. The 1980s had substantially shifted the balance of power between the oppressors and the oppressed. In Soweto, the political initiative was – for the first time since 1976 – in the hands of the population.

NEW BEGINNINGS

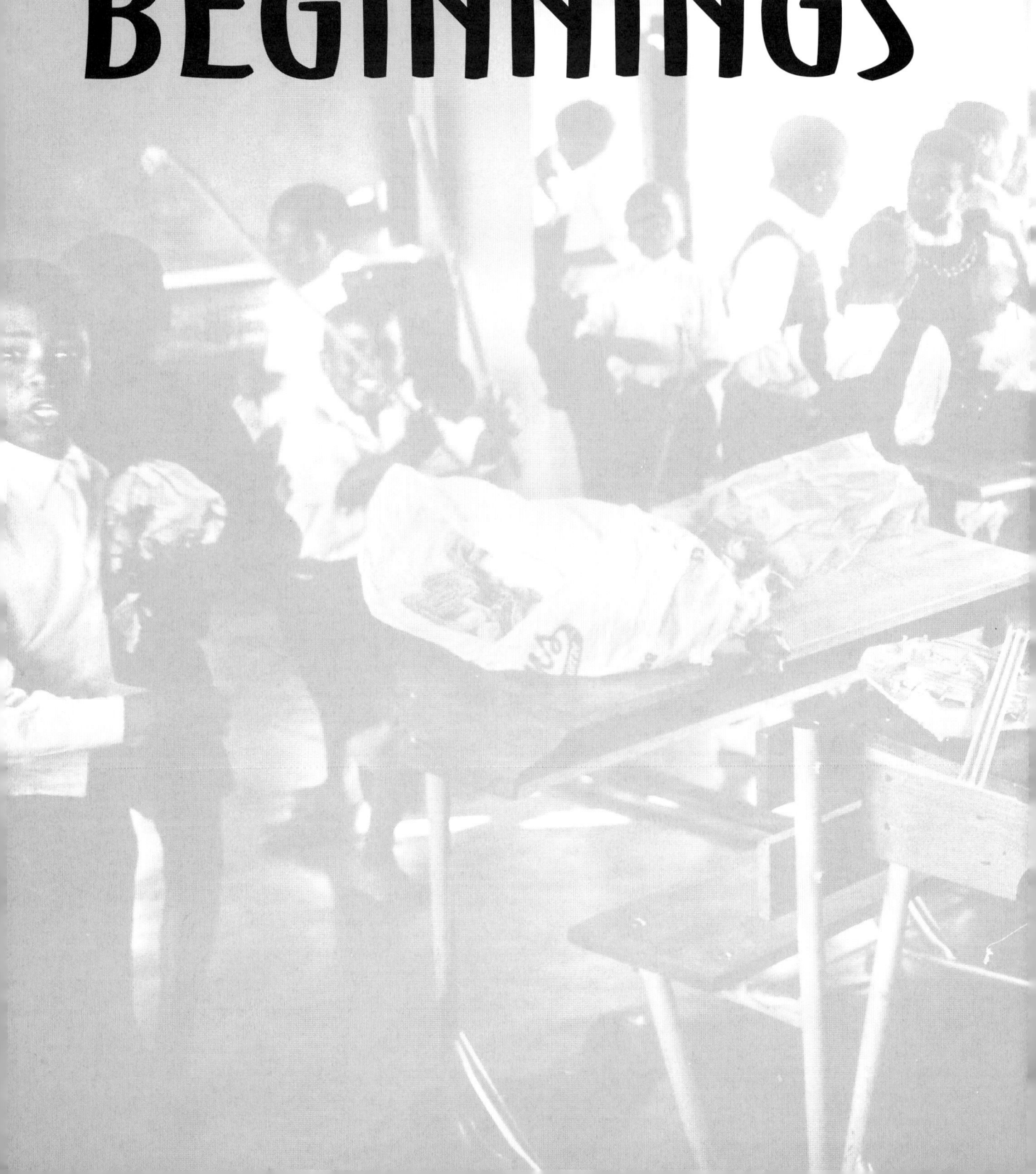

‘ *What happens in Soweto will determine what happens in the whole country; it has always been a catalyst. If Soweto were to be given autonomy today, the Government said, "right, you do with it what you want", then Johannesburg wouldn't last a month. We have the numbers and, I think, the economic clout to really determine the future of the country.* ’

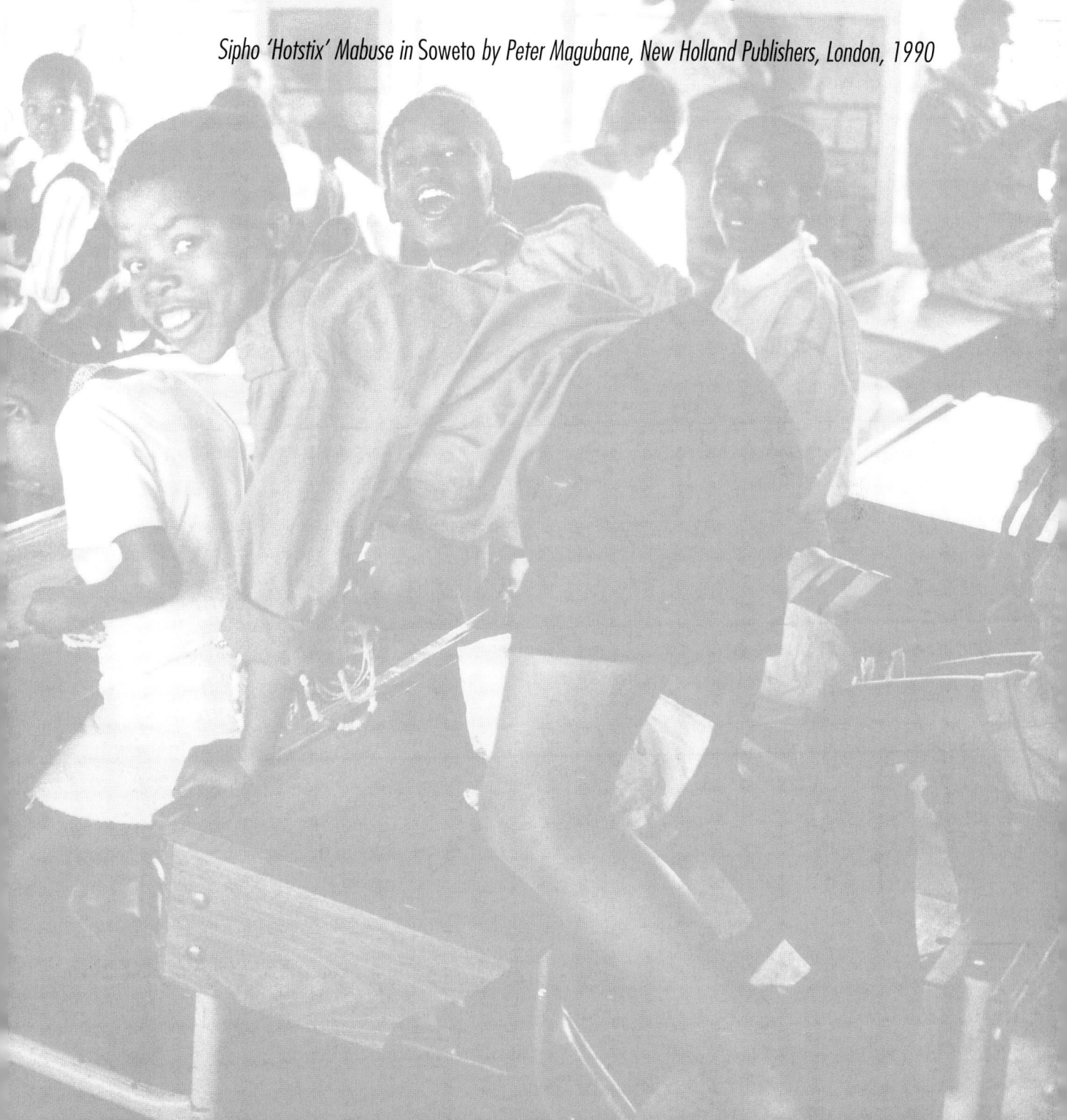

Sipho 'Hotstix' Mabuse in Soweto by Peter Magubane, New Holland Publishers, London, 1990

Soweto — A History

The tide of resistance that swept through townships across South Africa from 1984 sent a clear message to the government. Apartheid was in crisis. A reluctant Botha administration was once again forced back to the drawing board to reshape the system. In the late 1980s, the government thus passed reforms which were to prove far more meaningful than those of the earlier part of the decade. The infamous Mixed Marriages Act was repealed, so people from different racial groups could now be legally married to one another. Other 'petty apartheid' legislation was also removed from the statute books. Blacks could use the same beaches, transport, toilets, parks, and other public facilities as whites, and the notorious 'whites only' signs – which had been the hallmark of apartheid – gradually disappeared.

Although Sowetans and other township residents could now attend the same cinemas, use the same buses and swim in the same public pools as white people, the most significant reform was the abolition of the influx control system – and, along with it, the pass laws – in 1986. It was the pass laws, more than any other piece of legislation, which disfigured the lives of thousands of Sowetans and symbolised the evils of apartheid. An official commission of enquiry finally acknowledged that the government had lost the battle to keep black people out of the 'white' cities, and the endless pass raids, which had led to more than two million black people being arrested between 1975 and 1985 alone, ceased overnight.

Sylvia Dlomo, like most Sowetans, greeted the news with great joy and relief:

> *We were so happy to know that the pass laws were abolished. There were some celebrations in my street. People organised parties and they enjoyed themselves. Everybody was happy. There was really a difference after that. You would go freely wherever you want to go. Before, when you went from Soweto to the East Rand and you suddenly remembered you did not have your pass, you did not feel safe the whole journey. You thought that maybe a policeman would stop you and arrest you and throw you into jail and your family would not be told where you were. We now felt free. We could go wherever we wanted to go without worrying.*

Aerial photo of squatters in Soweto.

The new 'second-class citizens'

Although the repeal of the pass laws eased the day-to-day lives of township residents, this also created new problems for the people of Soweto. For the first time, black people could choose where to live and masses of people moved into Soweto. Squatter settlements, which had existed on a small scale in and around Soweto from the beginning of the 1980s, grew at a staggering rate. Fred Clark in Kliptown, Mdlaloseville in Dlamini, Mshenguville in Mofolo, Mandela Village in Diepkloof, People's Village in Diepkloof and Snake Park near Dobsonville were just some of the new neighbourhoods which sprang up. By 1989, there were an estimated 42 374 shacks in the township, and the face of Soweto was transformed. On every available piece of land stood groups of hovels and makeshift shelters.

'Hah, God, Soweto has changed!' exclaimed Linda Masemola who, for many years, lived in a house in Orlando East, the oldest township in Soweto and one of the areas most affected by squatters. 'There are times when I feel… that influx control was the best. Now anybody that feels like coming in here comes in… The squatters just go to a place and build their houses there. They [bring] their frustrations from the homelands into town. They fight against each other.'

'There is no longer space here in the location. Is there any? There's none,' added a worried Ndoza Sedise. 'Before, we used to play at the soccer grounds; we used to have the seesaws. They are no longer there. They have now put houses there. There are so many new people. We no longer all know each other. We are now so overcrowded.'

Sibongile Mkhabela, who was raised and still lives in Zola, felt a similar anxiety about the swelling squatter population:

❝ Obviously, with the relaxation of influx, people would move to metropolitan areas. But people within Soweto don't have houses and if you add to that population more homeless people, what do you expect? We are facing an open space and I'm scared that one day somebody will come and put their shack next to my yard. I'm an activist, I am political, I understand. But I definitely don't want a squatter camp next to my yard. ❞

Many township dwellers believed that the squatters were from the 'Bantustans' or from neighbouring countries such as Mozambique or Zimbabwe. The latter grouping were given derogatory names like *makwerekwere* and *magri-gamba*, which have no real meaning but which suggested that these people spoke languages that Sowetans could not understand. The squatters, however, were not 'outsiders', as many Sowetans believed. Because of the desperate shortage of housing in Soweto, the squatter camps also attracted hundreds of residents from within the township itself. Over the years, many people had been forced to live in corrugated iron shacks in the yards of people's homes. This situation, however, bred its own set of problems, as Neil Tobajane observes:

Typical shacks in a squatter settlement.

❝ There were often tensions between the people living in *mkhukhus* [backyard shacks] and home owners. The inhabitants of the corrugated iron shacks resented the high rents they were charged, especially given the overcrowded, and often unhygienic, conditions in the yards. But the real conflict started to emerge in the early 1980s when the rent boycott began. Those people in the backyards still had to pay rent whilst the owner of the house boycotted rent. A lot of people in the shacks said, "I'm not paying rent; you don't pay rent, so why should I?" But the shack dwellers were forced to accept their circumstances. Many lived in the township illegally and did not want to attract the attention of the authorities. Besides, there were few housing alternatives available. ❞

The repeal of the influx control laws gave people from the backyards a new freedom of movement for the first time in their lives. Many now chose to build shacks in the squatter camps. 'Living in a shack meant that they wouldn't be paying rent any more,' explains Neil Tobajane. 'It was now a "free-for-all" arrangement. It was unbelievable. Within one day, people felt a huge space to do as they pleased. The shack dwellers were sometimes joined by widows and divorced women who found it difficult to maintain their homes without the support of their husbands.'

The squatters were the most destitute, and even Soweto's poorest residents appeared relatively well off in comparison. In 1989, the average income of a household in Soweto was R900 per month. But some 20 per cent of shack households earned less than R300 per month. Those in employment usually performed unskilled work and received deplorable wages. Other squatters, mainly women, set up open-air shops where they sold fruit and vegetables, sweets, cigarettes and kip-kips (coloured popcorn) from rickety wooden stands on the outskirts of the settlement. These women rose early to get to the Johannesburg market by 7am and then travelled back to the township with their goods to set up their stalls and start business. Because the residents of the settlements were so poor, business was usually very slow.

The squatters also faced horrendous living conditions in the settlements. Most built their shacks out of an assortment of metal sheets, cardboard boxes, plastic cartons, sheets of canvas and pieces of junk. The shacks were sometimes referred to as 'five-in-ones' because the bedroom, lounge, bathroom, dining room and kitchen were all in one room. There were seldom any toilets or taps nearby and litter piled up in the dusty streets. In fact, the camps looked little better than Masakeng, the Shantytown set up by James Mpanza 40 years before. Township residents frequently accused the squatters of creating a health hazard in their midst. The inhabitants of Mofolo Township, for example, pleaded with the Soweto City Council to remove the massive Mshenguville squatter camp of over 3 000 families, and the residents sent a memorandum to the Council.

The Council eventually agreed to demolish the camp and the squatters were forced to move to plots many kilometres away at Orange Farm, near Vereeniging. Most of Soweto's other squatters also lived under the threat of being forcibly removed by the Council, and the squatters resented the insecurity. Phil Thabane, a resident of the Mandela squatter camp, asks:

MEMORANDUM TO: SOWETO CITY COUNCIL

- Residents cannot leave their homes in the evenings as they can be mugged or have their houses broken into – a very common occurrence.
- Mshenguville squatters draw water and use Mofolo residents' toilets without permission.
- Toilets at the squatter camp were placed on its outskirts where they affected Mofolo residents during hot days.

From: Residents of Mofolo Township

For heaven's sake. What can a man do, staying in a two-metre yard? You need a house out of the same small yard. You need a place to put your refuse. So I won't blame people who are staying in the shacks if they are filthy. Imagine a drunkard coming late at night singing an off-tune song. He takes his genitals and points them at your tin house and wee-wees just like that. You can't just beat him. You can't do anything. You just look at him and leave him. Tolerance comes first in the shacks.

Following an uproar by Soweto's established residents, the squatters of Mshenguville were moved to plots allocated to them in distant Orange Farm.

But not all residents reacted with hostility to the squatters. Neil Tobajane explains:

It would differ from area to area. In Diepkloof, for example, the squatters saw a need to actually participate in the democratic movement. Politically, it was okay for the residents of Diepkloof to accept the squatters and forge a link with them. In terms of the student struggles, a lot of those shacks were able to shelter activists in terms of hideouts and so on. In an area like Pimville, people were not politicised and would not see the political connection of such a settlement. In such an area, people would therefore resist the squatters, saying that they brought a lot of thugs and violence.

The grip of crime

Other insecurities plagued township life. The political upheaval of the 1980s and the lack of investor confidence in South Africa hampered the country's economic growth, and this economic slowdown was keenly felt by Sowetans. 'There were no jobs in Johannesburg any more,' comments Sylvia Dlomo. 'People were desperate. They started to look for work in Soweto itself. They looked for work as shopkeepers, or cleaning houses. Some started businesses in the areas where they stayed. I started selling food to schoolchildren. It was the only way of making enough money to live on.'

By 1990, only 20 per cent of new job-seekers in Soweto were able to find work.

School leavers were the main victims of the job crisis, and 70 per cent of the unemployed were under the age of 35. 'It was a kind of luck to find a job at that time,' remarks Thlokie Mofokeng. 'Most of the young people in the township felt that. They were very despondent. Some people turned to stealing as the main means of survival.'

The already extraordinarily high crime levels in Soweto continued to climb. 'By the 1990s,' comments Neil Tobajane, 'there were many crime syndicates in Soweto. Crime became far more organised and more sophisticated. There was more co-ordination between your syndicates of car-hijackers, thugs, shoplifters and so on.' In the first three months of 1990 alone, there were 319 murders, 414 rapes, 1 114 residential robberies and 760 armed robberies within the township, and many other crimes were not reported. With an average of four murders a day, Soweto was consequently dubbed the murder capital of the world.

New words entered the language of the township to describe the activities of the criminal underworld. Fulltime thieves were now referred to as *ba ya gintsa* (they rob and steal), while a *bariski* was a risk-taker and an *amagozo* was a person prone to violence. *Ukutabalaza* or *Ugucrivula* referred to the practice of 'doing all that is in your power to get money' and *Ukuspina* (literally, 'to spin') or *Ukuya eroundindi* – more specifically – referred to the practice of going out to steal or engaging in other crimes involving violence.

Pumlani, who grew up in Pimville and left school in Standard 7, turned to crime as a way of life and became one of the *ba ya gintsa*. Well-dressed and soft-spoken, Pumlani – who, for fear of victimisation did not want to be identified – explains how he came to join a criminal gang:

The number of hawkers in Soweto grew rapidly and stalls occupied virtually every street corner.

❝ *I was very affected by the life I was living in the township. When I grew up, I didn't grow up like other children. I grew up without clothes. I was wearing my sister's dresses without any underwear. My mother worked for a white lady and she used to tell me how her dishes were not put with her madam's dishes. They were put with the dog's dishes. It simply means a black man is a dog. When my uncle died, we didn't slaughter a cow because we didn't have money. We bought the meat at the butchery. I remember people laughed at us. I started thinking about other people who lived a good life. I tried at the school but it was still the same. Then I thought that to be a criminal is the better way. I started to join other guys who were dealing with cars, housebreaking and drugs. When I told my mother I had connections with criminals, she cried. But I just asked her whether she would give me the things that I wanted. We didn't talk because she knew why I decided to do those things.* ❞

Soweto — A History

The school crisis continues

The increase in gang activity in the township was also aggravated by the breakdown of the schooling system. By the end of the 1980s, teaching in Soweto had virtually ground to a halt. The inadequacies of Bantu Education, combined with a decade of boycotts, had deeply eroded the culture of learning and, in those few schools which were still functioning, the classrooms were in a state of complete disrepair.

Students sat in dark, unpleasant and grossly overcrowded classrooms. 'At a school in the location, the windows are broken. The doors are broken. The toilets are stinking,' says Pumlani who attended school in Pimville. 'At a school in the suburbs you're in heaven, but in the township you can't concentrate. When it is winter, you go to school in the morning but it is too cold. You just attend two or three periods and then the school is out. It made me angry.'

Those parents who could afford to, sent their children to private schools, schools in the homeland or else the new schools that were burgeoning in the centre of Johannesburg. In *Beyond the Headlines*, Nomavenda Mathiane remarks on the effects of this phenomenon:

Classrooms in disrepair became a visual symbol of an eroded culture of learning.

❝ When we first heard the call for "Liberation now, Education later", we were told that the students were going to stand united until liberation was achieved. What has happened is the opposite. The well-off children have left the township schools. The poor have stayed in the townships where they have long forgotten education and have now forgotten liberation too. There is no secondary education in Soweto and other main townships any more... In the old days, streets filled in the early morning with children dressed in black-and-white uniforms. Today, there are mini-buses ferrying children in the multi-coloured uniforms of the white private schools. ❞

The Department of Education and Training (DET) blamed the condition of schooling in Soweto on the boycotts of the 1980s, and insisted that it could not afford the estimated R30-million that it would cost to repair the classrooms. The attempts made by the DET to 'normalise' schooling in Soweto simply angered the students even further. The DET introduced strict enrolment criteria and a school quota system which allowed a maximum student/classroom ratio of 40:1. On the first day of school in Soweto in 1989, over 3 000 pupils were turned away. Most were matric students. Some were told that they could not register because they were not able to pay their school fees in advance. Others were informed that they were not wearing the correct school uniform or that they were over the age limit of 21 years.

Those students who were believed to be political activists were also denied admission, but the most common reason for students being refused admission was that they had failed the previous year. This policy was particularly harsh. In 1988, less than one third of those who had written the matriculation examination had passed.

The DET's new regulations thus re-ignited the anger of students. At the very moment that 47 schools in the white suburbs closed because their pupil numbers were dwindling, hundreds of Soweto students could not be accommodated. There were reports of outbreaks of violence all over the township and angry pupils who desperately wanted to be readmitted or allowed to repeat the matric subjects they had failed, petrol-bombed cars and school buildings. Teachers were taken hostage and principals were chased from the schools with death threats warning them not to return. As a result, frightened teachers refused to return to the classrooms and the schools simply remained empty. By June 1989, only half of Soweto's schools were functioning and had written mid-year exams. By the following year, nothing had changed.

Mr Peet Struwig from the DET, who had previously referred to Soweto as a 'model for education in the rest of the country', told the press, 'We do not want anyone left out in the cold. Everyone is given a second chance. We want open schools. The only limitation being put on schools was the widespread vandalism and destruction of school property.' (*The Star*, 26 January 1989)

By contrast, COSAS – which declared itself unbanned in 1989 and which still commanded a large following – placed the blame for the crisis firmly at the door of the DET. They argued that the authorities had failed to address any of the grievances voiced during the campaigns of the 1980s and that their 'gutter education' had remained the same.

For many students, however, it was the teachers – rather than the DET – who were the focus of their anger. 'It's very depressing at school. You get beaten up by teachers who are a law unto themselves,' recounts Thlokie Mofokeng. 'Most of the time they beat you up for a very silly thing. Our teachers were trained to beat a student who fails. They would use their stick to make you listen. That kind of violence created an environment where students felt they could retaliate if need be.' Students also claimed that girls were being sexually harassed by teachers and, during demonstrations in 1989, student demands ranged from calling for an end to teachers being drunk in the classroom to providing schools with enough teaching staff.

The situation, however, was far more complex than the students' complaints suggest. As quoted in Heidi Holland's *Born in Soweto*, a teacher at Phefeni Senior Secondary School defended the position of teachers and tells the following story to illustrate what the teaching profession was up against:

A student known to be a no-hoper in class came to me while we were marking papers. He apologised for bothering me, saying he was on his way to town and had just popped in to find out how things were going. As he spoke, he produced a lethal-looking hand gun and fiddled with it casually. I got the message. He was telling me that I either made sure he passed or I would suffer the consequences. I told him things were going well for him, although I knew he had performed hopelessly. After he left, I fiddled his papers to make sure he passed. I had very little option.

COSAS commanded a strong student following.

Teachers, as a whole, experienced great difficulty in teaching a generation of children who had not been in the classroom for four years. One headmaster went so far as to say that 'Soweto is Sodom and Gomorrah. This place must be razed to the ground and rebuilt afresh, and not with the present child. These children are poison'. (Nomavenda Mathiane, *Beyond the Headlines*, 1990) By 1989, Soweto was facing a social and political breakdown. Crime was out of control and schooling had collapsed. Tens of thousands of rebellious young people roamed the streets. Ungovernability had changed from being a slogan to a reality. Patrick Hlongwane describes what it was like:

> *If a student feels like going outside while the teacher is teaching, he can do so without telling the teacher and he returns smelling of dagga [marijuana]... After smoking mandrax, [a student] causes disorder because, if you tell him that he is wrong, he won't admit it. He's always right. There was nothing like this in the schools before.*

Nthato Motlana elaborates:

> *I knew one school where, over the years, the children went to school at 8 o'clock in the morning and were out of the classroom at 10 o'clock. And that was the pattern. When the date for registration of the exam is announced, they all go back to register. When the timetable is out, they all go back to write. They have not been at school; they have not done any homework for the whole year, and they know they are going to fail – and they all fail. Suddenly, everybody is aware that something is rotten when you get a white pass rate of 95 per cent and a black pass rate of 12 per cent. It is a national tragedy of enormous proportions, enormous implications.*

Problems of high failure rates, overcrowding, shortages and disillusionment plagued most of Soweto's schools but, ironically, it was the then Minister of Education, FW de Klerk, who radically altered the course of life in the township – for students and parents alike.

The ANC unbanned

Towards the end of 1989, FW de Klerk was elected as the new leader of the National Party and, subsequently, as the country's State President. De Klerk's appointment ended the tight control exerted by the security establishment under the Botha government.

Confronted by ungovernability in the townships, a grave economic crisis and intense pressure from abroad, the new president made a number of bold political moves. He allowed a series of protest marches to take place around the country, despite the fact that the State of Emergency was still in force.

De Klerk also released the group of ANC leaders who had been jailed during the Rivonia Trial in 1963. Amidst much excitement in the township, Walter Sisulu returned to his home in Orlando East.

It was on 2 February 1990, however, that the course of Soweto's history – and that of the rest of South Africa – changed forever. In his opening address to parliament, De Klerk announced that black political organisations were unbanned, the leaders of the ANC, SACP and PAC were to be freed, and that apartheid would be removed from the statute books by the end of the year. South Africa was to become, in De Klerk's words, a 'New South Africa'. FW told the opening session of parliament that 'the season for violence is over. The time for reconstruction and reconciliation has arrived'. Sowetans and the rest of the nation rejoiced.

Sylvia Dlomo remembers:

Euphoria swept the entire township of Soweto. I couldn't even move among the people in the streets that day. My mother is an asthmatic but she went out into the streets and was running around. She cried and screamed because she was so happy. That's the only day I've seen her face excited like that. I also cried – just out of happiness. My son told me that one day he'd die but that everything would then be OK. "I know very well my blood is a step towards freedom," I remember him saying to me. And he was right. People were everywhere – singing, cars were hooting. It was an exciting thing to know that we were free at last.

On 11 February, Nelson Mandela, who had been imprisoned for 27 years, walked out of Victor Verster Prison into the bright summer light of Cape Town with his wife Winnie by his side. Newspapers across the world described the historic day as one of 'triumph, signalling victory in the longest, most famous campaign for the release of a political prisoner'.

Soweto had been Nelson Mandela's home before his 27-year imprisonment and was the first place to which he returned after he was released from jail in 1990. In anticipation of his arrival in the township, throngs of people – young and old – threaded their way through the streets of Soweto towards his house, toyi-toying under ANC and SACP flags and loudly chanting 'Free At Last', 'Viva Mandela' and 'ANC! ANC! ANC!'

Rhoda Khumalo has vivid memories of how her daily routine was interrupted by the exuberant crowds of people ululating and celebrating in the streets:

I was inside the house; I heard the noise as if there is something banging the ground, so I called my daughter, "Daphne! Daphne!" We went out to find that everybody is running. The rain started to say "pshhh". The birds were singing. We started to run down to Mandela's house. It was an exciting day, I won't forget it.

Demonstrators call for the unbanning of the ANC.

The promise of freedom

'We were no longer activists that day,' says Neil Tobajane. 'Everybody was out. It was a people's celebration. There were ordinary Sowetans – big people, young people, everyone. There was no particular leadership.' Pheteni Khumalo spent that night 'sleeping at Mandela's house, toyi-toying outside the house of Mandela. I don't know how can I describe that joy. Even the people who were against the struggle were enjoying the night with us'. The sound of revolutionary chants and freedom songs could be heard in the calm night air for miles around. Thousands of television cameras and photographers jostled to capture the first image of Mandela's return to his home.

The carnival atmosphere in the township reached fever pitch on the day of the mass rally at Soccer City to welcome Mandela back formally to the streets of Soweto. Rhoda Khumalo tells how she prepared for the event: 'I took my material, I went to the other lady and I said, "Now, it's time. I must get the dress of the ANC." I showed her how to sew my dress because when we went to the stadium I wanted to wear this dress.' Hundreds of thousands of supporters, dressed in special outfits such as Rhoda's or in colourful green, black and gold ANC T-shirts, crammed onto every available vehicle to attend the celebration. 'Even old women wanted to go... Everybody wanted to be there,' says Sylvia Dlomo. Police vehicles, so often used to suppress street protest in the past, idly lined the route into the stadium as people poured in.

The stands were packed with a capacity crowd of over 120 000, all waving ANC and SACP flags and shouting and stamping their feet in anticipation of Mandela's appearance. Speaker after speaker bellowed, 'Viva the ANC, Viva Umkhonto we Sizwe, Viva the SACP', through the speakers. 'Long Live!' roared the crowd in response, thrusting their clenched fists into the air. The stadium erupted into applause and wild ululations when Nelson Mandela finally arrived by helicopter. 'I was crying tears of joy when I saw him,' says Sylvia Dlomo. 'I was thinking so many children have died, so many people have died for Mandela to be out. My child also died. Those people didn't care. They knew that when Mandela returned everything would be okay.'

'Today, my return to Soweto fills my heart with joy,' Mandela told the overflowing stadium. 'Apartheid has created a heinous system of exploitation in which a racist white minority monopolises economic wealth while the vast

Jubilant crowds welcomed Nelson Mandela back to Soweto.

Mandela on the podium at the mass rally held at Soccer City.

majority of the oppressed and black people are condemned to poverty... Our people need proper houses, not ghettos like Soweto.' Mandela ended on a note of goodwill. 'No man or woman who has abandoned apartheid will be excluded from our movement towards a non-racial, united and democratic South Africa based on one-person, one-vote on a common voters' roll.'

As the sun began to set, Nelson and Winnie Mandela returned to house No. 8115 in Orlando West. 'For me, number 8115 was the centrepoint of my world, the place marked with an X in my mental geography. It is the only home I ever knew as a man before I went to prison,' said Mandela of his four-roomed Soweto matchbox house that looked no different to any of the others in the street. 'When I saw it, I was surprised by how much smaller and humbler it was than I remembered it being. Compared with my cottage at Victor Verster, number 8115 could have been the servants' quarters at the back. But any house in which a man is free is a castle when compared with even the plushest prison.' (Nelson Mandela, *Long Walk To Freedom*, 1994)

Winnie and Nelson Mandela outside their Orlando West home.

Negotiations begin

The release of Mandela seemed to carry the expectations of township dwellers to new heights. In Neil Tobajane's opinion, 'Mandela's release pushed expectations beyond imagination. People thought that they were now free. Even as activists, we expected great changes the next day.' Thlokie Mofokeng agrees that 'the political consciousness of the people generally was that the world would change overnight. People expected the enemy forces to respect Mandela as though he was untouchable. I thought it was now time for me to look for an institution to go and study'.

Over the course of the next few weeks, however, this optimism began to fade. 'You'd wake up the next morning and there'd be no change,' continues Neil Tobajane 'and you'll go back to your thinking, "We're not free yet." People talked too much about the ANC being ready to govern, to come and assume office and run the affairs of the country. They expected a miracle of some sort. The whole problem began when that did not happen.'

Instead of the ANC assuming power immediately, a long, drawn-out process of multiparty negotiations began, and ushered in a period of both uncertainty and turbulence in the township. Political parties, eager to win a place at the negotiating table, set out to enlarge their power bases. Jon-Jon Mkhonza maintains that 'after the negotiation process began, you had a political contest to recapture the imagination and the support of the people'.

Both AZAPO and the PAC rejected the idea of negotiations and claimed that the ANC had 'sold out' to the white government. 'AZAPO and PAC were very strategic at the time,' recalls Thlokie Mofokeng:

> *They did not condemn Mandela but they were very much against negotiations. They tried to make people believe that Mandela was a genuine political leader but he was, unfortunately, surrounded by the ANC which was too influenced by whites. They also said that the very people who own the land cannot help to distribute it. They said, "You cannot negotiate to take back something that is yours. You must just take what belongs to you."*

The PAC's argument was, therefore, particularly attractive to the youth of the township. Pumlani says that he supported the PAC, 'because I hated the white man and the PAC were fighting the white man rather than talking with him'. However, although the PAC attracted a growing following among the youth, it was not a significant force in the township. The ANC and Inkatha, under the leadership of Chief Mangosuthu Buthelezi, emerged as the main contenders for power. Each party, however, faced their own particular obstacles in gaining support.

The return of the ANC

The ANC had operated clandestinely in Soweto for over 30 years, but Thlokie Mofokeng nevertheless believes that 'by the 1990s, the ANC enjoyed widespread support in the township. Everyone had so much loyalty and respect for the ANC especially because of the ANC's actions in the 1980s when they struck very hard at the enemy forces and the bombs went off at Sasol and other places. After the ANC was unbanned, people saw ANC cadres as saviours of some sort'.

Although the ANC may have had a strong support base in the township by the 1990s, it had no organisational structures. Its first task, therefore, was to transform itself from an underground movement with a commitment to the armed struggle, into a legal political party. This required rebuilding grassroots organisation and winning over those comrades who had expected victory on the battlefield and not at the negotiating table 'The ANC realised it had to regain the confidence of the youth,' says Neil Tobajane. 'People had to be convinced of the new route that was being taken – politically, with negotiations. Many still believed in a people's war bringing victory. Some understood the change of strategy. Others didn't. It was not easy to deal with.' One frustrated activist commented that 'we never thought one day President Mandela would be sitting with Pik Botha at the same table'. (Monique Marks, 'Organisation, Identity and Violence', 1993)

The ANC and the ANC Youth League (ANCYL) began to found branches throughout the township in order to replace UDF organisations and consolidate their support. Proudly displaying their banners – which were legal for the first time – members of the new branches held protest marches to call for a speedy end to white minority rule and the establishment of an interim government.

Sylvia Dlomo remembers the first ANC meeting she attended: 'We were really happy not to have to hide our ANC membership any more. It was very exciting to know that no policeman was going to come and interrupt you and ask, "Why are you here?" We could now have meetings without having to pretend that it was a church meeting.'

For the youth, the opening of new ANC branches was somewhat more problematic. 'The ANC changed the whole tradition of organisation in the township,' reflects Thlokie Mofokeng. 'There started to be a lot of bureaucratic things. In the past, you were a comrade as long as you were willing to chant and do certain things. But now the ANC insisted that you become a paid-up member of the organisation – with a membership card. They said that comrades needed to do specific tasks. We were saying, "No, I don't need a membership card to belong to a liberation movement. It's automatic." Despite these things, many youths did sign up.'

Protesters displaying ANC banners – now legal – took part in marches called by the newly formed branches of the ANC and the ANC Youth League.

Enter Inkatha

Unlike the ANC, Inkatha had been operating legally since its formation in 1975, but the organisation did not enjoy much popular support in Soweto. During the 1976 uprising, Buthelezi visited the township several times. On one such occasion, he called for peace between the students and the Zulu-speaking hostel dwellers and was seen as a moderator in the conflict that had erupted between these two warring factions. On a later occasion, however, he accused Soweto's youth of reckless behaviour and they, in turn, denounced Inkatha as 'the greatest enemy of black liberation'. The youth also attacked Buthelezi for accepting the position as leader of KwaZulu, a government-created ethnic homeland for Zulus. Thlokie Mofokeng elaborates:

In 1976, Inkatha was considered a serious problem by township youth but it died a natural death. By the 1980s, Inkatha was never really a significant force in Soweto except, perhaps, in the hostels. They organised few local campaigns. People knew it was only the apartheid leaders who supported Buthelezi as one of the country's leaders. They called Mandela a terrorist and made out that Buthelezi was the darling of the black people. That was a problem for most of the residents.

By the early 1990s, Inkatha's support beyond the border of KwaZulu-Natal was calculated to be as low as two per cent, and Buthelezi was now anxious to increase his political popularity in Soweto and other townships in the former Transvaal province. On 14 July 1990, Inkatha renamed itself the Inkatha Freedom Party (IFP) in an attempt to build a national profile and transform itself from a Zulu cultural liberation movement – based almost entirely in KwaZulu-Natal – into a national political party.

The repackaged IFP set out to canvas support in Soweto, and residents clearly remember Inkatha's reappearance. 'Inkatha became an issue in Soweto after the unbanning of the ANC. The first time they created a presence was when they became a Freedom Party,' says Jon-Jon Mkhonza. Pheteni Khumalo agrees that she only 'started to hear about Inkatha after the release of Mandela. I didn't know Inkatha before that'. Patrick Hlongwane sums up the situation at the time: 'Since the release of Mandela and the beginning of all these organisations, they are fighting for positions because everyone wants to see himself or herself getting into parliament.'

While the ANC and the ANCYL opened branches throughout Soweto, Inkatha built its support base mainly among Zulu migrants living in the hostels of Soweto, the most obvious place in which IFP could mobilise support. During the 1980s, the UDF and COSATU had made few attempts to include hostel dwellers in their campaigns. 'Not much work had been done by the Soweto Civic Association in the hostels. It was a very fertile ground for the IFP...' believes Thlokie Mofokeng. 'Moreover, many Zulu-speakers lived in the hostels.'

Inkatha's base in KwaZulu and its clear ethnic associations also appealed to the strongly Zulu traditionalist migrant population, and IFP leaders promised to preserve the hostels and protect Zulu identity in the townships. Ellison Mohlabe, a resident at Mzimhlope Hostel, describes how 'every night, when we were still busy cooking food, they called us to a meeting where they talked about Buthelezi being a good man and how he brought about changes in South Africa. They told us that they won't let the Xhosas rule the country because they haven't fought any war with the Boers or the English people. Mandela was a Xhosa. They said that the Zulus are the people to rule South Africa, not the Xhosas'.

Violence erupts

Before long, political competition between the IFP and the ANC began to slide into a cycle of violence. The first incident occurred in Sebokeng, a township to the south of Johannesburg. Residents reported that Inkatha went on the rampage and attacked people in their homes after a so-called peace rally at Evaton Stadium, while the IFP claimed that ANC supporters had tried to stop the rally and forced them to leave the stadium. The lives of 27 people were lost and, as the rumour of further attacks spread, suspicions were fuelled on both sides and fed directly into the conflict. One hostel dweller suggested that it was, in fact, rumours rather than concrete events that caused the subsequent violence. He said that the Xhosas were told that the Zulus were going to attack, and the hostel dwellers were told that the Xhosas were trying to have them 'abolished'.

By the beginning of August 1990, Soweto was also engulfed in the flames. The first major incident in the township occurred when 300 'impis', wearing red headbands and brandishing pangas, axes, spears and firearms, were reported by township residents as storming Inhlazane station in the Molapo Township. They attacked train commuters and hundreds of people failed to report for work that day.

These clashes sparked violence throughout Soweto and battles between residents and Inkatha-supporting hostel dwellers erupted on the streets of the township. After nine days of vicious fighting, the death toll in Soweto had risen to 122. By the end of August 1990, 512 people had died in townships across the Reef, the highest monthly death toll recorded during the long and turbulent years of political violence.

Heavy police presence at a train station.

Many residents were entirely bewildered by the sudden explosion and intensity of the violence. Samuel Ndebele from Mzimhlope Hostel says: 'I really don't know the reason for this fight between the hostel and township people. I can't tell who started it or why.' Thlokie Mofokeng makes the same point:

❛ *I can't say the violence started here and there, when or how. All I know is that it just surfaced.'* Neil Tobajane had a more firm opinion. *'The objective of Inkatha's campaign in Soweto,'* he argues, *'was organisational domination but it took on a violent form. Inkatha realised they couldn't contest the elections openly. They couldn't compete with the ANC for ownership of the people. This, therefore, caused an upsurge of violence.* ❜

Other residents offered their own, sometimes contradictory, theories about its causes. The most common explanation was that the incidents taking place on Soweto's trains – on which many Sowetans spent hours getting to and from work each day – were the main reason for the outbreak of violence. After the State of Emergency was called in the mid-1980s, train coaches were used as safe places to hold political meetings and certain coaches came to be known as *emzabalazweni*, meaning 'a place of struggle'. COSATU, in particular, developed a 'train sector' and shop stewards attempted to educate the employed and unemployed on trains and spread messages of boycotts and other political campaigns. Thlokie Mofokeng describes the scenario:

New Beginnings

❝ *Cosatu was known to have coaches which were theirs. And then you'd have others belonging to African religious churches where people would pray. In some coaches, people could just sit and relax and have nothing to do with singing or church or politics or anything. In early 1990, the ANC and COSATU were beginning to organise... inside the trains by singing, educating people and quoting those political slogans. The problem was that those who were singing in the coaches were always condemning Gatsha [Buthelezi] and this caused a lot of friction.* ❞

Thulani Ngubo, a member of Inkatha, believed that this was where the real conflict began: 'Those who were toyi-toying in the trains were cursing people – such as the leader of the Zulus and the Inkatha Freedom Party – and this led to an isolation of the Zulus and caused a conflict amongst commuters on the trains.'

But the violence soon spread well beyond the confines of the railway stations. Neil Tobajane believes that 'the train violence did not happen in isolation. Revenge attacks occurred from the initial attacks on the trains and they went on forever'. Indeed, from the first train attack in August 1990 until well into 1993, Soweto was embroiled in a vicious war between Inkatha- and ANC-supporting residents. Most of the violence took place in and around the seven hostels in Soweto – Diepkloof, Dube, Nancefield, Dobsonville, Jabulani, Merafe and Mzimhlope (also known as Meadowlands). Mzimhlope Hostel, the scene of the attack on township residents by hostel dwellers during the 1976 uprising, was once again the centre of some of the fiercest clashes, and it came to be known as the township's 'death hostel'.

The story of the events which took place in and around the sprawling Mzimhlope complex provides a graphic picture of how the violence was organised and the impact it had on the lives of Sowetans. Similar stories could be told about the other hostels in the township and the violence in the communities which surrounded them.

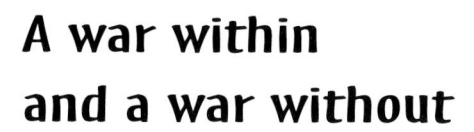

Women lead a prayer meeting on a train bound for Johannesburg.

A war within and a war without

The fighting in Mzimhlope began a few weeks after the initial outbreak of hostilities in Soweto. Hostel residents reported that hundreds of young warriors arrived from Natal and formed a 'military core' within the hostel and their movements – as well as those of the other inmates – were controlled by a 'warlord', who had established a quasi-military regime in the hostel and collected taxes from all residents to pay for guns and ammunition. He also mobilised people to fight and planned and executed the attacks carried out by the inmates. Rooms in the hostel were turned into weapons stores and arms factories. The 'warlord' reportedly stirred the wrath of the inmates by telling them that the ANC wanted to undermine the Zulu nation, its traditions and practices. His ability to exercise control over the Zulu inmates apparently owed a lot to his direct contact with the chiefs in the areas from which the hostel dwellers came.

But not all hostel dwellers who lived in Mzimhlope supported the 'warlord' and a struggle broke out between the inmates. Reports indicated that hostel dwellers were being murdered for being either Xhosa or ANC supporters. Non-Zulu-speaking hostel dwellers consequently fled their rooms and abandoned their possessions for fear of becoming victims, while others were forced to leave. Some Zulu-speaking hostel dwellers opposed the 'warlord' but stated that they had to go along with him in order to survive in the tightly controlled hostel environment. Edward Mashela, who lived at Mzimhlope Hostel, described the situation:

> *Most of us were like a blind person or a dog which follows the man who is pulling it by a chain. We did exactly as we were told... The youth were in the frontline and they did not respect or listen to us, their parents. They told us what to do. When I was a youth, I could never argue with my parents but, at that time in the hostel, if you tried to stop a young person from doing wrong, you were in trouble.*

Samuel Ndebele found himself in a similar situation: 'Our children no longer listened to us. Whenever I tried to talk, they would say, "Keep quiet, old man."' Those who refused to succumb to pressures to support the 'warlord' were attacked by his supporters and forced to flee, and many Zulu speakers were found savagely murdered within the hostels.

Inkatha-supporting hostel dwellers, called by some residents 'the redbands of death' because of the distinctive red headbands they wore, launched attacks on the communities surrounding the hostel. Pheteni Khumalo, who lives in Meadowlands, describes the horrors of one of the first attacks led by the hostel dwellers:

> *They went into one of the houses with their dangerous traditional weapons – they had things like pangas and axes. They went into the house which still had its lights on and hacked all the people in there. Only a woman who was breastfeeding her seven-day-old baby survived by hiding under the dressing table. We just watched the scene as we had nothing to help them with and no phone to call the police.' Pheteni goes on to say that 'most of the time, [they] attacked during the night or in the early hours of the morning when people were all fast asleep.*

'We are living in hell here,' said another terrified resident after several months of fighting. 'We go to bed with our clothes – ready for action. We bury victims every weekend.' Crossing Vincent Road – which separated Meadowlands and Killarney from the hostel complex – became a matter of life and death. Whitey Khanyeza reflects on what it felt like to be a Zulu-speaking resident in the area:

> *I am a Zulu, but I was not in the organisation of Zulus in the hostel. I was in the ANC. Not every Zulu is in Inkatha. You do get people who say, "You're Zulu, you're in Inkatha", but people gradually understood that it was not like that. You felt uncomfortable when people said you're Inkatha when you were not.*

Panic-stricken families fled the area and many simply abandoned their homes and left behind all their possessions. 'We didn't know if our house would still be there by the next morning,' said one fleeing resident, 'but at least we would still be alive.' The numbers of families in a similar situation swelled daily. Hundreds of signed affidavits from residents of Killarney, Mzimhlope and Meadowlands Zone 1 suggest that the bulk of the aggression in the area was initiated by the inmates of the Meadowlands Hostel. Their statements all indicated that the residents were not prepared to return to their original homes unless the hostel was demolished. Others simply could not return as their homes had already been destroyed. As more and more people left the area, an eerie no-man's land – dubbed the 'Ghost Town' – emerged between the hostels and those areas still occupied by residents. The residents who were left behind did not venture from their homes after nightfall.

New Beginnings

'Impis' brandish weapons during an Inkatha march.

In response to these new developments, the ANC found itself caught in a difficult situation. The negotiation process demanded that the organisation demonstrate its commitment to peace and non-violence. On the other hand, ANC supporters in the township expected protection for their violence-ridden communities and the youth felt especially betrayed by the ANC. Throughout the 1980s, they had romanticised the organisation as the great liberating force and the saviour of the black people. The young militants firmly believed that the ANC should reverse its decision of 6 August 1990 to suspend armed action. In their opinion, Mandela had fallen prey to De Klerk's 'sweet talk' while hundreds of people were being murdered in the townships. Mandela's assurances that 'the struggle is not over and the negotiations themselves are a theatre of struggle' failed to convince the youth. (Nelson Mandela, *Long Walk To Freedom*, 1994) 'The ANC has to give the people ammunition,' insisted one young schoolboy. 'So far, there is no time for negotiations – it is time for war.'

Violence was seen as the only means of self-defence and the youth took it upon themselves to launch attacks against hostel dwellers. Neil Tobajane maintains:

Policeman remonstrates with activist youngsters outside their school buildings.

❝ **You could see the youth saying, "We are the ones being put to the test of having to defeat the hostel warlords, the warriors who come and attack the township at night", and they started strategically locating themselves to respond to the violence.** ❞

Jon-Jon Mkhonza recalls: 'The people on the ground decided to fight. The leaders tried to stop them but they said, "No, we are going to fight." Then the war really started.' Pheteni Khumalo adds:

151

The involvement of the police

Residents repeatedly accused the SAP – who cruised the rutted roads of the township in their 'mellow yellow' vans bearing shotguns and R1 rifles – of openly siding with Inkatha. Days before the violence erupted in Soweto, newspapers reported that a white policeman went into the Meadowlands Hostel and told inmates that the ANC had vowed to exterminate Zulu hostel dwellers. He then apparently handed out weapons with the order, 'Go out and attack. You're a proud Zulu nation.' Over the next two years, residents throughout Soweto spoke of the police – nicknamed 'Iron Fist' or the 'A-Team' – escorting hostel dwellers through the streets or turning a blind eye to the atrocities carried out by them. 'The police always jump to Inkatha's aid and shoot teargas and bullets in our direction. They never do this to the Inkatha people when they burn and stone our houses,' one youngster told a television crew. 'Why do the police allow Inkatha people to come and attack us?' asked another. 'Why don't they go to the hostels and disarm those people? The minute we tried to defend our people the police started shooting at us.' Pheteni Khumalo recalls how 'one night, when we were patrolling the township, we heard that Inkatha was going to attack although we did not know where. As we were walking, we saw a hippo and we ran away because we thought it was the police. In fact, the hippo was loaded with Inkatha people'.

Loms Zikalala, who lived in Mzimhlope Hostel, believes that the situation was rather more complex:

> *The problem was that both parties believed that the police supported the other group. People in the township said that the police always shot at them and we said the same thing.' At the same time, he said, 'I think the police were protecting us because as soon as the people in the township started marching, the police would quickly come and tell us not to go out. We would then sit and wait because they would come to surround the hostel and they would tell us to stay.*

Writing on the township violence in his autobiography, Nelson Mandela says: 'It was becoming more and more clear to me that there was connivance on the part of the security forces. Many of the incidents indicated to me that the police, rather than quelling the violence, were fomenting it.' (Nelson Mandela, *Long Walk To Freedom*, 1994) In his autobiography, Mandela also accused the police of failing to conduct searches at the hostels and allowing hostel dwellers to parade around the streets openly bearing so-called traditional weapons. These included assegais, knobkieries, pangas and sharpened sticks. It was only after considerable pressure from the ANC that the government banned spears in areas designated as 'unrest areas'.

Several affidavits also alleged that the police picked up young people in the township and then abandoned them in the inhospitable and dangerous hostel environment.

Odyseus Harvey was also lucky enough to escape. According to the affidavit signed by Harvey in the Supreme Court on 22 March 1992, as he returned home from work one day, policemen stopped him and, without any explanation, bundled him into the back of a Casspir. They drove him into the heart of the hostel where he was ordered to get out. Harvey refused and clung desperately to the Casspir. One of the policemen took pity on him and persuaded his colleagues to drive out of the hostel with Harvey still in the back.

AFFIDAVIT IN THE SUPREME COURT OF SOUTH AFRICA

On Monday 16 March 1991, at approximately 10h30, I was sitting in my house in Killarney, Soweto. I was rudely surprised by about four policemen who barged into the house. They started to assault me by slapping and punching me. They forced me outside and put me inside a police vehicle parked there. There were a further six policemen outside. Residents had gathered outside demanding to know why I was under arrest. The police did not answer. All the police climbed onto the vehicle, which drove off. It drove directly to the Meadowlands Hostel. To my absolute dismay, the vehicle stopped in the middle of the hostel and one of the white policemen opened the door from inside. He told me to get out. He said to me, 'Dit is waar jy sal doodgaan.' (This is where you are going to die) Luckily, I fled the hostel grounds before being spotted.

Elias Smith, Killarney, 22 March 1992

In August 1991, newspapers finally revealed what was apparently hard evidence of a link between the police and Inkatha. They disclosed that the government had paid Inkatha millions of rand to fund rallies which had led to violence and the SADF admitted to secretly training Inkatha. These revelations, which seemed to confirm the long-held suspicions of township residents, forced De Klerk to accede to Mandela's demand that the Minister of Defence, Magnus Malan, and the Minister of Police, Adriaan Vlok, be dismissed from their posts.

Blood on the tracks

Evidence also began to emerge of a mysterious 'Third Force' either within, or else linked to, the police. This third force carried out random acts of terror in the hope of disrupting the negotiations between the government and the ANC. Neil Tobajane believed:

The aim of third-force activity was to exacerbate the fight, to take forward the tension and to make sure that the violence didn't stop. The most frightening aspect of third-force attacks was that they were carried out with a high degree of military precision. They went way beyond what either side, the ANC or Inkatha, would do as an organisation. All of a sudden, grenades were being used when, up until now, both sides had used petrol bombs. You knew that no amount of anger would make your own activists carry out such kinds of attacks.

The dead, after a train attack.

In Soweto, the train stations appear to have been the main target of shadowy third-force activity. The first incident was reported as early as 13 September 1990, a month after violence had erupted in the township. A gang armed with shotguns, pangas and knives attacked passengers on the crowded number 9346 train en route to Soweto. Survivors told how their 'journey of death' began when, without warning, a group of men pulled out weapons. 'They just started killing everyone. The attackers moved from carriage to carriage and shot, stabbed and hacked their way through the passengers, screaming "Viva, Viva!",' recounted one horrified eyewitness. Some passengers jumped from the train, while others tried to hide under seats. Twenty-six people died and more than 100 were injured during the rampage. The platform seemed littered with bodies.

Over the next two years, 20 such merciless and unprovoked attacks were recorded on the Soweto–Johannesburg line, and train coaches fast became dangerous chambers of terror. The attackers, however, seldom selected specific victims. In only one incident did passengers remember the attackers asking for 'mzabalazo people' or 'Mandela's children' as political activists were sometimes called. In fact, many victims were found lying dead or injured with a prayer book in their hands.

Soweto police spokesman Lieutenant Colonel Tienie Halgryn repeatedly denied the presence of a 'third force' on the trains, but there was not a single conviction for the train carnage in over 20 months. Halgryn said that, as a private company, Spoornet – which owned the railways – was responsible for the safety of commuters. He also claimed that it was too dangerous for armed policemen to patrol the trains. After an outcry from parties across the political spectrum, however, Spoornet posted security guards at Soweto stations. The men carried hand-held metal detectors and took the precautionary step of locking the doors linking train carriages, but these measures failed to stop the attacks. A newspaper article entitled 'No end to slaughter on the trains' claimed that 'the slaughter of train commuters has reached unprecedented levels despite the series of "safety measures" introduced. The murder yesterday evening of three people on a Soweto train brought the death toll for this year to 129'. (*The Star*, 23 April 1992)

As a result, some hostel dwellers chose to go to work by taxi – despite the fact that taxi fares were higher than train fares. Samuel Ndebele explains:

> One didn't really know what might happen if one went to the station. You took a big chance if you went there. I used taxis because I am now old and if I went to the station I knew I could be hurt. We were forced to pay R4.60 every day for taxis and were then unable to buy ourselves lunch. Now we struggle at meal time.

Thousands of commuters could simply not afford these extra costs. 'I was very scared but I can't afford to take a taxi,' explained a 28-year-old seamstress who worked in Johannesburg every day. Those who continued to use the trains travelled in fear of their lives and the mere rumour of an attack was enough to cause terrified commuters to leap from moving trains.

The costs of the war

Between August 1990 and the end of 1992, over 1 000 people lost their lives in political violence while many hundreds more were seriously injured in Soweto. This was the second highest death toll in any township in the country, but the bloody violence not only brought grief and heartache to Sowetans. It also damaged the image of political parties. Although most of the hostels were now IFP strongholds – West Rand IFP secretary, Humphrey Ndlovu, claimed that the level of IFP support in the hostels was close to 100 per cent by the end of 1991 – the party had failed to increase its support base among township dwellers. For many of the residents, the IFP had become associated with bloodshed and mayhem. But the ANC was not left unscathed by the violence, especially as the 1990s had brought only growing violence and despair. Freedom, as pledged by the ANC, felt like an empty promise.

Once again, it was the young comrades who were the most disaffected from the ANC. Although they still saw themselves as the guardians of their communities, they felt that they had been betrayed by the ANC. 'The ANC leadership is preoccupied with negotiations and gives people on the ground little guidance,' complained one youngster. Another lamented that 'when Mandela came out of jail, he didn't even thank us. He just seemed to think we only want violence. Comrades also felt distanced from the decision-making process'. Winnie Mandela, Nelson Mandela's estranged wife, became the most eloquent spokesperson for the frustrations of this group. In a television interview she said: 'Even if there is a war, at the end we have to sit down and talk. What I am opposed to is selling the masses. The answer does not lie with those who drink tea and eat biscuits in the corridors of the World Trade Centre [the venue for multiparty talks]. The answer lies with the people...'

Winnie Mandela, Nelson Mandela's estranged wife.

For Neil Tobajane, the main problem was a leadership vacuum: 'The early 1990s was a new ball game. Youth flocked into organisations. We did not have to go out and organise. But political education was not taken seriously. The experienced leaders were at the negotiating table and the new brand of leadership had no sense of being grilled in strategies and tactics. Organisational discipline was lost.' Without a strong leadership, targets became increasingly random and undefined. ANCYL secretary Rapu Mmolekane states that the youth now 'organised themselves around the ones who were brave and able to lead them in battle. We didn't have the same political leadership as before'. (*The Weekly Mail*, 4 June 1992) In fact, the ANCYL had no clear plan of action and found it difficult to hold onto its disillusioned members.

Killing in the name of the struggle

In the absence of clear-cut lines of organisational control, many youths who claimed to be members of political organisations became involved in criminal activities and were now motivated by personal gain. They were dubbed the 'comtsotsis', tsotsis or criminals pretending to be comrades. While claiming to be members of Umkhonto we Sizwe, the comtsotsis formed vicious gangs which burned houses at random, stole or hijacked cars, raped girls, and collected protection fees from households. 'If you are a comtsotsi, you can take from the community and pretend you want it for the struggle,' explains one youngster. 'You can run into a house in Soweto and say, "Come, Comrades, lend me your car. I have to go to a funeral with Comrade Mandela." They give you the keys because they must help the struggle. But you don't bring it back. You take the car and spin and spin and spin.' (Heidi Holland, *Born in Soweto*, 1994)

For Thlokie Mofokeng, the comtsotsis became a force to be reckoned with because they drew on the identity of comrades: 'The rise of the comtsotsis was because they felt secure to say, "I am a comrade." If you're a comrade, you can do certain things and nobody will say anything to you. But, at the same time, these people were tsotsis and their interests were those of a thug.' Neil Tobajane locates the problem of the comtsotsis more generally in the changing role of the comrades in the new political landscape of the 1990s:

During the 1980s, the comrades were seen as the heroes of the communities. The society gave them an elevated position. They were built into people who could resolve even family disputes. In the 1990s, the comrades were caught off-guard. They expected that, because they had sacrificed their lives for the political struggle, the ANC would understand their plight and they'd get access to jobs etc. A lot of people got frustrated when this didn't happen. A large number of youths were sort of disowned by the movement, unintentionally because of the political change. They had to resort to some kind of survival. A lot of them turned into gangs of comrades.

The arbitrary violence of the comtsotsis threatened ANC control and local branches were often unable to resolve what to do with a member who had become a comtsotsi. Some branches, in fact, split into warring factions over the issue, and the problem grew worse as ordinary criminals wreaked just as much havoc.

Guns circulate freely

The levels of violence in the township also increased as guns started to flood into Soweto. In the 1980s, MK soldiers were the main source of guns for the youth and the guns were only handed to comrades to fight the gangs that terrorised certain areas. Other guns were stolen from the white suburbs or in ambushes of policemen in the township, but both the control over guns and the number of them circulating in the township had changed radically by the mid-1990s. Many guns were brought from Mozambique where they had been distributed by the South African government to destabilise that country during the 1980s.

Patrick Hlongwane claims that 'the young people who had guns mostly used them to disarm and attack targets such as cold drink trucks, furniture and food trucks. If they managed to overpower the guard, they'd take it'. For Neil Tobajane, this behaviour was understandable: 'There was a general upsurge in undisciplined activities. You've got a weapon, there's no armed struggle any more and you're hungry. What else do you do? You have an instrument that can help you survive. Why not use it to survive? I would have done the same if I was unemployed.' A member of the ANCYL adds that 'in the eighties, if you had a gun, you didn't tell anyone. Now it's the fashion... Whereas thugs of the past could be disciplined by organisations, those of today are armed, dangerous and untouchable.' Like Sibongile Mkhabela, many parents despaired at this situation:

❝ What was really disgusting was that you'd find a 13-year-old pointing a gun at you and that makes you really angry. As a parent of a 13-year-old, you'd say, "This is my own child." Something in you rebels – you think, I just can't be told by a child what to do and what not to do. ❞

Ndoza Sedise summed up the situation:

❝ These youth of today are controlled by the fact that they've got guns. They fear nothing. They know that they will shoot and there is nothing you can do to them. These guys take drugs, they smoke dagga. When all these things get mixed in one's head, you can imagine... If I see my enemy, I won't mind shooting him. ❞

On the threshold

The unchecked tide of violence repeatedly threatened to derail the negotiation process. Neil Tobajane believes that 'what led to the solution of the [political] violence was organisation. As the violence got more serious, people got more organised and ploughed resources into their defence. The national peace accord also starting having an impact. The warring parties started talking at a round table and people on the ground started to respond to calls to end the violence'.

The negotiation process thus hiccuped and stalled but nonetheless went forward, and the chain of events set in motion by De Klerk created an unstoppable momentum towards liberation. After months of talks the multiparty forum at the World Trade Centre announced a date for the country's first nonracial, one-person-one-vote election. The date was set for 27 April 1994.

On the eve of South Africa's first democratic elections, Sowetans shared the mounting excitement that gripped the whole country. No Sowetan had ever voted in a national South African election and the prospect of that alone created a sense of expectation. Sowetans flocked to the polls in their thousands. Long queues wound through the dusty streets, and people waited patiently in the burning sun to cast their vote. One distinctive image that remains is of an old man being carried to the voting station in a wheelbarrow so that he could vote for the first time. The mood in the township was jubilant. 'What I remember that day is the excitement of the people because they knew now that they are going to get their real rights by voting, especially the old people who believed Mandela would now hear their grievances,' says Sylvia Dlomo.

Yet few Sowetans believed that things would change overnight once a new government was in power. The excitement of the elections was thus laced with a sober realisation of the scale of problems to be overcome. Ethel Leisa believes:

❝ Very little will be changed until after a long time because we are still the same people. The oppressors may change but that fear, that weight, is still hanging over us. Now it is just sort of an empty packet which, even if it falls on you, will not hurt you but – because you have lived under that fear all your life – it will take some time. ❞

Sibongile Makhabela also believes that things will not change overnight:

Perhaps I am pessimistic, but I'm trying to find a ray of hope to say that if a new government comes to power things will change; but when will that be? Maybe we'll have a black face instead of a white face, but is there going to be an essential change to the person in the street? For me, this future – whether in the old or new South Africa – looks pretty bleak for the ordinary person.

For Murphy Morobe, Soweto is a place that evokes contradictory feelings:

Soweto people can be fantastic. We've got a community spirit here. People live close to one another. Grannies look after grandchildren. Young people always know that there is always the extended family to look after, to fall back on in times of trouble. We all share whatever little we've got. And that's the one Soweto. But when you look at Soweto in social and political terms it's a different matter altogether – because you know that there is nothing really in those terms that makes Soweto a place to love. Given a chance, people don't actually like to live in the kind of hovels that they've been made to live in.

The end of the rainbow

In the months that followed after the election, life carried on in much the same way as before. On the weekends, there were the usual beauty contests, choir competitions, movies at the Eyethu Cinema in Mofolo, and action videos in makeshift shacks. Liquor flowed at the 'stokvels', kitchen parties and shebeens dotted throughout the township. People still shopped in the small family-owned, corner cafés or at the hundreds of spaza shops that dotted the streets of the township. Each Sunday, music blared, the streets were full, and the church services filled the air with hymns and prayers. The heavy pall of smoke from braziers and coal stoves – which is the hallmark of Soweto – still hung like a cloud over the township and was clearly visible for miles around.

And yet, while much has stayed the same, much has also changed. For Mongezi Mnganyi these changes are most visible among the youth:

It is impossible to compare today's 15-year-old kid with myself. It's like we are living in two different worlds. They can go into town at any time. Even a 10-year-old from Soweto can just board a taxi and find himself in Johannesburg. I didn't know how to go to Johannesburg on my own. Someone had to accompany me. Then there is also the style of life. The youngsters today just go to nice places where we couldn't go. There are no passes, so everyone moves freely... They just tell their parents what they want and what they don't want. I could never relate to my parents like that. It's like living on Mars.

Long queues waited patiently outside the polling stations in South Africa's first democratic elections.

BIBLIOGRAPHY

Amnesty International 'South Africa; State of Fear', Amnesty International Publications, London, 1992

Ashforth, A 'State Power, Violence, Everyday Life: Soweto', New School for Social Research, Working Paper Series, No. 210, March 1995

Bonner, PL 'The Politics of the African Squatter Movements on the Rand', *Radical History Review*, Vol. 46, No. 7, 1990

Bonner, PL 'The Russians on the Reef 1947–57. Urbanisation, Gang Warfare and Ethnic Mobilisation', in Bonner, PL, Delius, P, and Posel, D, *Apartheid's Genesis 1934–62*, Ravan Press, Johannesburg, 1993

Bonner, PL 'African Urbanisation on the Rand between the 1930s and 1960s: its Social Character and Political Consequences', *Journal of Southern African Studies*, Vol. 21, No. 1, March 1995

Brewer, J *After Soweto: An Unfinished Journey*, Oxford University Press, Oxford, 1986

Brooks, A and Brickhill, J *Whirlwind Before the Storm*, International Defence and Aid Fund for South Africa, London, 1980

Bureau of Information, 'The Young Revolutionaries', Government Printer, Pretoria, 1988

Calderwood, C 'Investigation into the Planning of Urban Native Housing in South Africa', PhD thesis, University of the Witwatersrand, 1953

Callinicos, A *Southern Africa After Soweto*, Pluto Press, London, 1978

Carr, W *Soweto: Its Creation, Life and Decline*, South African Institute of Race Relations, Johannesburg, 1990

Cawthra, G 'South Africa's Police', Catholic Institute for Race Relations Booklet, London, 1992

Chapman, M *Soweto Poetry*, McGraw-Hill, Johannesburg, 1982

Chapman, M and Dangor, A (eds) *Voices from Within: Black Poetry from Southern Africa*, AD Donker, Cape Town, 1982

Cobbett, W and Cohen, R (eds) *Popular Struggles in South Africa*, J Currey, London 1988

Cock, J *Colonels and Cadres: War and Gender in South Africa*, Oxford University Press, Cape Town, 1991

Coplan, D *In Township Tonight*, Ravan Press, Johannesburg, 1985

Counter Information Service *Black Soweto Explodes*, Russell Press, London, 1977

Crankshaw, O 'Race, Class and the Changing Division of Labour under Apartheid', PhD thesis, University of the Witwatersrand, 1994

Da Silva, M 'Black Hostels and Compounds in Johannesburg and Soweto', BA Hons dissertation, University of the Witwatersrand, 1983

Davenport, TRH 'The Beginning of Urban Segregation in South Africa: The Native (Urban Areas) Act and its Background' Institute for Social and Economic Research, Rhodes University, 1971

Davies, R, O'Meara, D and Dlamini, S *The Struggle for South Africa*, Volume 1, ZED Press, London, 1984

Delius, P 'Sebatakgomou: Migrant Organisation, the ANC and the Sekhukhuneland Revolt' in *Journal of Southern African Studies*, 15, 4, 1984

Diseko, N 'The Origins of Development of the South African Students' Movement 1968–76', *Journal of Southern African Studies*, 18, 1, March 1991

Dugmore, H 'Becoming Coloured: Class and Colour in Johannesburg's Malay Location', PhD thesis, University of the Witwatersrand, 1993

Eberhardt, JL 'Survey of Housing and Family Conditions: Orlando Township', MA dissertation, University of the Witwatersrand, 1949

Everatt, D and Sadek, S 'The Reef of Violence: Tribal War or Total Strategy?', Community Agency for Social Enquiry, March 1992

Financial Mail 'Soweto Survey', supplement to *Financial Mail*, 25 March 1983

Frankel, P 'The Dynamics of a Political Renaissance: The Soweto Students Representative Council', *Journal of African Studies*, Vol. 7, No. 3, 1980

Frankel, P et al. *State Resistance and Change in South Africa*, Croom Helm, London, 1988

French, K 'James Mpanza and the Sofasonke Party in the development of local politics in Soweto', MA dissertation, University of the Witwatersrand, 1983

Gerhart, G and Karis, T *From Protest to Challenge*, Vol. III, Standford Hoover, 1977

Glaser, C 'Youth Culture and Politics in Soweto 1958–76', PhD dissertation, University of Cambridge, 1994

Gorodnov, V *Soweto: Life and Struggles of a South African Township*, Moscow, 1988

Hart, D and Parnell, S 'Vukunzenzele: A History of Self-help Housing in a South African City', mimeo

Haysom, N 'Vigilantes: A Contemporary Form of Repression', Study of Violence Seminar, Paper No. 4, 1989

Hendler, P *Urban Policy and Housing*, South African Institute of Race Relations, Johannesburg, 1988

Hindson, D (ed.) 'The South African State and the Resolution of the African Urban Housing Crisis 1948–54', *Working Papers in Southern African Studies*, Vol. 3, Ravan Press, Johannesburg, 1983

Hirson, B *Year of Fire, Year of Ash. The Soweto Revolt: Roots of a Revolution*, ZED Press, London, 1979

Hlope, S 'The Crisis of Urban Living Under Apartheid Conditions' in Murray, M (ed.), *South African Capitalism and Black Political Opposition*, Cambridge, Massachusetts, 1982

Hyslop, J 'School Movements and State Education' in Cobbett, W and Cohen, R (eds) *Popular Struggles in South Africa*, J Currey, London 1988

Hellman, E *Soweto: Johannesburg's African City*, South African Institute of Race Relations, Johannesburg, 1967

Hellman, E 'Soweto', *Optima*, March 1973

Holland, H *Born in Soweto*, Penguin Books, London, 1994

Human, P 'Quality of Life in Soweto: A Sociological View', UNISA Department of Sociology, March 1981

Johnson, J and Magubane, P *Soweto Speaks*, AD Donker, Johannesburg, 1979

Kagan, N 'African Settlements in the Johannesburg Area: 1903–23', MA dissertation, University of the Witwatersrand, 1978

Kallaway, P and Pearson, P *Johannesburg: Images and Continuities. A History of Working Class Life through Pictures 1885–1935*, Ravan Press, Johannesburg, 1986

Kane-Berman, J *Soweto: Black Revolt, White Reaction*, Ravan Press, Johannesburg, 1978

Keeble, S 'The Expansion of Black Business into the South African Economy' MA dissertation, University of the Witwatersrand, 1981

Koch, E 'Doornfontein and its African Working Class: A Study of Popular Culture in Johannesburg', MA dissertation, University of the Witwatersrand, 1983

Kramer, J 'Death in the City: Burial Societies in Soweto', African Studies Institute Seminar Paper, University of the Witwatersrand, June 1974

Lebello, S 'Sophiatown Removals, Relocation and Political Quiescence in the Rand Townships 1950–65' BA Hons dissertation, University of the Witwatersrand, 1988

Lee, R and Schlemmer, L in *Transition to Democracy: Policy Perspectives*, Oxford University Press, Oxford, 1991

Lewis, PRB *A City within a City: The Creation of Soweto*, Johannesburg City Council, 1966

Lobban, M 'Black Consciousness on Trial 1974–76', African Studies Institute Seminar Paper, University of the Witwatersrand, August 1990

Lodge, T 'Children of Soweto', in *Black Politics in South Africa since 1945*, Ravan Press, Johannesburg, 1983

Lodge, T 'The African National Congress Comes Home', African Studies Institute Seminar Paper, University of the Witwatersrand, June 1992

Lodge, T 'South Africa: Democracy and Development in Post Apartheid Society', African Studies Institute Seminar Paper, University of the Witwatersrand, March 1994

Bibliography

Lodge, T and Nasson,,B *All, Here and Now: Black Politics in South Africa in the 1980s*, South Africa UPDATE series, Ford Foundation and David Philip Publishers, Cape Town, 1991

Luckhardt, K and Wall, B *Organise or Starve*, Lawrence Wishart, London, 1988

Lunn H 'Antecedents of the Music and Popular Culture of the African Post-1976 Generation', MA dissertation, University of the Witwatersrand, 1983

Mabin, M 'State Homes for Sale', *Work in Progress*, No. 26, 1982

Mafeje, A 'Soweto and its Aftermath', *Review of the African Political Economy*, 11, January–April 1978

Magubane, P *Soweto: Portraits of a City*, New Holland Publishers, London, 1990

Maguire, R 'The Peoples' Club: A Social and Institutional History of Orlando Pirates Football Club 1937–73', BA Hons dissertation, University of the Witwatersrand, 1991

Mandela, N *Long Walk to Freedom: The Autobiography of Nelson Mandela*, Macdonald Purnell, South Africa, 1994

Mandy, N *A City Divided: Johannesburg and Soweto*, MacMillan South Africa, Johannesburg, 1984

Manoim, I 'The Black Press 1945–63', MA dissertation, University of the Witwatersrand, 1983

Mapheto, A 'The Violence: A View from the Ground', *Work in Progress*, No. 69, 1990

Marks, M 'Organisation, Identity and Violence Amongst Activist Diepkloof Youth, 1984–93', MA dissertation, University of the Witwatersrand, 1993

Mashabela, H *Apartheid People on the Boil*, Skotaville, 1987

Mashabela, M *Urban African Cities of the Future*, South African Institute of Race Relations, Johannesburg, 1990

Mashinini, A 'The Black Bourgeoisie', *Sechaba*, February 1984

Mather, C and Parnell, S 'Upgrading the "Matchboxes": Urban Renewal in Soweto 1976–86', in Drukakis-Smith, D (ed.) *Economic Growth and Urbanisation in Developing Areas*, Routledge, London, 1990

Mathiane, N 'In Soweto: the Glowing Embers', *Frontline*, 9:3–9

Mathiane, N *South Africa: The Diary of Troubled Times*, Freedom House, New York, 1989

Mathiane, N *Beyond the Headlines: Truths of Soweto Life*, Southern Book Publishers, Johannesburg, 1990

Mayer, P 'Soweto People and their Social Universes', Human Sciences Research Council, Pretoria, 1977

Mokwena, SD 'The Dube Riots', BA Hons dissertation, University of the Witwatersrand, 1990

Mokwena, SD 'The Era of Jackrollers', Project for the Study of Violence Seminar Series, 1991

Molteno, F 'The Uprising of 16th June 1976', *Social Dynamics* (1), 54–89, 1979

Morris M and Hindson, D 'Political Violence and Urban Reconstruction in South Africa', mimeo, *Economic Trends*, Working Paper 3

Morris, M and Padayachee, V 'State Reform Policy in South Africa', *Transformation*, Vol. 7, 1988

Morris, P *Soweto: A Review of Existing Conditions and Some Guidelines for Change*, Urban Foundation, Johannesburg, 1980

Morris, P *A History of Black Housing in South Africa*, Johannesburg, South African Foundation, 1982

Moss, G 'Total Strategy', *Work in Progress*, No. 11, 1980

Moss, G 'Crisis and Conflict: Soweto 1976–77', MA dissertation, University of the Witwatersrand, 1982

Moss, G and Obery, I (eds) *South Africa Review*, Vol. 6, Ravan Press, Johannesburg, 1992

Mutloase, M (ed.) *Forced Landing Africa South: Contemporary Writings*, Ravan Press, Johannesburg, 1980

Mzamane, M *Children of Soweto: A Trilogy*, Ravan Press, Johannesburg, 1982

Parnell, S 'Johannesburg's Slums and Racial Segregation: 1910–37', PhD thesis, University of the Witwatersrand, 1993

Phillips, M 'The Politics of State Power in the 1980s', Centre for Political Studies, University of the Witwatersrand, July 1988

Phillips, M and Coleman, C 'Another Kind of War: Strategies in the Era of Negotiation', *Transformation* No. 9, 1989

Posel, D *The Making of Apartheid*, Clarendon Press, Oxford, 1991

Report of the Commission appointed by the City Council of Johannesburg to enquire into the causes and circumstances of the riots which took place in the vicinity of the Dube Hostel in the South Western Native Townships on the weekend 14–15 September 1957

Report on the Violence in Meadowlands, April 1991 to June 1992, compiled for the African National Congress

Rich, P 'Liberals, Radicals, and the Politics of Black Consciousness 1969–76', African Studies Institute Seminar Paper, University of the Witwatersrand, July 1989

Sapire, H 'Informal Housing in the PWV: A Case Study', Report for the Urban Foundation, October 1990

Sarakinsky, I 'State Strategy and Transition in South Africa', African Studies Institute Seminar Paper, University of the Witwatersrand, August 1988

Sarakinsky, I 'The State of the State and the State of Resistance', *Work in Progress*, 1990

Seekings, J 'Why is Soweto Different?', African Studies Institute Seminar Paper, University of the Witwatersrand, 1986

Seekings, J 'Quiescence and the Transition to Confrontation: South African Townships 1978–84', PhD thesis, University of Oxford, 1990

Seekings, J 'Trailing behind the Masses: The UDF and Township Politics 1983–84', *Journal of Southern African Studies*, Vol. 18, No. 1, March 1992

Shubane, K 'The Soweto Rent Boycott', Honours dissertation, University of the Witwatersrand, February 1983

Simpson, G, Mokwena, S and Segal, L 'Political Violence', *South African Human Rights and Labour Law Book*, Oxford University Press, Cape Town, 1992

South African Research Services (eds) *South African Review*, Vols 2 & 3, Ravan Press, Johannesburg, 1984

Stadler, AW 'Birds in the Cornfield: Squatter Movements in Johannesburg 1944–47', *Journal of Southern African Studies*, 6, 1, October 1979

Stubbs, A (ed.) *Steve Biko: I Write What I Live*, London, 1978

Swilling, M 'The Politics of Negotiation', *Work in Progress*, 1989

Swilling, M and Shubane, K 'Negotiating Urban Transition: The Soweto Experience' in Lee, R and Schlemmer, L in *Transition to Democracy*, Oxford University Press, Oxford, 1991

'The Social History of Soweto', prepared for IDASA by the Urban Research Services

Tlali, M *Footprints in the Quag: Stories and Dialogues from Soweto*, David Philip Publishers, Cape Town, 1989

Two Dogs and Freedom: Children of the Townships Speak Out, Ravan Press/Open School, Johannesburg, 1986

Van Onselen, C *Studies in the Social and Economic History of the Witwatersrand 1886–1914*, 2 volumes, Ravan Press, Johannesburg, 1982

Wilkinson, P 'The South African State and the Resolution of the African Housing Crisis in Johannesburg 1944–1958' in Hindson, D (ed.) *Working Papers in Southern African Studies*, Vol. 3, Ravan Press, Johannesburg, 1983

AUTHORS' NOTE

A number of sources and reference material provided a wealth of information and detail from which much of this publication was compiled. Of particular relevance here is the Central Archives Depot (CAD), and certain of the original documents and affidavits quoted on these pages may be found in the following files at the Archives:

- (Mpanza, page 22) CAD NTS 6470 File 51/313 (S1) Vol. 1 Affidavits
- (Henderson, page 25) CAD NTS 6471 File 51/313 (S1) Vol. 2
- (Mpanza, page 26) CAD NTS 6470 File 51/313 (S1) Vol. 1 Affidavits
- (Bantu Homelands Citizen Act, page 72) Access provided by Debora Posel

PHOTOGRAPHIC ACKNOWLEDGEMENTS

Cover illustration: David Goldblatt/South Photo Agency

ABPL (130; 140)

ANC (142)

Bailey's African History Archives (21; 36; 47; 53t; 59; 60; 61; 62t; 63b; 64 t+b; 66; 97; 103; 117)

The Cape Times (126)

City of Johannesburg Housing Division (18)

City Press (113b; 122b; 141)

David Goldblatt/South Photo Agency (40; 45; 62b; 63t; 65; 67; 105)

Die Transvaler (19)

Historical Papers Department, University of the Witwatersrand (12b; 14; 22b; 23)

Inkatha Freedom Party (147)

INPRA (144 t+b; 145; 146; 159)

Jurgen Schadeberg (153t)

Mayibuye Centre (24; 27; 38; 42; 49; 50; 51; 52; 53b; 73; 77; 85t; 86 t+b; 88t; 90 t+b; 92; 110; 112; 113t; 116; 131; 135; 136; 143; 153b)

MuseuMAfricA (9; 10; 11; 12t; 16t; 17; 20; 22t; 25 [TIMES Media Collection]; 26; 30; 33; 34; 37)

Paul Weinberg/South Photo Agency (115)

Peter Magubane (68; 84)

Rodney Barnett/South Photo Agency (133)

Santu Mofokeng (149)

SOWETAN (55; 69; 75; 107; 121; 122t; 151b; 155)

TIMES MEDIA LTD (16b; 39; 96; 108; 118; 127; 134; 137; 148; 151t)

The Star (48; 87; 94; 104b; 123)

Transvaal Weekly Illustrated (13)

The publishers also wish to thank the following:

Open School, Johannesburg, for the extract on p118

Jonathan Ball Publishers for the poems on p61, p72, p74, p75 and p100

Oxford University Press for the poem on p109

Historical Papers Department, University of the Witwatersrand for providing documents and various newspapers for extracts.

In certain instances, the publishers were unable to trace copyright holders
and would be grateful for any information in this regard.